WONDER WOMAN

EDITED BY COREY K. CREEKMUR, CRAIG FISCHER,
CHARLES HATFIELD, JEET HEER, AND ANA MERINO

Volumes in the *Comics Culture* series explore the artistic, historical, social, and cultural significance of newspaper comic strips, comic books, and graphic novels, with individual titles devoted to focused studies of key titles, characters, writers, and artists throughout the history of comics; additional books in the series address major themes or topics in comics studies, including prominent genres, national traditions, and significant historical and theoretical issues. The series recognizes comics of all varieties, from mainstream comic books to graphic non-fiction, produced between the late 19th-century and the present. The books in the series are intended to contribute significantly to the rapidly expanding field of comics studies, but are also designed to appeal to comics fans and casual readers who seek smart critical engagement with the best examples of the form.

WONDER WOMAN

BONDAGE AND FEMINISM IN THE MARSTON/PETER COMICS, 1941–1948

Noah Berlatsky

RUTGERS UNIVERSITY PRESS
NEW BRUNSWICK, NEW JERSEY AND LONDON

LIBRARY OF CONGRESS CATALOG ING-IN-PUBLICATION DATA
Berlatsky, Noah.
Wonder Woman : Bondage and Feminism in the Marston/Peter Comics,
1941–1948 / Noah Berlatsky
pages cm.—(Comics Culture)
Includes bibliographical references and index.
ISBN 978-0-8135-6419-7 (hardback)—ISBN 978-0-8135-6418-0 (pbk.)—ISBN 978-0-
8135-6420-3 (e-book)
1. Wonder Woman (Fictitious character) 2. Feminism in literature. 3. Women in literature. 4.
Bondage (Sexual behavior) in literature. 5. Comic books, strips, etc.—United States. I. Title.
PN6728.W6B47 2015
741.5'973—dc23
2014014279

A British Cataloging-in-Publication record for this book is available from the British Library.

For Marcy and Siah, in loving submission

CONTENTS

ACKNOWLEDGMENTS

As with any book project, this one could not have been accomplished without the aid of many people. Dirk Deppey's blog posts at *Journalista!* first introduced me to the Marston/Peter run on Wonder Woman, for which I am extremely grateful. Bill Randall, Ben Saunders, and Eric Berlatsky commented on various versions of the book proposal. Bert Stabler, Sharon Marcus, Peter Sattler, Monika Bartyzel, Ben Saunders, and Craig Fischer all read chapter drafts and provided helpful comments and advice, as did two anonymous reviewers. Andy Mangels (through the Comix Scholars listserv), Robert Stanley Martin, Jones, One of the Jones Boys, and Ken Alder all provided generous help with particular research questions and problems. Abigail Rine kindly shared her work on Irigaray and incarnation. My editor, Corey Creekmur, has provided useful comments and advice throughout the project and read more drafts than he probably cares to think about. Thanks are due also to Leslie Mitchner and Lisa Boyajian at Rutgers, who helped with the long process of shepherding the book to press, and to Andrew Katz for his careful copyediting.

This project began with, and was inspired by, writing about Marston/Peter on my blog, *The Hooded Utilitarian*. I am very grateful to readers and commenters on the site for challenging me and sharpening my thinking. In particular, I would like to thank Jones, One of the Jones Boys, Kelly Thompson, Sina, Sharon Marcus, Ben Saunders, Vom Marlowe, Richard Cook, Derik Badman, and Charles Reece for participating in a roundtable on Marston/Peter at HU, which generated many questions, ideas, and arguments that I have used in this book.

Finally, I want to thank my son, Siah, who quite likes the Marston/Peter comics (especially Etta Candy), and my wife, Marcy, who does not particularly but who has put up with this book anyway.

WONDER WOMAN

INTRODUCTION

Everybody knows about Wonder Woman, but not many people know about *Wonder Woman.*

Wonder Woman, of course, is the superhero. Most people are familiar with her from the 1970s television show, in which Lynda Carter put out her arms and spun herself into a big ball of light and a star-spangled swimsuit. Others may have seen her in the *Justice League Unlimited* television series, on the MAC cosmetics line, or (much less likely) in her own comics. She occasionally gets referenced on television shows such as *Bones* (where wonder sleuth Temperance Brennan dresses up as Wonder Woman for Halloween) or *The O.C.* (where Summer dresses up as Wonder Woman to titillate her boyfriend).

Wonder Woman has not been very successful for a long time— certainly not as successful as Batman or Spider-Man or other comic-book properties with major motion-picture series to their name. Still, she remains reasonably visible, if not exactly necessary. Among the hordes of strong women heroes, from Buffy to Katniss Everdeen to Dora the Explorer, Wonder Woman is notable mostly for wearing a sillier costume and for having more improbable weaponry (a magic lasso? bullet-stopping bracelets? an invisible plane?) Sometimes she is a bad-ass warrior; sometimes she is an avatar of peace; sometimes she is a feminist icon (as when she appeared on the first cover of *Ms.* magazine in 1972); sometimes she is a fetish symbol (as in a June 2011 spread for *Playboy* Mexico).[1] In general, though, she is what most pop-culture icons are—a placeholder for nostalgia and recognizability, whose image provokes strong emotions in some people and moderate amusement in everybody else. She is an unassuming brick in the postmodern bricolage, famous for being famous—like Paris Hilton but significantly more charming, not least because she is less real.

Wonder Woman the original comic book, on the other hand, though successful when it first appeared in the 1940s, is not well-known today. It rarely shows up in comics best-of polls and is not even necessarily ranked all that highly among the superhero comics of its own era. Will Eisner's *The Spirit*, Jack Cole's *Plastic Man*, C. C. Beck's *Captain Marvel*, and (for historical reasons) Joe Siegel and Jerry Shuster's *Superman* are probably the works from that time that are considered most important and that have the highest profile today.[2] *Wonder Woman* is second tier—though if it weren't for its historical standing as the first female superhero comic, it probably wouldn't even rate that.[3]

It is not just the public that tends to focus on Wonder Woman rather than *Wonder Woman*. It is scholars as well. There is remarkably little criticism that sees *Wonder Woman* as an aesthetically important or significant comic in its own right. Rather, most writing tends to focus on the historical or cultural significance of the book—which effectively means that it looks at *Wonder Woman* through the lens of Wonder Woman. Thus, Les Daniels's *Wonder Woman: The Complete History* and *Tim Hanley's Wonder Woman Unbound* examines the Marston/Peter run in the context of Wonder Woman's history as a cultural phenomenon. Mike Madrid's *Supergirls* is interested in the *Wonder Woman* comics primarily because of Wonder Woman's importance in the pantheon of superheroines.

The ascendency of Wonder Woman over *Wonder Woman* is partly a simple matter of popularity. *Wonder Woman* the Marston/Peter comic is old, and the interest in old pop culture is always going to be limited in comparison to the interest in a current pop-culture icon. However, especially among comics scholars and critics, I think the ascendency of icon over comic is also contradictorily linked to comics studies' interest in comics. Or, to put it another way, being too focused on comics in general can make it hard to see why you should talk about the Marston/Peter comics in particular.

That seems counterintuitive. An interest in comics, you would think, would make you emphasize the *comic*, not the icon. And yet that has not been the case. Again, books such as Les Daniels's history of Wonder Woman or Mike Madrid's *Supergirls*, which come from a comics-centered perspective, tend to see the early comics as important for their place in the history of comics—as significant because the character is significant or because she was one of the "archetypes that would define the female superhero" (Madrid 31). To find someone who cares primarily about the Marston/Peter comics in themselves rather than about the character, you need to turn to writers such as Lewis Call, whose book is focused on bondage, discipline, sadism, and masochism (BDSM) in science-fiction narratives, or to Ben Saunders, whose book *Do the Gods Wear Capes?* takes a theological approach to superheroes in comics and film.

Why do you need to take your eyes off comics in order to see Marston and Peter? The answer, I think, is William Marston, Wonder Woman's creator. Before he was a comic-book writer, Marston was an academic, a polyamorist, a feminist, a psychologist, a queer theorist, and a utopian. He saw his comics as a scheme to advance radical ideas and theories and dreams. As a result, looking at his comics from inside comics is a little like reading Freud for the plot. You tend to miss a lot of what is going on.[4]

What this means is that theoretical approaches—feminism, queer theory, psychology—are not something imposed on *Wonder Woman* from outside. Rather, they are intrinsic to the work's goals and commitments. For that reason, this book quite consciously privileges theory over comics' specific history. I do not provide much discussion of other female superhero comics of the time, for example, or (until the conclusion) about later versions of Wonder Woman. Instead, I talk about romance novels, Japanese urban incest legends, shell shock, and the Michigan Womyn's Festival. That is not because history does not matter. Rather, it is because to me the way to be truest to the historical Marston is to grant him his theoretical breadth and ambition. Marston meant his ideas about gender, sexuality, and peace to be widely applicable and, indeed, widely transformative. He wanted his ideas to be big, which means you need to take a step back, in various directions, if his achievement is going to come into focus.

What follows, then, is not aimed at Wonder Woman fans—though I certainly hope they will find something to like in this discussion of the Amazon princess. Nor is it aimed, necessarily, at comics or superhero enthusiasts, though I will inevitably talk a good deal about their interests as well. Rather, it is aimed at anyone who cares about Marston's passions—about gender, about equality, about peace, about bondage, about love, and about God(ess). It is aimed at folks who think, like Marston, that comics should change the world.

The book is organized into three chapters focused on three of *Wonder Woman*'s most important themes. These are, in order, feminism, pacifism, and queerness—or, if you prefer, bondage, violence, and heterosexuality. For Marston, these topics were all inextricably intertwined; his feminism was based on his pacifism, his queerness on his feminism, his pacifism on his queerness, and on and on, in every multiple combination. The exact order of the chapters is in some sense arbitrary; each relies on the others and builds on the others. The book presents not so much a linear argument as a braided exploration, in which the same ideas and obsessions recur in slightly different combinations and from slightly different perspectives. In this sense, at least, the book is something like the deliriously recursive *Wonder Woman* comics themselves, with their heroines and villains forever tying up and being tied up in an endless ecstatic fever dream of dominance, submission, enslavement, and release. The conclusion will return again to the difference between Wonder Woman and *Wonder Woman* and look at some of the specific ways in which the first has diverged from the second.

THE STORY AND THE CHARACTERS

Wonder Woman—in the original comics and in most other iterations of the character—is a princess from an all-female community of Amazon warriors who live on Paradise Island. She is the daughter of Hippolyte, the queen. The Amazons have lived on the island since the time of the ancient Greeks, watched over by their patron, Aphrodite, the goddess of love.

The Amazons' idyllic existence is interrupted when Steve Trevor, an American pilot, crash lands on their shores. Diana is smitten with him and volunteers to return with him to man's world in order to fight for peace against the Axis. Besides her superstrength, superspeed, superendurance, and other physical prowess, she also has bracelets that she can use to block bullets, an invisible plane, and a magic lasso that compels obedience to her commands (in later iterations, the lasso's power is often downgraded so that it forces people to tell the truth rather than forcing them to obey any command).[5] In man's world, Wonder Woman takes on the secret identity of Diana Prince, eventually becoming the secretary to Steve's boss and often working with Steve on missions for army intelligence.

Besides Hippolyte and Steve, the other most important supporting characters are the Holliday girls, sorority members at Holliday College. Led by the short, squat Etta Candy, the girls often aid Wonder Woman and Steve in foiling Axis espionage plots or (especially after the war's end) in pursuing other fantastical adventures. Etta and the Holliday girls are generally written out of the Wonder Woman mythos by later creators, but in the original comics, they are a constant, central presence, ensuring that Wonder Woman is surrounded with women in man's world, as well as on Paradise Island.

THE CREATORS

I will discuss aspects of the biography of William Marston and artist Harry Peter as they are relevant in the text. However, I think it would be helpful to give an initial outline of their careers here. In addition, I will briefly discuss some issues of auteurism raised by the inevitably collaborative nature of corporate comics.

William Moulton Marston (May 9, 1893–May 2, 1947)

As I have mentioned, Wonder Woman is the brainchild of William Moulton Marston—a man who had a very unusual background for a comics creator. Most writers and artists in the comics field in the 1940s were pulp writers and artists. They often came from working-class or lower-middle-class backgrounds and had little formal education beyond high school. Many of them were Jewish. Marston, on the other hand, was a member of the WASP elite. A psychologist with a law degree and a Ph.D. from Harvard, he wrote a number of articles and two full-length books describing his psychological research.

Marston's research was quite idiosyncratic. As Geoffrey Bunn has said, Marston "consistently disregarded the apparent boundaries between academic and popular psychology, between science and values, and between the legitimate and the illegitimate" (92). Marston set out on the ambitious, crank-tinged goal of finding the most basic elements of human consciousness, or what he called the "simplest normal emotion elements" (Marston, *Emotions* 5). Chief among these were the binary emotions dominance-submission—through a close understanding of which, Marston believed, psychology could open the way for human liberation (Bunn 93). Marston encapsulated this in his DISC theory, which referred to Dominance, Inducement, Submission, and Compliance. According to Marston, favorable relationships were based on inducing submission, unfavorable ones on inducing compliance. Or, as Hanley summarizes, "Harsh dominance led to forced compliance, while kind inducement led to willing submission" (15).

Marston had little influence on mainstream academia, but his theories have had a long-lasting impact on pop psychology. The DISC personality test is based on Marston's categories and work (AM Azure Consulting 4). Marston is even better known, though, for his work on the technology used in polygraph machines. On the basis of this research, he dubbed himself "the inventor of the lie detector" (Bunn 95).

As such self-promotion suggests, Marston was, among his other accomplishments, a shameless carny—or, as Ben Saunders more kindly puts it, a "public professional" (42). Rather than pursuing an academic career, Marston supplemented his fame and fortune with endorsements and stunts. He used his polygraph to demonstrate that blondes were less emotional than brunettes and wrote up the results for magazines. He penned pop-psychology books with titles such as *Try Living!* and worked briefly as a consulting psychologist for Universal Pictures. In his role as media advocate and general hype man, Marston wrote a laudatory article about comics in 1939 that brought him to the attention of the publisher of All American Comics, M. C. Gaines. Gaines, who was eager to increase comics' respectability, contacted Marston about being on an advisory board. Marston quickly parleyed that into a full-time gig, and under the pen name of Charles Moulton, he wrote Wonder Woman's adventures from her first appearance in *All Star Comics #8* in 1941 until his death in 1947.

Marston's audacity was not confined to his professional endeavors: his personal life was if anything more startling than his career. Beginning in the late 1920s, he and his wife, Elizabeth, lived in a polyamorous relationship with Olive Byrne, a woman Marston had met while doing research at Tufts. Marston had children by both women. After his death in 1947, Elizabeth and Olive lived together for another four decades.[6]

Harry G. Peter (March 8, 1889–1958)

Harry G. Peter's biography has been much less well documented than Marston's, though he had a long career as an illustrator prior to his run on *Wonder Woman*. He worked on *Mutt and Jeff*, a well-known comic strip, and also did cartoons for humor magazines such as *Judge*. Philip Sandifer, whose chapter on Peter appears to be the fullest consideration of the artist in print, notes that Peter also worked drawing Gibson Girls, early twentieth-century pin-ups with, as Sandifer says, "feminist leanings"—they were generally portrayed as educated, strong, and independent (137–138). Sandifer argues that the eroticism and the feminism probably appealed to Marston. So too, perhaps, did Peter's stylistic similarities with Victorian and Edwardian pornography—Sandifer points out that there's at least one nude Peter drawing of Wonder Woman extant (140).

Peter was over sixty years old when Marston personally hired him despite the opposition of the editor Sheldon Mayer (Daniels 23–24). Peter continued to work on the series after Marston's death in 1947 but was finally fired in 1958 by the editor Robert Kanigher. He died a few months later (Daniels 102–105).

Other Creators

Marston had a great deal of control over *Wonder Woman*; as mentioned earlier, he selected Harry Peter as the artist on the book and paid him himself. Nonetheless, there were many others who contributed to the writing in one way or another. Chief among these was Joye Hummel Murchison, Marston's assistant, who was for practical purposes the coauthor of many scripts after 1945, when Marston began to be seriously ill (Daniels 73–74). Murchison is credited with some scripts in the *Wonder Woman Archive Edition* (for example, with *Wonder Woman #12*), though the exact criteria for attribution is not explained. Besides Murchison, other writers may also have been involved to varying degrees; for example, Marston's children contributed plot ideas with some regularity (Daniels 43).

Similarly, while Harry Peter was the credited artist on all but a handful of Marston's *Wonder Woman* scripts, he was rarely if ever the sole illustrator. Assistants (often apparently women) would work on backgrounds and lettering, while Peter would do the figure work (Daniels 47–48). The remarkable coloring on the series was also anonymous; there is no way to know whether Peter even supervised it.

For the purposes of simplicity, I have with some exceptions treated Marston as the writer and Peter as the artist of the *Wonder Woman* comics. I will usually attribute the comic as a whole creation to Marston and Peter, though at times when it seems appropriate, I may simply attribute it to Marston.

AUDIENCE

Exact sales figures for *Wonder Woman* are not available. Still, the consensus at the time and since is that the original *Wonder Woman* sold extremely well in the 1940s during a period when comics, with millions of sales to their credit, were truly a mass medium. Daniels, for example, writes that "Wonder Woman . . . was a smashing success. By summer 1942, only a few months after her debut, a new *Wonder Woman* comic book was launched, making the Amazon one of only a handful of characters considered strong enough to carry her own publication" (37). Bradford Wright says that in 1940, shortly before Wonder Woman debuted, an average DC comic sold about eight hundred thousand copies an issue (14). If Wonder Woman was a hit, she must have been selling more, and probably significantly more, than that. Marston in his *Family Circle* interview with Olive Byrne said that *Wonder Woman* outsold all other DC titles, which Tim Hanley suggests would put its readership at over five million—though Marston may well have been exaggerating the success of his book (Hanley 17). In any case, it seems reasonable to suggest that at least some issues of *Wonder Woman* sold in the seven figures. As a point of comparison, the average DC comic in April 2012 sold 35,264 copies, according to Marc-Oliver Frisch, a reporter at the comics news site *The Beat*.

Besides the question of how many people read *Wonder Woman*, there is also the question of who those people were. Were the readers girls? Were they boys? How old were they? Gerard Jones, in *Men of Tomorrow*, argues that *Wonder Woman* sold "mainly to preteen and teenage boys." He cites a "customer survey" indicating that 90 percent of *Wonder Woman*'s audience was male (211). However, Jones provides no date for the survey, no information about where it was conducted, no details about how the question was phrased, and no explanation of where he saw it or who told him about it. As such, though his figures are often referenced, it is difficult to know how seriously to take them. On the other hand, Trina Robbins, in a 2006 essay, argues that there is strong anecdotal evidence indicating that *Wonder Woman* had a substantial female readership. She points to statements by Gloria Steinem and Jane Yolen, as well as to her own memories. In her essay, "Wonder Woman: Lesbian or Dyke?," she writes, "When I was a young girl, my girlfriends and I all read and loved Wonder Woman."

Given the comic's popularity, it seems reasonable to believe that *Wonder Woman* was read by substantial numbers of both girls and boys. Whether or not this was the case, I think that Marston aimed the comic at girls and boys—and that his stories deliberately encouraged boys, girls, and everyone else to identify across gender lines. Throughout the book, therefore, I assume that Marston's audience included, and was deliberately seen as including, all genders.

THE COMIC

I have been referring to the original Wonder Woman comics as *Wonder Woman*, but that is somewhat deceptive. In fact, Wonder Woman was so popular in the 1940s that she was given several titles. After her first appearance in 1941, she became the regular lead feature in *Sensation Comics*, which first began running monthly in 1942. The *Wonder Woman* comic, which varied between bimonthly and quarterly, began running six months later. Wonder Woman also appeared beginning in 1942 as one feature in *Comics Cavalcade*, a quarterly anthology. There was also a *Wonder Woman* comic strip that ran for less than a year in 1944, and there were various other stories in other comics.[7]

Unfortunately, there is no good, faithful, complete reissue of the Marston/Peter *Wonder Woman* comics. DC Comics has a couple of archive projects covering some of the relevant issues in various forms, often with recoloring. The DC Archives has reached seven volumes; the *Wonder Woman Chronicles* has reached three. Neither has finished reprinting all the Marston/Peter stories—and both skip the stories from *Comics Cavalcade* (the first few of which are reprinted in the single DC Archives *Comics Cavalcade* collection). The entire runs of each title have been made available in various forms illicitly online, but obviously that is not an ideal solution for most readers. Since there is no definitive, or even decent, collected edition of these comics, I have decided throughout the book to cite the number, date, and page number of the original comics rather than referring to collections.

A NOTE ON THE BLOG

I first began writing about the Marston/Peter *Wonder Woman* in 2009 on my blog, *The Hooded Utilitarian*. I put together dozens of posts comprising in total tens of thousands of words. Most of this book is new material, but I have inevitably used some ideas and posts from the blog as well. In cases where it seemed necessary or useful, I have cited my own posts or articles; in other cases, I have simply adapted small sections of my own text. If you complete the book and want to read more of what I have to say about Wonder Woman, you can find my writing on the topic here: http://hoodedutilitarian.com/tag/wonder-woman/.

CHAPTER ONE

THE PINK BONDAGE GOO OF FEMINISM

The Marston/Peter *Wonder Woman* comics were both feminist and filled with bondage imagery. This chapter tries to explain how that was possible. Though some critics and feminists see fetishized bondage as disempowering to women, I point out that representations of disempowerment are popular in women's genre literature such as the romance and the gothic. Images of disempowerment, then, may be popular with women because they mirror women's actual disempowerment.

I then discuss *Wonder Woman #16*, perhaps the greatest Marston/Peter story (co-written by Joye Murchison). *Wonder Woman #16* is in many ways a gothic story. It also deals directly with women's disempowerment by exploring themes of rape and incest. I relate the treatment of these issues in *Wonder Woman #16* to discussions of incest by Sigmund Freud and Judith Herman in order to show the extent to which Marston/Murchison/Peter sympathize with and try to empower female (and male) victims.

However, the comic's identification with victims does not prevent it from also fetishizing those victims. Using *Twilight* and Gale Swiontkowski's argument that incest fantasies can sometimes be empowering for women, I argue that Marston/Murchison/Peter not only fetishize women but also give women the opportunity to be the fetishizers/objectifiers. *Wonder Woman #16* sympathizes with victims but refuses to see women solely as victims or solely as reacting (with heroism or violence) to victimization. Instead, Marston, Murchison, and Peter insist that condemnation of sexual violence can, and must, coexist with an embrace of sexual fantasy.

BONDAGE AND EMPOWERMENT

In an introduction to a 1972 collection of Marston and Peter Wonder Woman stories organized by *Ms.* magazine, Gloria Steinem declared,

> Looking back now at these Wonder Woman stories from the forties, I am amazed by the strength of their feminist message. . . .
>
> Wonder Woman symbolizes many of the values of the women's culture that feminists are now trying to introduce into the mainstream: strength and self-reliance for women; sisterhood and mutual support among women; peacefulness and esteem for human life; a diminishment both of "masculine" aggression and of the belief that violence is the only way of solving conflicts. (Introduction to *Wonder Woman* [1972] n.p.)

For Steinem, then, Wonder Woman was a symbol of the power and independence of women—which is why an image of the heroine graces the cover of the first stand-alone *Ms.* magazine in July 1972.[1]

It is not hard to see what Steinem is talking about or why feminists such as Trina Robbins and Lillian Robinson have also expressed enthusiasm for Marston and Peter's version of the character. All you have to do is read a story like *Wonder Woman #13*, published in summer 1945 (and partially reprinted in the 1972 *Ms.* collection). The comic opens with a crisis on Paradise Island, where many young Amazons have started to doubt their own abilities to perform superfeats. Wonder Woman races to the rescue and shows the Amazons how to jump 150 feet in the air, snap the heaviest chains, and lift giant boulders. "You see girls, there's nothing to it!" she declares. "All you have to do is have confidence in your own strength!" And sure enough, as Marston tells us in a text box, "Under Wonder Woman's inspiration, the Amazon girls pass their strength tests with flying colors" (3A–5A). Or, as singer Judy Collins said in her introduction to the first *Wonder Woman Archive* volume, "I am sure that the energy and certainty of women that they can do anything is due in part to Wonder Woman's great example" (7).

But even in this story, one of Marston's most schematically ideological feminist lessons for girls, there is a moment or two that has to make even the most forgiving reader wonder whether feminism is really the focus. In one particularly striking panel, the Amazon girls, all dressed in short, flirty skirts, are shown winding ropes and chains around the (as always) be-swimsuited Wonder Woman, tying her fast to a wooden pole; Peter draws some swooping, energized, inky motion, filling the scene with an additional joyful oomph (5A). Everyone looks like they are having a great time, and obviously it is all in the name of sporty athletics and raising women's self-esteem. But why does raising women's self-esteem require bondage imagery exactly? Isn't there a way we could get the feminist message without the cheerful-yet-kinky sexual charge?

The answer to that last question, at least for Marston and Peter, is no. We can't, and we won't, have the liberation without the bondage. Gloria Steinem and Judy Collins focus on the feminism and avoid the other thing, but one has to think that even they noticed at some point that the Marston/Peter *Wonder Woman* is a wall-to-wall bondage-fetish romp. In fact, according to Tim Hanley, fully 27 percent of the Marston/Peter *Wonder Woman* included bondage, compared to only 3 percent for *Captain Marvel*, another character who got tied up quite a bit (46).

As an example, let's look at the first few pages of the last script Marston ever published, *Wonder Woman #28*, written in collaboration with Joye Murchison while he was dying of cancer.[2]

> The cover and splash page are notable in that no one is tied up.
> Page 2A: Wonder Woman is shown binding a whole horde of evil Saturnians. The male Saturnians get sent away, so only the women are left, presumably because Marston and Peter don't really care about men. In any case, the Saturnian women then have Venus girdles strapped on them—magic metal belts that compel "complete obedience to loving authority."
> Page 3A–4A: The Saturnian leader, Eviless, is shown variously bound with her hands behind her back and/or the Venus girdle around her waist, but despite these impediments, she cleverly plots to escape.
> Page 5A: Eviless escapes and immediately ties up her jailer, "Mistress" Mala.
> Page 6A: More tying up Mala (these things take time). There are

some scenes of prisoners begging not to be freed from their
Venus girdles.

Page 7A: There are lots of people in prison clothes on this page,
which I'm sure Marston enjoyed, but technically the narrative is
devoted to freeing people rather than putting them in chains.

8A–9A: After Eviless frees a bunch of supervillains, they all team
up to capture Wonder Woman's mother, Hippolyte, and of
course tie her up from head to toe. (Peter gives us a tall, half-
page dramatic panel to better see her in her full bondage glory.)
Then the villains paralyze all the other Amazons and put Venus
girdles on them (Marston loves paralysis).

10A: More business with Hippolyte tied up, compelled by Wonder
Woman's lasso to betray her daughter. Marston throws in some
begging and pleading to add spice.

11A: Not even a hint of bondage here, believe it or not.

12A: One villain (in male drag) tries to hypnotize Wonder Wom-
an, which is kinky but doesn't work. Finally, the villains show
Wonder Woman her mother tied up, causing her to surrender.
Then she is also tied up. End of chapter.

I could go on, but I think you get the idea. And just to underline this
wasn't simply a deathbed interest for Marston, figure 1 shows one of
the most arresting sequences from *Wonder Woman #18*, cover date of
July–August 1946 (page 10C). In case you can't quite parse the image,
or simply can't believe your eyes, what we have here is a minister dissolving into pink ectoplasmic ropes of phallic goo and binding Wonder Woman and the entire wedding party from top to toe. As Wonder
Woman says, "Even an Amazon can't break ectoplasm." It's difficult to
avoid wondering if Marston (who worked on this issue in collaboration with Joye Murchison) might not be imagining his ideal marriage
night here; what, after all, could be better than a good round of bondage tentacle sex? Certainly, Peter seems to have drawn the detached
ectoplasmic bit in the lower left with a kind of bulbous, frolicsome
trembling, redolent of suppressed cheer and passion.

Not surprisingly, many critics have looked at this sort of thing—
the bondage, the hypnosis, the mind-control girdles, the tentacle sex,
the bondage—and have concluded that Marston (and perhaps Peter as

FIGURE 1. *Wonder Woman #18* (1946)

well) had an unhealthy and decidedly unfeminist interest in our heroine. Douglas Wolk, for example, says that Wonder Woman was "very
specifically an excuse for stories about sexual domination and submission" and suggests that it was only in the 1970s that the character
became a vehicle for feminist content (98). Bradford Wright notes that
Marston tried to include positive messages for women but concludes
that "there was a lot in these stories to suggest that Wonder Woman was not so much a pitch to ambitious girls as an object for male
sexual fantasies and fetishes" (21). Harshest of all, perhaps, is Richard
Reynolds, who calls Marston's feminist pretensions disingenuous and
argues that the comic was actually "developed as a frank appeal to
male fantasies of sexual domination" (34). In his distaste, he echoes
Josette Frank, a member of the Child Study Association of America
and of the initial *Wonder Woman* advisory board, who pointed to
women wrestling wild boar and turning into cheetahs and concluded,
"Personally I would consider an out-and-out strip tease less unwholesome than this kind of symbolism" (qtd. in Valcour 107).

ONE OF THOSE ODD, PERHAPS UNFORTUNATE MEN

Ben Saunders insists, in his groundbreaking chapter on Wonder
Woman in *Do the Gods Wear Capes?* that these critics are misguided.
By looking closely at Marston's psychological writing, Saunders concludes that, in *Wonder Woman*, there is no necessary contradiction
between bondage and feminism. Instead, Saunders argues that for
Marston, women are superior to men precisely because they are more
loving and more submissive (62–63). Men must learn from women the
virtues of love and of submission. When they do, and when women
rule, the millennium will arrive (59).

I am very sympathetic to Saunders's argument and, indeed, in many
ways to Marston's, and I will explore both, in one form or another,
through most of this book. For the moment, however, I want to take
a slightly different tack and acknowledge the force of the criticisms
made by Wolk, Wright, Reynolds, and others. Saunders is clearly
correct when he points out (quite gently) that none of these writers
appears to have really engaged with the full extent of Marston's theories or (at least in Reynolds's case) even with the comics themselves
(57). Their reading is in many ways a superficial one. But superficial

readings are not necessarily wrong. These were after all comic books for children. Most of the original eight- to ten-year-old readers would not have been aware of Marston's psychological work.

In fact, we have evidence that at least one reader of *Wonder Woman* took the comics in precisely the way that Wolk, Wright, Reynolds, and Frank suggest. In 1943, a staff sergeant wrote to Marston to thank him for his Wonder Woman stories. He said, "I am one of those odd, perhaps unfortunate men who derive an extreme erotic pleasure from the mere thought of a beautiful girl, chained or bound, or masked, or wearing extreme high-heels or high-laced boots,—in fact, any sort of constriction or strain whatsoever. Your tales of *Wonder Woman* have fascinated me on account of this queer 'twist' in my psychological make-up" (qtd. in Bunn 94). Marston's publisher, M. C. Gaines, after seeing this letter, told Marston, "This is one of the things I've been afraid of without quite being able to put my finger on it" (qtd. in Bunn 94).

Gaines is not the only critic who has had trouble putting his finger on the really remarkably obvious. As I have already mentioned, Gloria Steinem has written a number of essays about Wonder Woman and feminism but never pointed out what struck our staff sergeant at once. Similarly, feminist comics scholar and Marston/Peter fan Trina Robbins insists that there was no more bondage in *Wonder Woman* than in any other comic from the period (a claim Hanley's research conclusively refutes). Robbins concludes unconvincingly that "some heroes get tied up more than others," which is no doubt true but seems to rather dance around the question of why that variation exists and why this hero in particular gets tied up with such frequency, variety, and enthusiasm (Robbins, *Great Women* 13). Moreover, as Saunders points out, it ignores the fact that Marston's narrative constantly centers bondage as a political theme and an evangelical good (58).[3]

The reason for this ringing round of reticence is obvious enough. The bondage aspects of *Wonder Woman* are embarrassing. They are embarrassing to a publisher who would like to think he is providing wholesome entertainment to children. They are embarrassing to feminists such as Steinem and Robbins who want to celebrate the comic's message of empowerment.[4] But, embarrassing or not, there it is . . . and there . . . and there . . . and, good lord, over there is he actually having a bunch of sorority girls tie up a female gorilla?

There is no way around it: Marston's bondage imagery is an obsession. More than that, it is a fetish, and men like the enthusiastic staff sergeant are going to consume it as such, yea, even unto the gorilla bondage (in *Wonder Woman #9*, 5A, if you must know). Thus, *Wonder Woman* provides images of constricted women (and even female apes) for men's sexual aggrandizement. The comic not only allows but encourages males—and females too—to take sensual pleasure in women's disempowerment. If feminism does not mean speaking out against that, what does it mean?

"THE MOST POPULAR FANTASY PERVERSION"

Many second-wave and radical feminists have asked this very question and have concluded, emphatically, that feminism must reject the sexualized subjugation of women. John Stoltenberg, for example, sees the "humiliation and exploitation, chaining and bondage" in gay pornography as embodying the "values that male supremacists [gay or straight] tend to have—taking, using, estranging, dominating—essentially sexual powermongering" (96). For Stoltenberg, bondage imagery such as that used in *Wonder Woman* validates and promotes an ethic of sexual dominance, teaching those who consume it to treat women as "utterly submissive masochists who enjoy pain and humiliation and who, if they are raped, enjoy it" (114). The mainstreaming of "sexualized beating, mutilation, bondage, dismemberment" is part of a process of "eroticized injustice," which, Stoltenberg believes, normalizes sexual violence against women (114).

Susan Brownmiller comes to similar conclusions in her classic 1975 feminist discussion of rape, *Against Our Will*. After a harrowing discussion of sexual assault in the slaveholding American South, Brownmiller says this:

> The master-slave relationship is the most popular fantasy perversion in the literature of pornography. The image of a scantily clothed slave girl, always nubile, always beautiful, always docile, who sinks to her knees gracefully and dutifully before her master, who stands with or without boots, with or without whip, is commonly accepted as a scene of titillating sexuality. From the slave harems of the Oriental potentate, celebrated in poetry and

dance, to the breathless description of light-skinned fancy wom-en, *de rigueur* in a particular genre of pulp historical fiction, the glorification of forced sex under slavery, institutional rape, has been a part of our cultural heritage, feeding the egos of men while subverting the egos of women—and doing irreparable damage to healthy sexuality in the process. The very words "slave girl" impart to many a vision of voluptuous sexuality redolent of perfumed gardens and soft music strummed on a lyre. Such is the legacy of male-controlled sexuality, under which we struggle. (169–170)

The adamant antiporn and antimasochism arguments made by Stoltenberg and Brownmiller have been challenged by many writers. As just one pertinent example, Lewis Call has argued that the bondage imagery in *Wonder Woman* is not violent but on the contrary empha-sizes consent, play, and equality in a way that directly challenges the nonconsensual, patriarchal sexualities that Stoltenberg decries (27).

For my part, I'd like to point out a perhaps unavoidable structural issue raised by Brownmiller's discussion of slave harems. Namely, in order to condemn the history of eroticized bondage, Brownmiller is forced, however briefly, to participate in it. In that paragraph about the evils of images of disempowerment, Brownmiller presents us with scantily clothed slave girls, with docile, exotic bodies, with boots and whips and nubile beauty. Indeed, toward the conclusion of the quoted passage, she directly acknowledges that, whether she will or no, her use of language means that she has no choice but to work to some degree in the genre she is rejecting. "The very words 'slave girl,'" as Brownmiller says, "impart to many a vision of voluptuous sexuality." To say the phrase is to participate in the narrative.

Brownmiller argues that this dilemma is due to the legacy of "male-controlled sexuality"—a legacy that she is struggling against. But struggle doesn't necessarily mean freedom, at least not instantly. Before you are free, you are not free. Or, to put it another way, there is no way to imagine liberating yourself from bondage without imagin-ing bondage, with all its connotations. Wonder Woman can't break her chains if she isn't tied up in chains in the first place.

In this context, it's interesting to note that Brownmiller acknowl-edges having had rape fantasies herself. She explains that as a girl she saw a World War I propaganda poster depicting a German Hun raping a beautiful woman, who stood for Belgium. Brownmiller explains,

> This was the middle of World War II, the German Army had marched through Belgium a second time, and I was a Jewish girl growing up in Brooklyn. I could not help but conclude that the Hun and the Nazi were the same and, therefore, I had to be Belgium. In the next year I fantasized myself to sleep at night with a strange tableau. A tall and handsome Nazi concentration camp guard stood near a barbed-wire fence. He did not menace me directly—after all, I had no idea what the actual menace involved. For my part, I lay there motionless, at a safe distance. I was terribly beautiful. (311)

Brownmiller goes on to say about this image, "[It] struck me as peculiar and dangerous even as I conjured it up, and I soon rooted it out of my fantasy life" (311). Such rootings are complicated endeavors, though, and I mean no disrespect to Brownmiller when I suggest that the little girl who fantasized confusedly about rape may have a causal relationship with the woman who spent four years of research and four hundred pages of prose anatomizing the ways in which rape has been used to systematically oppress and terrorize women. Similarly, it seems that there may be a link between that long-ago fantasy about Nazis and Belgium and the feminist who insisted, with such brilliance, that rape during wartime is not an accident or an unfortunate inevitability happening off to the side but is instead one of the central, hideous truths of war.[5] Brownmiller argues that *"The rape fantasy exists in women as a man-made iceberg. It can be destroyed—by feminism"* (322; italics in original). Her own prose, and her own fantasy, however, seem like they point to a more complicated conclusion. Imagining rape is not, or not only, a false consciousness that must be destroyed by feminism. It is also, or can be also, a feminist consciousness—a way of naming and thinking through oppression.

My aim here is not to exculpate Marston and Peter, nor is it to condemn Brownmiller. Rather, the point is that there can be a logic, or logics, to stories of masochism, bondage, and feminism and that there are various ways in which those stories can have something to offer to women and to feminists. To ignore the bondage in Marston and Peter, then, is to miss the comic's appeal not only to men but to women— and is also to ignore an important part of the feminist message.

There is no shortage of evidence that women are interested in nar- ratives of disempowerment, as well as narratives of empowerment. If you want examples, you need only look to the most popular female- oriented publishing megaphenomena of the past few years. In Stephe- nie Meyer's massively successful vampire-romance *Twilight* series, the heroine, Bella, is infatuated with a powerful, sexy, exciting vampire who also behaves like a controlling stalker, sneaking into her house at night to watch her sleep and disabling her truck to prevent her from seeing another male friend. In E.L. James's *Fifty Shades of Grey*, which was directly inspired by the *Twilight* books, Christian Grey not only behaves like a crazed control-freak stalker but also indoctrinates the hapless, virginal Ana into the joys of bondage and sexual discipline. Finally, in Suzanne Collins's dystopic-future *Hunger Games* series, the heroine, Katniss, is repeatedly, almost compulsively, subjected to sus- tained traumatic violence for the pleasure of a television audience and, by extension, of the readers.

Many writers have criticized *Twilight*, *The Hunger Games*, and *Fifty Shades of Grey* for their retrograde, unfeminist views.[6] And yet, if sales figures are any indication, these series—with their themes of trauma, control, and voyeurism—have connected strongly with the lives of girls and women. Perhaps, then, these themes matter to women, not because they don't understand their own lives but because they do. And perhaps *Wonder Woman* mattered to the girls who read it (and to the boys) not just because it showed liberation but because it showed disempowerment—a state of being that girls (and boys) often under- stand all too well.

ZOMBIE REVOLUTION

In thinking about the appeal of mass culture for women, a useful start- ing point is the writing of Tania Modleski. At various points, Modleski has identified two distinct ways of approaching pop-culture criticism. First, there is what I would call the "it's all good" approach, which assumes that popular works are automatically and necessarily libera- tory simply by virtue of their popularity or by virtue of the fact that we (whoever "we" may be) like them. Pop culture, in this view, is a heady, seething stew of subversive impulses—not only will the revolution be televised, but staring at the tube is itself a revolution. In an online interview at the *Lazy Scholar*, Modleski acidly paraphrases this view as "I enjoy *The Real Housewives of New Jersey*; I am a feminist; therefore the program must be feminist" ("Q&A").

On the other hand, there is what might be termed the "it's all bad" approach, which assumes that pop culture is debased crap or, from a more leftist perspective, that it is more or less deliberately manipulated in the interest of our hegemonic overlords. Individuals under capitalism, from this perspective, are little more than blind and drooling drones, ideologically programmed for political quietism, regressive gender roles, and endless consumption. The moldering, shopping zombies in George Romero's *Dawn of the Dead* are a metaphor for us all—though, presumably, that film too, as capitalist exploitation fodder, does not so much provide a critique as distract us from the real work of revolution. In these "tedious" discussions, Modleski says, mass art is generally opposed to high art, "thereby demonstrating the political and/ or aesthetic superiority of the latter" (*Loving with a Vengeance* 110).

The division here is perhaps best seen as a description of tendencies in scholarship rather than as hard and fast philosophies with firm adherents.[7] In *Loving with a Vengeance: Mass-Produced Fantasies for Women*, Modleski, for her part, prefers the it's-all-bad to the it's-all-good approach. As a result, defenders of the romance have criticized her for being overly negative.[8] Still, Modleski, like many writers on pop culture, ultimately tries to figure out a synthesis. Thus, she argues that mass culture for women is neither innately progressive nor innately repressive. Instead, for her, pop-culture narratives "both stimulate and allay social anxieties, both arouse and symbolically satisfy the 'properly imperishable' desires and fantasies of women" (19).

For Modleski, in other words, the literature she examines—Harlequin romances, gothic romances, and soap operas—appeal to women because they address and analyze women's problems and women's oppression. Or, as Sherrie Silman (from a more unambivalently pro-romance perspective) says, "Within romance literature are subtle and overt lessons about power, including representations of the strange lies that each gender is taught within the normalizing forces of tradition."

Because the novels consider power and oppression seriously, they are important and often insightful. This is the case even though romances and soap operas are rarely, in Modleski's view, directly subversive. They speak to and illuminate women's dilemmas under patriarchy, even if the solutions that Modleski feels they offer to those dilemmas (find the perfect man! buy more romances!) are not ones that she would endorse.[9] For Modleski, mass fantasies for women are not feminist parables. But they *are* a way to see what is going on in women's heads. Thus, she describes the typical plot of gothic romance:

> The heroine comes to a mysterious house, perhaps as a bride, perhaps in another capacity, and either starts to mistrust her husband or else finds herself in love with a mysterious man who appears to be some kind of criminal. She may suspect him of having killed his first wife . . . or of being out to kill someone else, most likely herself. She tries to convince herself that her suspicions are unfounded, that, since she loves him, he must be trustworthy and that she will have failed as a woman if she does not implicitly believe in him. Often, but not always, the man is proven innocent of all wrongdoing by the end of the novel, and the real culprit is discovered and punished. (*Loving* 51–52)

For Modleski, to simplify somewhat, this narrative points to the basic untrustworthiness of men in patriarchy. In the gothic, women are victims—and women in real life are victims. In the gothic, women are in the power of men—and in real life, women are, in fact, in the power of men. The analysis is correct, even if the comforting conclusion (the loved one is innocent; true love triumphs) is not.

As I said, this is a simplified version of Modleski's argument. Her actual discussion of the gothic is significantly more subtle than this one-to-one analogy suggests. For instance, Modleski points out that, while men in patriarchy are often untrustworthy, they "are *not* often lunatics and murderers" (53). The gothic is paranoid—and Modleski argues that it is that paranoia itself that is true to women's experience. In particular, she singles out social isolation as a major contributing factor in paranoia. She argues that the gothic was established in the eighteenth century, at a time when at least middle- and upper-middle-class women were becoming more isolated in their husbands' homes, as well as significantly more idle (54). Thus, the gothic mirrors a reality in which social changes and patriarchal demands were placing some women in a situation of increasing powerlessness. The hyperbolic dangers of the genre are false when applied to individual men (who are mostly not murderers or lunatics). But they express a truth about the social order in which men and women exist: a social order in which patriarchal power can, and often does, appear both rapacious and overwhelming.

Again, this is not the end of Modleski's analysis, and I'll discuss a number of her other insights in the remainder of this chapter. However, the point I want to emphasize here is that even Modleski, who is skeptical about the value of mass literature, does not take that skepticism as grounds for blanket dismissal. The fact that *Wonder Woman* is about sex and submission does not mean that it is worthless, just as the fact that romance is (arguably) about sex and submission does not mean (even for Modleski) that it lacks insight, feminist and otherwise. With that in mind, I'd like to return now to the Marston/Peter *Wonder Woman* and specifically to the story of theirs that adopts the most elements from the gothic. As it happens, this is also, in my opinion, the high point of Marston and Peter's run and one of the strangest, most beautiful, and most moving comics I've ever read. The issue is *Wonder Woman #16*, titled "In Pluto's Kingdom," with a cover date of March–April 1946. It was co-written by Joye Murchison.[10]

SUPERHERO GOTHIC

As is typical of Harry Peter's covers, *Wonder Woman #16* is colorful and optimistic. Pluto is represented as a white-haired, flamboyantly bushy-eye-browed, hairy-legged man looking over his shoulder in surprise as Wonder Woman lassoes him and pulls him from his magnificent, leaping black horse. Pluto is shown in his moment of defeat; his butt is in the air and his feet are higher than his head. He looks ridiculous. To make his plight even sillier, Peter has so positioned him that his trident looks like the pole of a merry-go-round, and the circle at the end of it seems to be fastened to the horse. Rather than a dark and powerful god, Pluto ends up looking like a silly, naughty boy who won't come in from the playground. You half expect Wonder

FIGURE 2.
*Wonder
Woman* #16
(1946)

Woman to spank him when she gets ahold of him. The cover suggests
that Pluto is not a real threat and that the comic will include adventure, excitement, and (naturally) bondage but no real danger. In fact,
though, *Wonder Woman* #16 is perhaps the darkest comic that Marston, Murchison, and Peter ever created.

    As was so often the case with early *Wonder Woman*, the story here is anchored in Greek myth. In this instance, the story focuses on one of the many Greek narratives of gendered violation: the rape of Persephone.[11] According to the myth, Persephone, daughter of Demeter, is kidnapped by Pluto, separated from her mother, and dragged down to the underworld to be his queen. Marston, obsessively concerned with themes of female empowerment and disempowerment, chose with Murchison to focus this story on the signal myth linking sexual violence to abandonment, powerlessness, and despair.

On page 4A of the comic, the creators provide a two-panel synopsis of the Greek narrative. This retelling, thanks in large part to Peter's art, is pervaded by a feeling of overripe wrongness. In the first panel, Persephone is shown kneeling amid expressively undulating, mostly red-tipped flowers. She clutches a bouquet in her left arm as her right hand reaches out in a claw to pick a demurely nodding yellow bud. She has not seen Pluto yet, but his shadow lies across her; the darkness turns her red skirt to a dark, bloody crimson. Off to the side, Persephone's three companions flee, shouting to her to escape. They are placed against a background without horizon line, so that ground and sky merge into a single flat yellow; the figures almost seem to be running suspended in space. Coupled with the angled shadow, the entire image ends up looking disjointed and disconnected, as if Persephone has been cut loose from the earth.

This sensation is only heightened in the next panel, where Peter's idiosyncratic use of perspective turns the scene into a depthless funhouse. Pluto, positioned at an angle to the panel's lower left corner, grasps Persephone in one arm. Her top half seems too small, and her legs even smaller, so she dwindles in his grasp. She throws her right arm out in terror, her left hand still sadly, instinctively clutching her bouquet. Off to the right, in close-up, is a squiggly, monstrous, red, and suggestively feminine flower that would make Georgia O'Keefe blush. Further back in the image, a team of weirdly tiny, black horses pull a curved chariot with a black interior like a pit. Peter has placed a few swift motion lines to suggest Pluto's movement, but because he dominates the scene and because his exact motion is ambiguous, they end up making the whole image appear to twist and rotate. "Lovely one, you shall bring light to dark Hades," Pluto declares, and against

FIGURE 3. *Wonder Woman #16* (1946)

the disorienting background, every courtly word sounds like a death knell. Perhaps the most telling detail in the panel, though, is what is left out. Only Pluto gets a speech bubble—Persephone's mouth is open, but no sound emerges. There could not be a more eloquent way of saying that she is completely in his power and already in hell.

In the comic, the story of Persephone is a flashback. It is related by Aphrodite to Wonder Woman and her mother, Hippolyte. Aphrodite also tells the two women that the rape of Persephone was not an isolated event. Pluto is still around, and he is still kidnapping and abusing women. In particular, he has abducted a Holliday college girl named Lorrie, whose kidnapping opens the comic. As we have seen, Persephone's abduction is presented in an almost surreal dreamscape. Lorrie's fate, on the other hand, is in a much more conventional melodramatic register. We first see her in the inset of the splash page. She is in bed, a shaft of light illuminating her, the covers pulled childishly up to her face as she shrieks, "Eeek! Go away from me! Help!" On the next page, the other Holliday girls, led by Etta, rush in to aid her. She insists, "a giant shrouded in black reached for me!" (2A). She goes on to describe a classic gothic scene: "He came in a jet-black chariot drawn by four black horses, leaped through my window, and stood over me with an enormous pitchfork!"

The other girls, though, are not convinced. Instead of believing Lorrie, they behave like parents whose child has had a nightmare. Etta tucks Lorrie in and tells her she must have been dreaming. Lorrie's reaction to this dismissal is hyperbolic. In the center panel of the page, she breaks down in tears, one hand clutching her blue blanket, the other dabbing at her eye. "No one 'sob' cares what happens to me anyway. When Dad 'sob' learns I've flunked my exams, he'll disown me. No one would even care 'sob' if I was kidnapped! 'Sob' I wish 'sob' I were dead!" Etta pooh-poohs her, standing at the door like a diminutive mother and assuring her that everything will be "kopasetic in the morning!" But it is not. When they come into her room the next day, she is gone, and all that is left behind is a trident so heavy that Etta can't pick it up.

As I said earlier, Tania Modleski links gothic romances for women to anxieties about the disempowerment of marriage. From that perspective, Lorrie's panic could be seen as a paranoid reaction to a wedding, a fear of leaving the world of mother and female friendships for the uncertain and darker realm of the husband and patriarch. While wife-husband tensions may be in play to some extent here, though, I think the comic as a whole is focused on some of the other possibilities of the gothic. In particular, I think Lorrie's kidnapping is a very thinly disguised metaphor for incest.

Father-daughter incest was in fact one of the prevalent themes in gothic novels aimed at adolescent girls. According to James Twitchell in *Forbidden Partners: The Incest Taboo in Modern Culture*, "the iso-lated female protagonist and the isolating older male" are two of the staples of the gothic romance genre. Twitchell elaborates:

> The ingénue is often orphaned or of mysterious parentage, always virginal, adolescent, and sensitive. In confinement, she is con-fronted with this older man, perhaps a wanderer, priest, landlord, robber, noble, or even a creature from another world. . . . He is driven by desire, sexual desire which he may or may not be able to control. In either case, he does not *want* to control this desire. He is rarely ashamed of himself or of his actions. He is almost totally unselfconscious. Often he is more than capricious. He is demonic and evil precisely because he enjoys these illicit desires, these unmentioned urges, precisely because he has refused to sublimate. What becomes progressively obvious, as you con-sume more and more of these novels, is that this central relation-ship is essentially that of father-daughter from *both* their points of view. (148)

Twitchell's description fits the narrative in *Wonder Woman* #16. Pluto is an old, white-bearded man, capriciously driven by desire. His victims are young innocents. And the father-daughter intimations are perhaps even more explicit than in the gothic novels Twitchell dis-cusses. When Persephone is abducted, Peter's haphazard foreshorten-ing makes her look tiny, as if Pluto is carrying a child.

Even more telling, when Lorrie breaks down and weeps like a baby, her mind instantly turns to her unsympathetic, punishing father. Daddy is going to hurt her, and no one cares—not even Mama Etta, who doesn't believe her story. And if any doubt remains that this is a

FIGURE 4. *Wonder Woman* #16 (1946)

narrative about abuse, you can skip ahead a few pages to one of Peter's large dramatic panels in which Wonder Woman and the Holliday girls, after traveling to the planet Pluto to rescue Lorrie, plunge through a crack in the ice (9A). As they fall down, "black sinister hands," disconnected from any visible body, reach up and grab hold of them, spinning them round and round. The underworld is seen as a vision of manipulation and disorientation, of being handled against your will. As with Persephone, the Holliday girls and Wonder Woman have their mouths open, but no sound comes out. They may be screaming, but nobody hears them.

As Modleski said, when the gothic is taken as a metaphor for marriage, or for the behavior of men or lovers in general, it seems paranoid and hysterical. All men are not rapists, and (though Modleski does not say this specifically) all men certainly do not have the kind of fearsome dark power that lurks in the more vampiric reaches of gothic storytelling. However, when the gothic is connected to incest, as in the Marston/Murchison/Peter story, both the paranoia and the massive power disparities become less unbelievable and more uncomfortably apt. Elizabeth Ward in *Father-Daughter Rape*, for example, quotes one incest survivor as stating, "I felt that it wasn't only sex, it was my whole life he had control over" (13). Lorrie's over-the-top reaction to being disbelieved—"'Sob' I wish 'sob' I were dead!"—may seem like typical comic-book melodramatic silliness at first. But it looks somewhat different if Lorrie is an incest survivor begging for, and not receiving, help.

Lorrie's hyperbolic reaction would not have been a surprise to at least one researcher: Sigmund Freud. In fact, in his 1896 essay "The Aetiology of Hysteria," Freud addressed the essentially melodramatic or excessive nature of trauma reactions: "The reaction of hysterics is only apparently exaggerated; it is bound to appear exaggerated to us because we only know a small part of the motives from which it arises" (278; italics in original). Freud argued that "at the bottom of every case of hysteria there are *one or more occurrences of premature sexual experience*" (263). Further, Freud made it clear that this "premature sexual experience" amounted to violent rape. As he said, such experiences involved

> on the one hand the adult, who cannot escape his share in the mutual dependence necessarily entailed by a sexual relationship, and who is yet armed with complete authority and the right to punish . . . and on the other hand the child, who in his [sic] helplessness is at the mercy of this arbitrary will, who is prematurely aroused to every kind of sensibility and exposed to every sort of disappointment. . . . All these grotesque and yet tragic incongruities reveal themselves as stamped upon the later development of the individual and of his [sic] neurosis. (276)

Freud summed up his view in a December 22, 1897, letter to his close friend Wilhelm Fliess, saying that the "new motto" for psychoanalysis should be "What has been done to you, you poor child?" (Freud, *Complete Letters* 289). This is a motto that *Wonder Woman #16* emphatically agrees with.

FREUD OF FUTURE PAST

It appears, then, that Marston, Murchison, and Peter shared much common ground with Freud in their approach to incest. Or at least they did until Freud changed his mind. That reversal had major impli-cations for psychoanalysis. It also illuminates ongoing debates in our culture about sexuality and violence and underlines the uniqueness of *Wonder Woman #16*'s achievement. To understand what's at stake, it's necessary to examine Freud's theories about incest, and the controver-sies surrounding them, at some length.

To start with, as I've said, in the essay "The Aetiology of Hyste-ria," Freud argued that adult hysteria was caused by childhood sexual abuse. This theory is usually referred to as the "seduction theory," though "rape theory" seems like it would be more appropriate. In any case, whatever it is called, the theory was extremely controversial, both at the time and since. Jeffrey Moussaieff Masson argues in his own much-contested book *The Assault on Truth* that the German psychiat-ric and medical establishment was horrified at Freud's findings—not because of the revelation of rape but because of the accusation of it. Doctors, Masson says, had no intention of letting sick women accuse well-respected men—their patrons and friends—of perversion and brutality (134–138). Freud was repudiated and isolated, and eventually, in what Masson believes was "a loss of courage," he reversed himself (134). In a September 21, 1897, letter to Wilhelm Fliess, Freud declared that "surely such widespread perversions against children are not very probable" (*Complete Letters* 264). Freud cited no new evidence; he had simply decided to stop believing in abuse. Instead, he eventu-ally concluded that it was not fathers who lusted after their daughters but daughters who lusted after their fathers. No real rape occurred; instead, daughters were fantasizing about sex with their fathers and mistaking the fantasies for reality. Or, as Etta tells Lorrie in *Wonder Woman #16*, "You're either dreamin' babe or nuts!" (2A)[12]

Freud's decision to treat incest as fantasy in his later work is espe-cially striking because of the rhetoric of "The Aetiology of Hysteria," in which he set out his seduction theory. Again and again through-out the paper, initially delivered as a lecture, he anticipates his audi-ence's skepticism. After telling them that hysteria is based in sexual experience, he notes, "From previous experience, I can foresee that it is precisely against this assertion or against its universal validity that your contradiction, Gentlemen, will be directed" (259). Later he asks rhetorically, on his audience's behalf, "Is it not very possible either that the physician forces such scenes upon his docile patient, alleging that they are memories, or else that the patients tell the physicians things which they have deliberately invented or have imagined and that he accepts those things as true?" (264). He then goes on to cite his clinical experience and especially to point out instances in which he says his diagnosis of early rape was confirmed by other evidence.

Thus, Freud, as Masson argues, seems to have already anticipated and answered his own future objections. "The Aetiology of Hysteria" ends up sounding for all the world as if Freud is arguing against his future self—as if future Freud has fallen backward in time, back to the day before past Freud, so that his predecessor had to try to negate him before he even existed.

Nor is the argument through time confined simply to Freud's past and present. As I mentioned earlier, the argument around "The Aetiology of Hysteria" has continued unabated and remains extremely contentious. Masson, as noted, has taken the position of early Freud, arguing for incest as the basis of trauma. Other writers such as Allen Esterson, however, have insisted that, while some of Freud's patients did say they were abused, most did not (16). Instead, Esterson says, in most cases, Freud diagnosed abuse on the basis of patients' symptoms and then pressured them into "remembering" (3). Esterson also disputes Masson's contention that Freud's findings were received with horror by the medical community or that Freud was pressured to change them (12).

Esterson's arguments do call into question the certainty of Masson's conclusions. But it is interesting that, as David H. Gleaves and Elsa Hernandez state, Esterson's arguments are "similar to the original reaction that Freud received" (324)—the reaction that Freud responded to in advance. The debate about abuse seems doomed to repeat itself backward for all eternity.

This conflation of chronology, the way that future and past wrap around each other into an inseparable jumble, recalls Freud's own description of the intertwined chains of trauma and memory from "The Aetiology of Hysteria":

> If we take a case which presents several symptoms, we arrive by means of the analysis, starting from each symptom, at a series

of experiences the memories of which are linked together in association. . . . From a single scene, two or more memories are reached at the same time, and from these again side-chains proceed. . . . In short, the concatenation is far from being a simple one; and the fact that the scenes are uncovered in reverse chronological order . . . certainly contributes nothing to a more rapid understanding of what has taken place. (258)

For Freud, you do not experience trauma and then experience symptoms. Rather, you experience trauma, and that trauma spreads out throughout your life, not just as a single memory but as a web of memories. As a result, the future often occurs, in some sense, before the past—A then B then C then A again and then C then B—so time is constantly tying itself into a knot of trauma. Freud suggests that the role of the analyst is not so much to undo the chronological jumble as to codify it into a narrative in which the ending precedes the beginning. The analyst uncovers the truth in reverse, so that the past only becomes visible in the future. You do not put the trauma behind you; rather, you hurtle toward it. And when it is at last before you, Freud maintains, you can confront it. Though Freud's own backward-talking cure, in which he first uncovered trauma and then (or previously?) convinced himself to forget, suggests that the knots he sought to untie may have been even more tangled than he was willing to admit—as does Esterson's argument that at least some of the fantasies Freud was confronting were his own rather than his patients'.

Marston/Murchison/Peter, on the other hand, seem to have understood the tangle very well. They also understood Freud's dictum that hysteria appears exaggerated because we do not know its motives—or perhaps more precisely, because its motives are chronologically displaced. Thus, as discussed, on the second page of the comic, Lorrie, who has seen something in her bedroom, has a panicked and even ridiculous reaction, in which she worries that her father will disown her for failing her exams and prays for death. It is only *after* her outburst that she is justified, first, by her disappearance, second, perhaps, by the intimations that she is responding (metaphorically? diegetically?) to incest, and, third, by the actual image of her kidnapping, placed later in the story, when Wonder Woman and her mother look back through time using a magic sphere (5A).

However, Lorrie is only the beginning—or possibly (if we see the story as specifically about her trauma) the end. Either way, the sequence of hysteria followed by (rather than preceded by) trauma is repeated over and over again throughout the comic. Wonder Woman brings the trident left in Lorrie's room to the goddess Aphrodite—and Aphrodite, the calm, all-powerful goddess of love, freaks out. "How darest thou encroach upon the love sanctity of my temple by bringing the fate fork of King Pluto, vicious ruler of the dark planet," she shouts. It's only after this inexplicable outburst that she narrates the rape of Persephone (3A). Persephone's silent scream, then, is displaced backward several panels; through Aphrodite, she voices her terror before she is terrified. The trauma occurred before it occurred.

This pattern repeats throughout the comic. On page 7A, Etta accidentally launches a rocket to Pluto with herself and the other Holliday girls inside. Steve is generally a heroic sort, fairly calm under pressure, but in this instance, he, like Aphrodite before him and like Lorrie before *her*, completely loses his cool. We are given a close-up panel specifically to watch the hero dissolve into helpless terror. Peter shows Steve with his head tilted back and his hand raised toward his face in a familiar gesture of overwhelmed Victorian femininity. Sweat drips from his brow, his mouth and eyes are agape, and his eyebrows slide expressively across his forehead in an elegant agony of terror. Steve's reaction, then, is stereotypically hysterical. And though it takes a while, it, too, is eventually linked to a traumatic cause. Toward the end of the comic, Steve, who was left on Earth while Wonder Woman went to Pluto to help the Holliday girls, is still berating himself. He sits at the desk in his small office, where, thanks to Peter, all the angles are askew—and through the window, one hairy leg extended, comes Pluto, to bear Steve away just as he once took Persephone (4C).

Marston, Murchison, and Peter make a peculiar storytelling choice here (5C). Instead of staying with Steve and Pluto, where the action is, the perspective shifts outside the office, where Steve's secretary hears a struggle through the intercom. She opens the door to investigate. And then, on the next page, she sees Pluto leaving through the window, with the unconscious Steve over his shoulder. The desk falls over as

Pluto leaves, and Peter shows it tipping with a semicircular motion line. The motion line, however, intersects the secretary's head, so that it seems to be indicating her dizziness or her panic or even suggesting that the desk itself is hurtling toward her. In the next panel, Steve's boss, Major Darnell, rushes in, and the secretary tells him what's happened.

And then in the next panel, Wonder Woman shows up. Darnell is hugging the secretary to comfort her, and Wonder Woman (who has after all seen a lot of semi-incestuous sexualized violence in the preceding pages) clearly thinks she's stumbled on an illicit tryst. Darnell reassures her, though: "Oh—uh—Wonder Woman! Ahem—Steve's secretary is hysterical—she imagined she saw Steve being kidnapped." And then the secretary tells her story *again*, this time in a full close-up reminiscent of Steve's hysterical moment. Like Steve, her hand is raised toward her face; like him, her mouth and eyes gape—though she cries where Steve sweated. She's even blond like Steve, her hair spun into tight whorls of stylized anxiety as she looks straight out at the reader, her dialogue punctuated by sobs just as the also blond Lorrie's was at the beginning of the story.

Narratively, there is not much reason to have the secretary there at all; surely Wonder Woman (who was racing back to protect Steve from Pluto) could have figured out what was going on without the secretary's panicked (re)recitation. But thematically, the secretary is necessary because we are talking about uncovering trauma, and for that you need not only the rape but also the witness to the rape—not only the (child) abuse but also the traumatized child-adult left behind.

OEDIPUS AND PERSEPHONE

The secretary in *Wonder Woman #16* perhaps serves another purpose as well. By having her echo, and even adopt, Steve's trauma, she emphasizes the fact that, despite his male body, his trauma is structurally linked to Persephone's and Lorrie's. His kidnapping is not just a kidnapping; it is also (metaphorically) rape and incest. Though he is a man, he is (as many male children are) the violated, not the violator. It's as if the creators are trying to make sure that any male readers do not switch allegiances as Freud did. In this context, it seems especially important that Darnell—humorously, but still—is shown as a potential sexual aggressor or transgressor at the same moment that he denies the truth of his secretary's story. In fact, this sequence of substitutions can be seen as an almost deliberate undermining of Freud's progress/regression in his dealings with incest. Most commenters agree that Freud's central insights, the major edifice of psychoanalysis, came about because of Freud's rejection of his seduction/rape theory. In a letter to Masson, which he quotes in his book, Anna Freud—who believes Freud was right to reject the seduction theory—insists that if Freud retained the seduction theory, he would have had "to abandon the Oedipus complex, and with it the whole importance of phantasy life, conscious or unconscious phantasy. In fact, . . . there would have been no psychoanalysis afterwards" (113).

Thus, at first Freud believed his patients were abused. Later, he decided that they were not. If there was no abuse, he had to figure out why they had sexual memories. He decided that they had those memories because they had sexual fantasies—fantasies that seemed to start very early in life. This indicated that very young children had sexual desires. Contemplating infantile sexuality in turn led to the male-centered Oedipal drama, in which the son lusts after the mother, precipitating the trauma of (fantasy) castration. Or, to sum up:

- Fathers do not rape.
- Daughters must want to be raped.
- Children are sexual.
- Children must be guilty and fear being punished for their sexuality.
- Sons worry about castration.

When Freud's logic is reduced to this schematic form, one of the most startling things about it is the way that concern for the trauma of daughters (and of some sons), which Freud originally saw as central to psychoanalysis, is, without any real explanation, replaced by concern for the trauma of sons alone. As Elizabeth Ward says, "The 'sexual shock' of girl-children (like the fate of Jocasta) has by this stage been quite forgotten as Freud reels under the existential agonies of his (the Father's) frustrated desire for his mother" (112). Ward is correct that girls have been forgotten, but, as Freud should know better than anyone, forgotten does not necessarily mean gone. The trauma of incest may be denied, but that doesn't mean it has disappeared. On the contrary, I would argue that the plight of female victims becomes the displaced emotional center of Freud's edifice—the anguish fueling the otherwise fairly ridiculous male whining about not being able to have intercourse with everything and everybody, up to and including the mother.

One of the main ways in which Marston, Murchison, and Peter diverge from (later) Freud is that they insist on making childhood incest about the iconically feminized (though not solely female) experience of rape, rather than about the iconically masculine experience of the Oedipal complex. This is perhaps most clear, paradoxically, when Marston, Murchison, and Peter confront male trauma. In the scene in which Steve is abducted, we see Pluto standing over his victim with his great trident raised, one of its two prongs pointed at Steve's head. "Your time has come earthling! King Pluto has come for you!" the patriarch declares, as if it is a moment that Steve has been waiting for all his life (4C). Given the giant pointy weapon, the sense of an intimate encounter long anticipated, and the fact that Pluto has come after Steve specifically to revenge the loss of his female slaves, it seems pretty clear that this is an Oedipal castration scene. The Holliday girls and Wonder Woman have escaped; Pluto will punish Steve and prevent the son from having what is rightfully the father's.

But, as I noted before, structurally this castration scene is an imitation of, or an echo of, the father-daughter rape of Persephone and of Lorrie. This link is further emphasized, again, by the manner in which Steve's secretary becomes the voice of his trauma. For Marston, Murchison, and Peter—as surreptitiously for Freud—castration is a secondary male reworking of an essentially female primal scene. Whereas Freud went on to erase the female prototype, though, Marston, Murchison, and Peter insist on remembering it. When fathers commit violence against sons, Marston, Murchison, and Peter say, they are simply treating sons the way that, historically, daughters have always been treated. If castration anxiety is horrible, it is because it causes men to feel what women have long known—the terror of disempowerment and of sexualized brutality. Castrated, Steve joins a painful sisterhood.

Joining the sisterhood, though, does not mean leading it. Marston,

Murchison, and Peter take some care to indicate that, contra Freud, Steve's castration is not *more* important than father-daughter rape. Rather, the castration is understandable and articulable only through the history and experience of violence against women. If child rape (of boys as well as of girls) is to be taken seriously, then the experience of girls must be taken seriously. If girls are not allowed to speak, then boys who have experiences statistically and culturally linked to girls will not be allowed to speak either. This is why, in *Wonder Woman #16*, the secretary must find Steve and tell his story. It is also why the narrative takes care to show that, despite patriarchal disbelief, what the secretary says about patriarchal violence is true. If Steve's trauma is to be validated, the female voice telling it has to be validated as well. Freud, like the father himself, treats the daughter as his property—he uses her to assuage his own desires and to suit his own purposes. Marston, Murchison, and Peter, on the other hand, insist that the daughter's experiences be recognized, that both men and women, sons and daughters, must place themselves with the (female) victim, not the rapist, with the (female) child, not the father. For Marston, Murchison, and Peter, it is not the blinded Oedipus who is universal. It is the Persephone he refuses to see.

MOTHER DOUBLES

Marston, Murchison, and Peter, then, want men to be women, not patriarchs. Moreover, by upending traditional gender identifications, they are directly challenging the logic of incest and rape.

The link between patriarchy, gender identification, and incest is also central to Julia Herman and Lisa Hirschman's groundbreaking study *Father-Daughter Incest*. First published in 1981, the book continues to be cited and used to understand why incest occurs and what effect it has on victims.[13] Moreover, I believe, Herman and Hirschman share with Marston, Murchison, and Peter a focus on, and sympathy with, victims and an explicit feminism. As a result, Herman and Hirschman's book is a useful lens through which to view and think about what Marston, Murchison, and Peter are doing, and vice versa.

One of the most striking ways in which Herman and Hirschman's feminism colors their analysis is in their evaluation and discussion of abusers. On the basis of their research with incest victims, Herman and Hirschman argue that incestuous families do not pervert traditional family structures but rather follow them through to their logical culmination.

> Whereas male supremacy creates the social conditions that favor the development of father-daughter incest, the sexual division of labor creates the psychological conditions that lead to the same result. Male supremacy invests fathers with immense powers over their children, especially their daughters. The sexual division of labor, in which women nurture children and men do not, produces fathers who are predisposed to use their powers exploitatively. The rearing of children by subordinate women ensures the reproduction in each generation of the psychology of male supremacy. It produces sexually aggressive men with little capacity to nurture, nurturant women with undeveloped sexual capacities, and children of both sexes who stand in awe of the power of fathers. (62)

Thus, Herman and Hirschman argue, incestuous families are not unusual families but hyperusual ones. Fathers in these families do not fail in their roles as head of the household; rather, they are "perfect patriarchs," who are generally perceived as good, competent providers, respected both at work and in the community (71).

Like these incestuous fathers, *Wonder Woman #16*'s Pluto—king of the underworld, raper of Persephone—is a kind of superpatriarch, master of all he surveys. In one telling panel, for example, Peter shows the white-bearded, grotesquely grinning king seated on his throne. He holds the shaft of his trident in one hand and an apple in the other, while all around him multicolored, glowing women in diaphanous gowns offer him trays of fruit or pour wine into his glass (5B). Pluto appears, then, as both despot and despoiler, receiving from a plethora of younger, radiant women domestic ministrations that are also, as the none-too-subtle apple indicates, sexual favors. Just to emphasize the point, in the next panel, we see the apple in the foreground with a bite taken out of it, clutched in Pluto's swollen, hairy, too-large hand.

Pluto's patriarchal powers go beyond the mere physical, however. They extend into the very selves of the women he controls. Again, after the Holliday girls and Wonder Woman arrive on Pluto, the king of the realm sends his trident to break the ice on which they stand. They fall into a chasm under the ice and are grabbed by black hands that spin them "round and round," as the text says (9A; see figure 4). Then, in the next panel, "Suddenly another weird phenomenon occurs—the color is drained from Wonder Woman, forming a color body and leaving her physical form entirely black." You can just imagine Peter reading that description and thinking, "How the heck am I going to draw that?" But he does his best. In a narrow panel, we see Wonder Woman at full length suspended in the air, with spinning motion lines curled all around her. Behind her, there are a series of jagged, incongruous multicolored flashes of lightning: pink, yellow, orange. Wonder Woman herself is a pale orange. She also looks remarkably calm: her head turned to one side, her body forming a subtle s, her legs together. The overall effect is of a diva illuminated by a spotlight, the motion lines suggesting a controlled pirouette even as they hug her like a shimmering gown.

The image is so striking that you can almost miss the uncanny touch in the lower right. There we see Wonder Woman's shadow—but its pose is wrong. Wonder Woman's arms are both at her side, but the shadow has one arm raised; Wonder Woman's legs are both together, but the shadow's are spread apart, its body tipping backward as if it is about to fall. The truth is that this is not a shadow at all but, as the caption says, a body drained of light. There are two Wonder Women—one illumined and radiant, rising up; one dark and almost unnoticed, tumbling down.

Again, Pluto's caricatured patriarchal power is consistent with the theme of incest. His ability to affect the bodies and souls of the women in his control can be seen as an extension of that power. But still—light bodies? Dark shadow bodies? What does any of this have to do with rape or abuse or incest?

It is possible that the story is simply incoherent; maybe Marston and Murchison just thought up the light-body/dark-body split and threw it in for the hell of it. Before dismissing the imagery, though, I think it is worth remembering that doubling—the encounter with another or second self—is a characteristic theme of the gothic. Since incest is also a common gothic trope, it seems like there should be a way to read, or think about, gothic doubling in terms of gothic incest. For a start, let's go back to Tania Modleski's discussion of the gothic romance. In *Loving with a Vengeance*, Modleski talks a great deal about gothic doubling and relates it to Freud's notion of the uncanny. For Freud, Modleski says, the uncanny is linked to castration anxiety and/or repetition. Since women are, according to Freud, not subject to castration anxiety, that should mean that women do not experience the uncanny in its full intensity. But, Modleski points out, gothic romances for women (such as *Wonder Woman #16*) are filled nigh to bursting with uncanny doubling; the heroines can't spit without hitting themselves. The prevalence of the theme of doubling indicates that Freud, in linking the uncanny to castration, was suffering (as happened not infrequently) from gendered confusion. But if the uncanny is not about fear of castration, then what is it about?

Modleski offers an answer. She points out that doubling in the gothic generally involves a woman from the past who has suffered. "Usually [the heroine] feels a strong identification with a woman from either the remote or the very recent past, a woman who in almost every case has died a mysterious and perhaps violent or gruesome death" (*Loving* 61). The doubling is, then, a doubling through time, a link between an older woman and a younger woman—a mother and a daughter. Thus, Modleski reasons,

> It is not only that women fear being *like* their mothers, sharing the same fate, but also that, in an important sense, they fear *being* their mothers—hence the emphasis on identity in physical appearance, the sensation of actually being possessed, the feeling that past and present are not merely similar but are "intertwined," etc. In each case, the heroine feels suffocated—as well as desperate and panic stricken in her inability to break free of the past. (62)

Modleski goes on to suggest that Freud's castration fear is "part of a deeper fear"—specifically the fear of not separating from the mother, of not becoming an autonomous individual. Boys fear castration because they fear it will make them like their mothers; "castration is perceived as threatening in part because it would deny this difference"

(63). Girls, though, have no anatomical difference to separate them-selves from their mothers—and, indeed, in patriarchal society, they are expected, unlike sons, to repeat in their own lives their mother's claustrophobic experiences of service, childrearing, and disempower-ment. Thus, Modleski concludes, "If my speculations are correct and the uncanny has its chief source in separation anxiety, then it follows that since women have more difficulty establishing a separate self, their sense of the uncanny may actually be stronger than men's" (63). In a tour de force, Modleski uses her interpretation to connect Freud's two sources of the uncanny, arguing that both doubling and repetition point to a helpless backward slide, an involuntary return to the mother and a consequent loss of self.

You could perhaps make Marston/Murchison/Peter's gothic tale fit into Modleski's interpretation with a bit of work. After all, as I've already (repeatedly?) discussed, the narrative includes relentless rep-etition. Persephone, Lorrie, Steve, and the secretary relive the same hysteria and the same trauma. The mythic victim Persephone, then, could be seen as a kind of ur-victimized mother, whose inescapable fate both sons and daughters are doomed to helplessly recall. The shadow body in this reading could be Persephone or the mother, the dark fate that looms beside every light daughter.

In the end, though, while Modleski's analysis may make sense for the gothic romances that she studied, I think there are problems with extending it to a gothic incest story such as *Wonder Woman #16*. In the first place, Modleski is essentially locating uncanniness in the mother; it is from the mother that both boys and girls want to escape. In the context of an incest narrative, Modleski would then be suggesting that abused children are more afraid of their mothers than they are of the fathers who are abusing them. That seems confused.

Another problem is that, as noted earlier, there is good reason to think that, in the historical development of male castration anxiety as a concept, it was a distortion or projection of the trauma caused by abuse of girls. The fear of castration, from this perspective, is, like hysteria, not hyperbolic. On the contrary, the uncanniness in *Won-der Woman #16* seems decidedly muted if it is seen as a stand-in for actual sexual abuse. Freud rejected the idea that his patients had been assaulted; castration anxiety was a way to explain their anxiety, their fear, and their sense of wrongness. Modleski similarly tries to explain the paranoia of gothic romances by looking to a fear of a lack of autonomy. But Marston, Murchison, and Peter's narrative suggests (as Freud did at first) that the anxiety, the fear, and the sense of wrongness are linked, not to inner emotional events but to real physical threat. Children—boys or girls—who fear that powerful forces will harm them are not making things up. The powerful forces called "adults" sometimes do just that. Moreover, the fact that adults (and especially fathers) sometimes really do harm children (and especially girls) has implications even for those who are not abused. As Ward argues, "such stories touch all women in terms of our own suppressed childhood memories, and in terms of our lifelong existence as potential rape victims." She adds that acknowledging that fear is to admit the existence of an uncanny world where "the unknown yawns like a void" (166).

Finally, and most directly, Modleski's equation of castration and the uncanny with loss of autonomy simply doesn't fit well onto the narrative that Marston, Murchison, and Peter have constructed. It is possible, again, to see the shadow as threatening the light body—but only if you ignore the entire rest of the narrative, in which the creators show repeatedly that uncanny doubling is not caused by being bound to an inescapable shadow. Rather, it is caused precisely by *escaping* from one's shadow. The trauma is in being split from one's shadow, not in being tied to it.

I've already discussed the scene in which Wonder Woman is lifted out of her physical shadow body. The next panel shows the Holliday girls being spun out of theirs (10A; see figure 5). In this image, the whipping motion lines, with a jagged slash of lightning off to the side, visually transform the underground cavern of Pluto into a gothic, storm-racked landscape. As the Holliday girls' light selves move upward, the bottom of the panel shows their physical bodies as dark silhouettes being pulled downward by disembodied black hands. There is claustrophobia here, certainly, but it is not precisely a claustrophobia of insufficient autonomy or of merging. Rather, it is a claustrophobia of severing—of watching as your (real? your truest?) self is taken away from you and locked forever beneath the ice. As one incest victim told Herman and Hirschman, "I used to think I was one step beyond . . . in another world from the others. I dreamed once about a

FIGURE 5. *Wonder Woman #16* (1946)

little girl who fell under the bed. They looked for her but they couldn't find her. She was in another dimension. She was upset and crying. She screamed, but nobody heard" (97). If the gothic doubling does indicate a split between mother and daughter, then, the anxiety that Marston, Murchison, and Peter are focused on is not the fear of being unable to separate from the mother but rather the fear of losing her and of being lost by her in turn.[14]

SUPERMOTHERS AND PLUTONIC SERVANTS

Anxieties of losing the mother and being lost by her are precisely those experienced by incest victims, according to Herman and Hirschman. Just as the father in an incestuous family is almost a caricature of patriarchal power, so Herman and Hirschman argue that the mother is often a caricature of feminine weakness and self-effacement:

> While the fathers of our informants preserved a façade of competent social functioning, the mothers were often unable to fulfill their traditional roles. Over half of the informants (55 percent) remembered that their mothers had had periods of disabling illness which resulted in frequent hospitalizations or in the mother's living as an invalid at home. Over a third (38 percent) of the daughters had been separated from their mothers for some period of time during childhood. The separations occurred because

their mothers either were hospitalized or felt unable to cope with their child care duties and temporarily placed their daughters in the care of relatives. Three mothers died before their daughters were grown, one by suicide. Another mother committed suicide after her daughter left home. (77)

The daughters of these women did not need to worry about separating from their mothers. Rather, their mothers effectively disappeared into their own brutalization and trauma. Mothers of incest victims tended to have little education and little work experience. They generally had large families, in part because of multiple pregnancies, which, Herman and Hirschman say, were often "more or less imposed on women who felt helpless to prevent them" (77). "In short," Herman and Hirschman conclude,

> even by patriarchal standards, the mother in the incestuous family is unusually oppressed. More than the average wife and mother, she is extremely dependent upon and subservient to her husband. She may have a physical or emotional disability which makes the prospect of independent survival quite impractical. Rather than provoke her husband's anger or risk his desertion, she will capitulate. If the price of maintaining the marriage includes the sexual sacrifice of her daughter, she will raise no effective objections. Her first loyalty is to her husband, regardless of his behavior. She sees no other choice. Maternal collusion in incest, when it occurs, is a measure of maternal powerlessness. (49)

With mothers sidelined, daughters did in fact gain a kind of autonomy by taking on the roles their parents had abandoned. "Before the age of ten, almost half (45 percent) [of the incest victims surveyed] had been pressed into service as 'little mothers' within the family" (79). They cared for siblings, cooked, and cleaned. And, of course, many were expected to perform sexually for their fathers as well, taking their mother's place in bed as they did in the home.

The Marston/Murchison/Peter story follows this pattern through with an eerie exactitude. After the Holliday girls lose their physical shadow forms, they become perfectly frilly and feminine—even the dumpy, heavy Etta is transformed into a pink sylph (see figure 5). In one panel, Peter shows her suspended above the closing chasm, her hair floating up, her arms extended as if balancing in the air (10A). She looks like a dancer or a skater, poised and still amid the delicate rush of Peter's by-now-familiar cocoon of spinning motion lines. There is probably no other point in the series at which the butch Etta appears so graceful or so feminine.

Usually femininity is a positive characteristic in Marston/Peter. Here, though, it's more ambiguous. No sooner have the ethereal, glowing Holliday girls gotten to the surface than they're drawn hypnotically to Pluto's "weird castle," as Wonder Woman calls it. Once inside, they become literal decorations; Pluto straps them to chandeliers and pillars, where they provide light and ornamentation. "Ha!" observes Pluto, speaking villainously in the third person. "Soon King Pluto's realm will be the most beautiful in the universe!" (11A). The Holliday girls, abandoned by their physical anchor, their mother-selves, become entirely father focused. They are his ornaments and his servants; they live to please. Ward's description of incest families seems to fit: "The Mother, so cowed as to be hardly visible, is like the Queen in many fairy stories, absent from center stage. . . . The Daughter exists only for her Father's pleasure; allowed no playmates, no closeness with her Mother, no freedom, she is contained within a world where to be female is to be a sexual slave" (194). The daughter, like the mother, is then a servant or a thing. And sure enough, Pluto has two kinds of servants. The light, ethereal daughters become his ornaments and bring him fruit, but most of the drudgery is done by black-robed, faceless, and apparently genderless "Plutonic servants."

We never learn exactly where these servants come from or what they are. There are hints, however. In one sequence, Pluto captures Wonder Woman's color body. In a close-up, Pluto—all shifty eyes, bulbous nose, fuzzy white hair, and knotted fingers—strokes his beard and thinks, "Hmm. That girl looks familiar—I know—she's the Amazon Princess! Ha Ha! Once her color body is dead her other self will be my slave, and with her strength there will be no limit to the evil deeds she can perform for me! Ha! Ha!" (12A). This seems to suggest that Pluto's black-robed servants may be the shadow-bodies of women he has kidnapped. If this is the case, the mother-daughter roles are flipped. The light body becomes the mother brutalized, marginalized, and even killed by the father, while the shadow body becomes the daughter who, without the mother to give her light, enters a nightmare world of slavery.

I don't think there's any contradiction in seeing the mother/daughter roles as symbolically reversible. After all, the whole point of a double is that it's a double; the self is both the self and the other. As Ward says, "All mothers have been daughters: we/they have much to share" (180). And, indeed, there is one sequence in *Wonder Woman #16* in which the line between the "we" and the "they" is deliberately crossed, recrossed, and muddled.

Wonder Woman and the Holliday girls, having escaped Pluto's clutches, attack a group of Plutonic servants and knock them out. They then don the black robes in order to sneak through the castle and reunite with their lost physical dark bodies. The girls don't realize, however, that a real Plutonic servant has sneaked in among them. Thus, while light is imitating dark, dark is also imitating light imitating dark. The two panels in which this takes place are set underground, and you can see little except for the outlines of robed figures, black against the blackness. Besides Etta, who is distinguishable by her shortness, there is no way for the reader to tell the difference between Holliday girls and Plutonic slaves, any more than the servants and the girls can tell the difference among themselves (3B). It seems significant, too, that when the Plutonic servant/spy sneaks away to tell Pluto that the Holliday girls are coming, she (or possibly he?) is reprimanded for speaking before kneeling. Whether dark or light, cowed collaborators or struggling victims, everyone in Pluto's castle is crushed beneath his despotism (5B).

As I've indicated a couple of times now, one of the most interesting mysteries around the Plutonic bodyguards is their gender. They are never explicitly referred to as either male or female, and while the Holliday girls see them without their robes, we never do. Pluto does mention one more time that he makes slaves of dark shadow bodies, and it makes sense to think that the Plutonic slaves may be those dark bodies, which suggests that they are women (or at least that they come from women). But on the other hand, at one point a Plutonic servant chains Wonder Woman's bracelets together, rendering her helpless. Wonder Woman is only supposed to lose her strength when a man chains her bracelets—ergo, the Plutonic bodyguard is male. However, Marston and Murchison never explicitly explain the logistics. Though we have no way to tell if the Plutonic servant is a man or a woman, and though it is important to the plot to identify the servant as a man, Marston and Murchison refrain from doing so.[15]

In part, the confusion around the Plutonic servants may be a function of Marston and Murchison's casual relationship to diegetic consistency—these are not tightly constructed narratives. However, I think the lacuna can also be seen as a tension or an ambiguity in the material itself. Daughters—especially daughters who are the victims of incest—often have extremely conflicted views about mothers. On the one hand, girls and mothers in incestuous families tend to have hostile relationships; according to Ward, the daughters "often feel angrier with their Mothers than with the Fathers" (164). "At best," Herman and Hirschman say, "daughters [in incestuous families] viewed their mothers ambivalently, excusing their weakness as best they could" (81). In many cases, though,

> the relations between mother and daughter were marked by active hostility. Many of the daughters remembered their mothers only with bitterness and contempt. They described the women who had borne them as selfish, uncaring, and cruel. In their moments of despair, these daughters felt the absence of the most primary bonds of caring and trust. They believed they had been unwanted from the moment of their birth, and they cursed their mothers for bringing them into the world. (81)

Marston, Murchison, and Peter's narrative seems to mirror this dynamic in a number of ways. For example, in one of Peter's shadowy panels, Etta is confused in the dark and reaches out for someone to guide her. We can make out the diminutive, childlike Etta in her robe holding on to another dark, robed figure—a figure so wicked it cackles even in its thought bubble: "Ha Ha! If the 'Woo Woo' girl only knew that she's holding on to a *real* Plutonic bodyguard! Ha Ha Haaaaa!" (3B). If Etta is the child here, the bodyguard is the evil mother, so utterly under the thrall of her husband that she destroys her own daughter. The fact that we do not know if the bodyguard is male or female can perhaps be seen as a sign of the depths of her betrayal and (given Marston's belief in the superiority of women) the completeness of her corruption. The Plutonic bodyguards have abandoned their own gender in order to become faceless and subservient patriarchal pawns.

While victims of incest often have deep (and understandable) resentment toward their mothers, they also want and need their mothers' help. According to Herman and Hirschman, every woman in their study of incest victims "longed for a mother who could be strong, competent, and affectionate" (90). Moreover, Herman and Hirschman's study suggests that the incest victims had analyzed the situation correctly. Strong mothers were in fact the key to preventing incest. Again, Herman and Hirschman argued that incest tended to occur in families in which the mother is weak. But Herman and Hirschman also did research on families with incestuous dynamics, in which the father expressed sexual interest in the daughter but no actual incest occurred. Looking at these families, Herman and Hirschman concluded, "The families in which mothers were rendered unusually powerless, whether through battering, physical disability, mental illness, or the burden of repeated childbearing, appeared to be particularly at risk for the development of overt incest. In families where a more nearly equal balance of parental power was preserved, overt incest did not develop, even though the fathers' sexual interest in their daughters was quite apparent" (124). Herman and Hirschman add that while daughters in families with what they call "seductive fathers" experienced emotional trauma and long-term consequences, the effects of overt incest were much more harmful. Strong mothers kept their daughters from being raped, and that in turn helped their daughters to be stronger, happier, and less ruled by the trauma of their childhoods. Herman and Hirschman concluded, "At present too many girls learn by observation that oppression is their destiny and that to love a man is to be enslaved. If daughters are to be protected, they must learn from their mothers' example that they have the ability to fight and the right to defend themselves. When daughters see in their mothers an image of dignity and self-respect, they can more easily find in themselves the courage to resist abuse" (207).

Marston, Murchison, and Peter, working from similar feminist commitments, also believe in the heroic force of strong mothers. They cannot, of course, create flesh-and-blood strong mothers. But they certainly did their best to create imaginary ones and to show daughters that they have "the ability to fight and the right to defend themselves." Again, Aphrodite, the ur-mother figure for Marston, goes into an uncharacteristic rage when Pluto's trident is merely brought into her presence. Pluto raped Persephone, and in response, Aphrodite censures him absolutely. There is no question that, as a mother, she will side with daughters (3A–4A).

Just as Aphrodite takes Persephone's part, so the rest of the comic—as, indeed, with most of Marston/Peter's comics—is devoted to images of women saving each other. One of the most striking sequences occurs after Wonder Woman's light body is captured by Pluto. She is placed with the green light body of Lorrie, the girl Pluto initially kidnapped, in a giant Bunsen burner (somewhere the creators of the *Batman* television show were reading). Peter draws the burner in a large panel, with the green-glowing Lorrie and the orange-glowing Wonder Woman facing each other inside the tube. Smoke boils up around them, while the dark Plutonic bodyguards tend the fire below. It's an image of mad scientist's laboratory as hell (12A–13A). The melodrama is enhanced by a close-up of Lorrie's green face, surrounded by smoke so that it looks like she's adrift in clouds. "Oh Wonder Woman, we are doomed!" she sobs. "Soon the test tube will be filled with boiling water and we shall melt like color tablets!" The means of her death—evaporation—emphasizes her utter helplessness and insubstantiality. Before Pluto's wrath, she can do nothing but dissolve (12A).

But that's not going to happen with Wonder Woman around. The Amazon breaks her bonds and then seizes Lorrie and swings both of them out of the top of the test tube (13A). This is accomplished in three wordless panels—the first time in the *Wonder Woman* comic that Marston, Murchison, and Peter let an action sequence stand alone without narration. The result is lushly riveting; the panels—one long rectangle and two square panels stacked beside it—turn into a single rush of action and color, Peter's motion lines sending Wonder Woman and Lorrie up and up in a exuberant ascent.

The lack of text also emphasizes Lorrie's passivity. In the first panel, she is stiff and staring in Wonder Woman's arms, her eyes wide and her mouth open, with no sound emerging. In the next panels, she is also mute; her body is bent double as Wonder Woman holds her around the waist, her green diaphanous dress and the scribbled mass of her hair both hanging limply down. Whether stiff or boneless, she comes across as a doll—and dolls are the surrogate daughters of daughters. Wonder Woman can then be seen as the daughter identifying with the mother saving the daughter—a girl's image of herself as the woman she would like her mother to be.

There is a thematically similar sequence later in the comic when the light bodies of Wonder Woman and the Holliday girls finally locate their physical shadow bodies. Peter shows the light bodies gathered around what looks like a frozen pond. The diminutive Etta, pink and glowing, kneels on the lip of the ice, staring down, while the others lean over to see their own silhouettes trapped and frozen (9B). They are outside themselves—an experience analogous to the dissociation experienced during trauma. Such traumatic experiences are described by Herman and Hirschman: "In situations of helpless terror, some people spontaneously enter an altered state of consciousness. In this 'dream-like' state of numbness and detachment, people feel disconnected from their own sensations, emotions, or awareness of what is happening to them" (226). Wonder Woman, then, when she picks up a giant rock and breaks through the ice, can be seen both as a mother saving her daughter and as a self reintegrating—a daughter saving herself, perhaps. And, again, since there is reason to think that the dark shadow bodies are at various points seen as mothers, Wonder Woman could also be seen as a daughter simultaneously returning to and liberating her parent. Daughters need mothers to provide them with strength and protection, but mothers also need daughters to release them from the past and show them a way out of patriarchy. Women divided will be ruled by Pluto; it's only when mothers and daughters come together that they can be free.

This feminist vision is at the heart of much of Marston and Peter's comics—and in illustrating it, Peter creates a phenomenal double-page spread (10B–11B). In a tall upper-left panel, he shows Wonder Woman and the Holliday girls lying against an almost abstract background of jagged colors. Each of them is spinning around and around as their light bodies and dark bodies are fused together—again, the motion lines around each body make it look like they are all wrapped in cocoons. In the next panel, on the upper right, the girls and Wonder Woman burst from the cavern in a graceful arc and then race off in pursuit of Pluto. On the next page, the pursuit continues, with Wonder Woman pulling the Holliday girls along with her magic lasso and Pluto flying away in his chariot—the motion lines flow across the page like great fluid, rushing waves. It is as if the reintegration of light and dark, mothers and daughters, releases a force that can't be contained in narrative but must be released in a kind of pop abstract-expressionist enthusiasm, with Peter's pen racing and swooping across the page while Pluto, the evil father, flees before it.

Alas, Pluto isn't really vanquished—not with the release of the Holliday girls at the end of that chapter and not, despite further struggle, at the end of the comic either. Children are still raped, as Marston, Murchison, and Peter surely knew. The last panel of *Wonder Woman* #16, then, has a bitter edge (11C). Wonder Woman kneels before Aphrodite, who, seated on her throne, reaches out one hand to bless her: "Princess Diana, through thy great courage and wisdom, thou hast rid the earth of an unseen enemy who, through the centuries has been responsible for the disappearance of countless humans whose terrible fate had never been traced!" But even if this is hope rather than triumph, surely that hope is itself a political act. In imagining Pluto's demise, in thinking of a world without him, Aphrodite paradoxically makes him visible, just as in speaking of the victim's traceless doom, she gives Persephone back her voice. This is one instance in which speaking about women's experiences is itself a feminist stance. I can see Marston and Murchison nodding in agreement with the last line of Susan Brownmiller's *Against Our Will*: "My purpose in this book has been to give rape its history. Now we must deny it a future" (404).

MAMAS, LET YOUR DAUGHTERS GROW UP TO BE FATHERS

I hope I've demonstrated at this point that, in one comic at least, Marston, Murchison, and Peter's themes of rape, slavery, and bondage were not simply exploitive or titillating. On the contrary, they used themes of rape, slavery, and bondage because they were creating a comic about the exploitation and trauma of women and their chil-

FIGURE 6. *Wonder Woman #16* (1946)

dren. Gothic romances show women in sexual peril not to enjoy the sight of women in sexualized peril but rather because women often are in sexualized peril and want to read books that address their experiences. Similarly, Marston, Murchison, and Peter do not show the rape of Persephone because the rape of Persephone is a stimulating thing to see. They show it because girls (and boys too) face incest and rape, and stories addressed to them must therefore face those things as well.

Or so I've been arguing. The truth though is perhaps a little less clear-cut. Marston, Murchison, and Peter in *Wonder Woman #16* are writing about incest and rape, and they are doing so from a consciously feminist perspective. But that doesn't mean that they can't get off on fetishized bondage too. After all, Marston's correspondent who "derive[d] an extreme erotic pleasure from the mere thought of a beautiful girl, chained or bound," would find no shortage of provocative material in *Wonder Woman #16*.

As just one example, a particularly arresting panel shows a cage full of female light bodies (9C; see figure 6). The multicolored, glowing women are all in advanced stages of panic as Pluto is readying to electrify and destroy them. Their hands grip the bars futilely, their mouths open fetchingly, their dresses curve and drape as if in a fashion illustration. Bright, pretty, animated, and framed, they "connote *to-be-looked-at-ness*," in Laura Mulvey's phrase (837).

Outside the cage, Pluto stands, hands on hips, mouth open, nose bulbous—a cartoonish, guffawing caricature reveling in all the trapped graciousness before him. "Ha Haa! What great entertainment! This will be an unsurpassed color spectacle!" he declares. The emphasis on viewing female bodies as entertainment, and indeed as consumption, is self-referential. We are supposed to condemn Pluto for his looking, but at the same time, we are definitely with him, and presumably with Marston (and Murchison), staring into the cage at all these delectable, constrained bodies. Indeed, it is easy to see Pluto here *as* Marston, instructing Peter (his Plutonic servant?) to provide a cage full of lovelies for his delectation.

Wonder Woman #16 is, then, arguably not only a sensitive portrayal of the trauma of incest and rape—it is also a way to show women in cages, or women enslaved, for the enjoyment of male viewers. From this vantage, even the weird image of Wonder Woman and the Holliday girls being spun around by the black hands starts to seem potentially lascivious. The female bodies tied up in the strands of Peter's motion lines, the one Holliday girl's skirt lifting slightly off her legs—whose hands are those reaching out to grasp them, anyway? Do we identify with the Holliday girls in their panic and fear? Or are we (is Marston?) relishing the view, our gazes reaching out like shadowy, roving hands? (9A; see figure 4).

I don't think the answer has to be one or the other. Herman and Hirschman, after all, note that men, and not least male therapists, often "become excited by the victim's narrative of forbidden sexuality" (186). In fact, it is, as Herman and Hirschman say, "not uncommon" for male therapists to sleep with incest victims—effectively replicating the abuse (187). Marston, Murchison, and Peter present incest as trauma and as tragedy. But they also present, and utilize, it as fetish.

This is an uncomfortable revelation, to put it mildly. Fetishizing bondage is one thing; fetishizing father-daughter rape is a whole different level of distasteful. It is unpleasant if Marston is catering to a male audience (and to himself) by presenting incest as an exciting, sadistic fantasy for men. But it is arguably even more unpleasant if Marston and Murchison are encouraging their female audience to identify with their fantasy abusers—not least because actual incest victims often *do* identify with their actual abusers. Herman and Hirschman report, for example, that incest victims frequently admire the "competence and power" of their fathers. They also speak with at least ambivalent enjoyment of being a daddy's girl, somewhere between daughter and lover (82–83). Incestuous fathers exploit and encourage this "special relationship" in order to bind their daughters closer to them and to make it more difficult for them to escape. When incest victims identify with their fathers, in other words, that identification is part of the abuse. If Marston, Murchison, and Peter encourage girls to identify with Pluto, they are not getting daughters out of the cage; they are putting them in it.

VAMPIRES AND DAUGHTERS

To see how father identification and abuse are intertwined, it is useful to take a short detour and consider one of the most popular current narratives for girls: *Twilight*. I discussed *Twilight* briefly earlier and noted that it is often seen as encouraging, or romanticizing, abuse. What I did not note, though, is that that abuse takes place in the context of barely sublimated incestuous desires.[16]

Many critics have seen incest themes in vampire stories, and *Twilight* definitely seems to fit into that unwholesome tradition.[17] To begin with, Bella calls her father "Charlie"—his first name—and after she moves back in with him at the beginning of the series, she cooks for and takes care of him more like a wife than like a daughter. Edward's vampire family is even more flagrantly incestuous. The "father," Carlyle, lives with his "children," all of whom reside together as brothers and sisters—and, at the same time, as paired husbands and wives. Even Carlyle himself and his wife appear no older than their "kids"—kids they create not by having sex with each other but by biting (i.e., having sex with) the children themselves. Father, mother, brother, sister—the familial roles are all, for the vampires, arbitrary, interchangeable, and interpenetrated with sex.

If vampires are both daddies and lovers, Edward is certainly no exception. In fact, much of Meyer's incomprehensible plotting is suddenly clarified once you start to view Edward as a father surrogate. Edward is much, much older than Bella (while still being, also, magically, nineteen). And his relationship with Bella is defined by his overwhelming desire to protect her, not merely from others but from himself. As mentioned earlier, he essentially stalks her, and this creepy stalking is specifically explained as a paternal desire to keep her from harm—he disables her car, for example, to keep her from being hurt by the werewolf Jacob. Meyer also is oddly fascinated with scenes in Bella's bedroom—scenes in which Edward does not have sex with Bella but rather spends hours watching her sleep, like a doting father. Edward's continual refusal to have sex with Bella, and/or to turn her into a vampire, is also consistent with his role as father. He loves her, but incest/sex would be so right/wrong. Eventually, however, the relationship is consummated—and Edward's strength and power is such that after coitus Bella is covered all over in bruises. In the end, Bella gives up her college plans and, indeed, her purchase in the human world to join Edward as his vampire bride/daughter. She chooses, in other words, to spend her whole life in the twilit, cloistered world of the sealed patriarchy—to never grow up and to be daddy's girl, lover, and victim forever.

Again, many feminist critics have been horrified by *Twilight*, and no wonder.[18] The series seamlessly integrates fantasies of love, abuse, and domesticity. Bella identifies so strongly with her Pluto that she eagerly rushes into his cage, beckoning millions of tween girls to join her in life-in-death before she locks the door.

This is not the only way to look at *Twilight*, however, or, indeed, at incest fantasies for girls. Gale Swiontkowski, for example, argues that, while actual incest is traumatic and disempowering, symbolic imagery in writing does not have to be. Discussing the poetry of Sharon Olds, who often uses incest imagery, Swiontkowski suggests, "An advocacy of incest by men, as in pornography, is a regressive move toward social and psychological hoarding that enslaves women to men's desires, especially if it is taken as a literal enactment of the right of males in patriarchy. The advocacy of symbolic incest by women is an enlightening and advancing move because it breaches the social restrictions on women that determine their subservience in a patriarchy" (136). For Swiontkowski, male incest fantasies are about a patriarchal apotheosis of enslavement—like Pluto laughing over his caged daughters/victims. Female incest fantasies, on the other hand, can be about women gaining the father's power—symbolically fucking over the patriarchy in the person of the patriarch. As such, for Sharon Olds, and perhaps for other creators and readers, female incest fantasies can be empowering.

It is certainly possible to read *Twilight* as a male incest fantasy of enslavement. But I think it is also possible to see it as one of Swiontkowski's symbolic female incest fantasies. Again, Meyer's world is one in which the incest taboo is destabilized; fathers are brothers are husbands; siblings are lovers. The result of this is not (or not necessarily) restriction but instead the opening up of possibilities—and particularly of the possibility that daughters can be, or can seize the power of, fathers. Edward is Bella's lover and her father—and he is also Bella's self. Edward's paternal desire to keep Bella safe is ultimately accomplished not by stalking her or controlling her but by making Bella into Edward: by turning her into a vampire who is (the text is careful to note) stronger than Edward himself. Marrying her father makes Bella a free, empowered sire too—and she has the phallus/fangs to prove it.

RAPE FANTASIES

The question, then, is whether, in Swiontkowski's terms, Marston, Murchison, and Peter are presenting a male incest fantasy or a female incest fantasy—or perhaps (given the male and female collaboration in writing) both. Is the male gaze here, the voyeuristic scopophilia, defined and consolidated as a patriarchal right to the bodies of daughters? Or is that gaze, connected to that incestuous power, presented more openly, as a position that women can occupy as well as men—and thus as a way for women to safely, symbolically, participate in the power of the father? In answering this question, it is useful to consider other instances in which Marston, Murchison, and Peter present parallel voyeuristic, sadistic scenarios. For instance, consider a panel from *Wonder Woman* #28, in which two evil villainesses menace Steve Trevor (5C; see figure 7).[19] Clea and Giganta, clustered shoulder to shoulder at the left, merge into a single malevolent four-armed, two-headed feminine deity of castration. Their mouths are twisted into identical sneers of fury, their awesome Peter eyebrows are flexing, and that blade is aimed right where it's aimed, with some adorable little effect lines to make sure we watch the point. Meanwhile, Steve, at the right, with his shirt stripped off, is presented as a big slab of sexualized beefcake. "Go ahead and have your fun," he tells them. Indeed.

Gloria Steinem could have been looking at this panel when, in an introduction to a 1995 collection of *Wonder Woman* covers, she gently

FIGURE 7. *Wonder Woman #28* (1948)

chided Marston for being too masculinist: "Instead of portraying the goal of full humanity for women and men, which is what feminism has in mind, [Marston] often got stuck in the subject/object, winner/loser paradigm of 'masculine' versus 'feminine,' and came up with female superiority instead" (Introduction to *Wonder Woman* [1995] 12). If you compare the image of Steve in chains to the scene of Pluto looking at the glowing light bodies in the cage, you can see that it does exactly what Steinem says it does (see figure 6). That is, it doesn't undo the subject/object binary but simply flips it. Clea and Giganta occupy the place of the brutal father Pluto on the left; Steve occupies the position of the sexualized, restrained women on the right. The parallel is even more exact if we return to the idea that castration anxiety is historically a displacement of the traumatic abuse of young girls. The threat of castration here—the sword, the threat of blinding—becomes a direct metaphor for sexual abuse and violence. The two women looming over Steve and promising to unman him are in the position of the father. They are, moreover, preparing to treat him as fathers treat their daughters—and sometimes their sons as well.

The image, then, offers a masochistic investment for male readers—one that can be seen as structurally and ambivalently related to Pluto's hoarding of his colorful daughter-slaves. On the one hand, the masochist is putting himself in the position of, and identifying with, the plight of women. On the other hand, he is claiming women's experience as his own—replacing female abuse with castration, as Freud did. In this sense, Steve-as-masochist is inhabiting and taking control of women's bodies through a technology of fantasy much more advanced than Pluto's crude cage.[20]

Marston's use of castration allows men to identify with, or to take the place of, daughters. But it can also surely be seen as allowing women to identify with, or to take the place of, fathers—and specifically of fathers inflicting sexualized violence. In this sense, Marston, Murchison, and Peter take the incest fantasy for women a step further than *Twilight* does. In *Twilight*, Bella may take the position of the father, but she never actually uses those phallic fangs herself—we never see her biting another human being. Instead, Meyer is careful to tell us that Bella has greater control over her hunger than any of the other vampires do. Bella's incest fantasies are carefully segregated—she is raped by the father, and she is herself the father, but she never imagines herself as the father doing the raping. Marston/Murchison/Peter, in contrast, provide a fantasy of women as castrator—of women as the father in the act of committing incest.

At first, it may seem odd to suggest that women, like men, might enjoy imagining themselves in the role of rapists. Indeed, there is barely a terminology to discuss such desires. If you say, "women have rape fantasies," after all, you're talking about something quite different. Still, there's no shortage of evidence that women can and do, in fact, enjoy imagining themselves inflicting sexualized and sadistic violence. Nancy Friday in her (in)famous *My Secret Garden* records at least a couple of women fantasizing about being on top (143, for example). And then there is this concluding passage from Brownmiller's *Against Our Will*, in which she describes her self-defense class:

> We women discovered in wonderment that as we learned to place our kicks and jabs with precision we were actually able to inspire fear in the men. We *could* hurt them, we learned to our astonishment, and hurt them hard at the core of their sexual being. . . .
>
> Is it possible that there is some sort of metaphysical justice in the anatomical fact that the male sex organ, which has been misused from time immemorial as a weapon of terror against women,

should have at its root an awkward place of painful vulnerability. . . . How strange it was to understand with the full force of
unexpected revelation that male allusions to psychological defeat,
particularly at the hands of a woman, were couched in phrases like
emasculation, castration and ball-breaking because of that very
special physical vulnerability. (403–404; italics in original)

Brownmiller explicitly—even gleefully—makes the connection between rape and castration, positioning the second as the mirror image of the first. The penis as "weapon of terror" becomes the penis as
wound, and the woman as wound becomes the woman as weapon of
terror. Women can inflict on men a harm "at the core of their sexual
being" analogous to the harm that men inflict on women.

Brownmiller's book, with its lengthy discussion of rape and its concluding gestures toward violent retribution against men, can be seen
in some ways as the scholarly forerunner of the trashy, feministsploita-
tion rape-revenge genre. In this context, it is interesting to note that
rape-revenge films are, according to Carol Clover (156–159), characterized by a surprisingly fluid relationship between gender and bodies and by an often systematic effort to encourage viewers to identify
across genders. Clover particularly identifies the homosexual male
rape in *Deliverance* as the prototype of female rapes in films such as
I Spit on Your Grave (154). In that sense, the rape-revenge genre runs
Freud's castration complex backward, replacing male trauma with
female trauma. In light of this interpretation, it is perhaps possible to
see Clea and Giganta's attack on Steve as appealing not just to masochistic men, and not just to sadistic women, but rather to people of
any gender who might enjoy, for a moment, thinking of themselves as
assaulted, assaulting, both, or neither.

JUMP THE PLUTONIC GUARDS!

If identification is fluid, it should not necessarily be surprising to discover that desire is as well—and that women may have fantasies that involve
sexual dominance of other women. Sharon Marcus in *Between Women*
argues, in fact, that such fantasies were widely current across numerous
genres in Victorian England. Marcus discusses doll stories for children,
in which girls were presented as "imperious mistresses," disciplining

their dolls for naughtiness or just out of caprice (151). Marcus also points to a remarkable debate about birching, or beating, daughters, conducted by correspondents to *Englishwoman's Domestic Magazine*:

> Whether writing for or against corporal punishment, correspondents provided detailed accounts of inflicting, receiving, and witnessing ritual chastisements in which older women restrained, undressed, and whipped younger ones. Letters described mothers, aunts, teachers, and female servants forcing girls and young women to remove their drawers, tying girls to pieces of furniture, pinning back their arms, placing them in handcuffs, or requiring them to count the number of strokes administered. Some letters were written from the point of view of mothers and guardians who had to impose discipline, others from the perspective of those reminiscing about having been disciplined. Many provided testimonials that began with recollections of having "screamed, and shrieked and implored" to no avail and ended by celebrating the moral benefits of chastisement. (140)

There seems little doubt from Marcus's description that Victorian women and girls took pleasure in looking at, revealing, and controlling other female bodies.

Marston would certainly have been (extremely) interested in the birching debates, but he would not have found them surprising. On the contrary, in his psychological treatise *Emotions of Normal People*, Marston argued that the two "'normal,' strength-giving emotions" were "dominance" and "submission" (3).[21] He based this conclusion in large part on observations gathered at sorority rituals—rituals that were, perhaps needless to say, organized around female-female chastisements. It's worth quoting his discussion at some length:

> In the spring of the freshmen year, the sophomore girls held what was called "The Baby Party," which all freshmen girls were compelled to attend. At this affair, the freshmen girls were questioned as to their misdemeanors and punished for their disobediences and rebellions. The baby party was so named because the freshmen girls were required to dress like babies.

At the party, the freshmen girls were put through various stunts under command of the sophomores. Upon one occasion, for instance, the freshman girls were led into a dark corridor where their eyes were blindfolded, and their arms were bound behind them. Only one freshman at a time was taken through this corridor along which sophomore guards were stationed at intervals. This arrangement was designed to impress the girls punished with the impossibility of escape from their captresses. After a series of harmless punishments, each girl was led into a large room where all the Junior and Senior girls were assembled. There she was sentenced to go through various exhibitions, supposed to be especially suitable to punish each particular girl's failure to submit to discipline imposed by the upper class girls. The sophomore girls carried long sticks with which to enforce, if necessary, the stunts which the freshman were required to perform. While the programme did not call for a series of pre-arranged physical struggles between individual girls ... frequent rebellion of the freshman against the commands of their captresses and guards furnished the most exciting portion of the entertainment according to the report of a majority of the class girls.

Nearly all the sophomores reported excited pleasantness of captivation emotion throughout the party. The pleasantness of their captivation responses appeared to increase when they were obliged to overcome rebellious freshmen physically, or to induce them by repeated commands and added punishments to perform the actions from which the captive girls strove to escape. . . .

Female behaviour also contains still more evidence than male behaviour that *captivation emotion is not limited to inter-sex relationships*. The person of another girl seems to evoke from female subjects, under appropriate circumstances, fully as strong captivation response as does that of a male. (299–301; italics in original).

It seems clear that, in Marston's view, not just Pluto, and not just male readers, but female readers as well could enjoy controlling, dominating, and caging women.

To summarize, then, I think we can conclude that Marston,

Murchison, and Peter in *Wonder Woman* deliberately created a series in which both men and women were intended to identify with and desire both victims and victimizers of both genders. In *Wonder Woman #16*, in particular, this led to a sincere and even subtle identification with and analysis of the plight of victims of sexual abuse. But it *also* led to a lascivious investment in the sexualized power of the abuser. And, again, for Marston, Murchison, and Peter, these positions of victim and victimizer are not, or not necessarily, gendered. Daughters are sexually abused, but sons can be as well; fathers are the abusers, but women can also participate in that sense of power.

This is illustrated in a panel from near the end of the issue, which is in some ways the mirror image, or the conclusion, of the picture of Pluto laughing at the girls in the cage (10C; see figure 8). It shows Pluto's downfall and the release of the light bodies. On the left, as Pluto reaches for an electric switch that will kill his prisoners, Steve leaps on him from behind. Steve's arm goes around the king's neck just as Pluto's arm was wrapped around Persephone's during the narrative's ur-rape scene. Steve's lower half is lined up with Pluto's hind end; when our hero lands, it looks like crotch and rear will collide. The sensual "thunk" of that meeting is further emphasized by the swivel in Pluto's hips; Peter has drawn him midstride, and the folds in his belted, dress-like robe highlight the tight pull of the fabric across his right buttock. Meanwhile, on the right, Wonder Woman stands where Pluto once stood, before the trapped light bodies. Instead of laughing and engaging in a round of scopophilia, though, she pulls apart the cage, the bars twisting into graceful, flaccid curlicues as she makes an opening. Two light bodies stand waiting to be released. One looks gratefully toward her rescuer; the other looks down demurely, with a virginal modesty. Along the bottom of the pane, wires connect the cage to the generator, linking the two halves of the picture—and, I'd argue, emphasizing the sexualized content of both. Steve is in a position to rape Pluto as Pluto raped Persephone (and, indeed, as Pluto raped/castrated Steve). The homoerotic connotation turns Wonder Woman's forcing of the cage into a double entendre. Similarly, Wonder Woman is in a position to voyeuristically gaze on the trapped women just as Pluto did, and that sadistic metonymy implicates Steve's violent assault in the economy of desire. And, as if that were not enough, the next panel shows Etta with mouth gaping ridiculously wide as she shouts, "Woo woo! C'mon, keeds! Jump the Plutonic guards!" After this, Wonder Woman seizes Pluto's enormous trident, runs outside, and smashes it against the ground to create a great, gaping crack in the ice in order to reach the trapped female shadow bodies below.

Is Wonder Woman in this sequence the daughter? Or is she the father? You could certainly see her as taking the weapons of patriarchy—the sadistic gaze, rape itself—and using them in the interest of women's liberation. Or, conversely, you could see her as simply perpetuating the logic of patriarchy. Marston is so invested in that logic, you might argue, that freeing women from the father's control can only be seen, or only be pleasurable, through the analogy and structure of sexualized violence. These are criticisms that could also be leveled at Brownmiller's joyous paean to kicking men in the balls. There's no doubt that the father's power is seductive and not to be trusted. Aphrodite is not wrong when she bans the trident from her presence. But, at the same time, it's hard to blame Wonder Woman for picking the thing up in order to rescue her sisters. And if she's going to rescue them, why shouldn't she have a good time doing it? That is to say, for Marston, Murchison, and Peter, there is no necessary contradiction between confronting the reality of rape and abuse (for women and also men) and indulging in a sexually charged BDSM romp (for everyone). For Freud, childhood rape and children's fantasies of rape could not both be real. He could not imagine both at once. But Marston, Murchison, and Peter could.

FIGURE 8. *Wonder Woman #16* (1946)

That remains a rare ability and an extremely precious one. Most of us, most of the time, are more like Freud than like Marston. We can condemn child abuse or we can acknowledge children's sexuality, but we have enormous difficulty doing both at once. Freud downplayed the abuse in emphasizing child sexuality; arguably, today, we tend to downplay child sexuality to emphasize the reality of abuse.

Steven Angelides makes this case in a 2004 article. He argues that the feminist reconsiderations of incest in the 1980s—epitomized by writers such as Herman—were based on denying children sexual agency and sexual power (153). The result, Angelides argues, is that childhood sexuality is seen as radically different from adult sexuality, and children's sexual desires are seen as being utterly divorced from their sexual experiences. Angelides argues that this can hinder therapy and recovery, since children feel (rightly) that they have some power and because it denies the role of children's fantasies in their trauma. "It . . . assumes . . . that reality and fantasy can be definitively disentangled," Angelides concludes (160).

Angelides's critique is well taken, not least because he too falls prey to this desire to disentangle reality and fantasy. Thus, he repeatedly praises Freud for his focus on childhood sexual fantasy, as if that focus in itself ensures that Freud did not ignore actual evidence of sex abuse.[22] Similarly, Angelides insists that he himself is not discarding feminist interpretations of incest (142). And yet actual abusers—or, for that matter, adult sexual desires—are barely present in his argument. To read his piece, you'd think that the greatest danger children face is not rape and abuse but antisex feminists. Presented with the plight of children who encounter crushing power inequities and abuse, he responds by insisting that all sexual relations include power imbalances and that children sometimes exercise control over their parents—points that are both true and an evasion of the issue (152).

Angelides then, like Freud—and, for that matter, like Herman—finds it immensely difficult to give theoretical weight to both incest *and* child sexuality, to both rape *and* rape fantasies. This collective failure makes Marston, Murchison, and Peter's achievement all the more remarkable. In *Wonder Woman #16*, incest and rape are evil—Pluto is presented as perhaps the single most heinous villain in Marston and Peter's run.[23] That evil is overwhelming and unforgivable; Aphrodite, the highest authority in Marston's world, demands that it be utterly condemned and banished. But, at the same time, even the worst abuse of power, even the most unjust submission, doesn't change the fact that power and submission are also pleasures, for adults and most definitely for children. Marston, Murchison, and Peter want to provide those pleasures for everybody, even, or perhaps especially, to the most oppressed and the most wounded. Contra Angelides, contra Herman, contra Freud, Marston, Murchison and Peter insist that confronting Pluto does not erase child sexuality. *Wonder Woman #16* makes the case that the prescription for trauma is kink.

ONE THING AFTER ANOTHER
That kink is not just a sexual twist; it is also a narrative. Laura Mulvey famously connected sadism with Hollywood's linear storytelling and with its focus on a central male protagonist who drives the action and, along the way, looks at female bodies. Men are the ones who look and the ones who make the narrative move; women are the ones looked at, tending to freeze the narrative in fetishistic contemplation:

> The split between spectacle and narrative supports the man's role as the active one of forwarding the story, making things happen. The man controls the film phantasy and also emerges as the representative of power in a further sense: as the bearer of the look of the spectator, transferring it behind the screen to neutralize the extra-diegetic tendencies represented by woman as spectacle. This is made possible through the processes set in motion by structuring the film around a main controlling figure with whom the spectator can identify. As the spectator identifies with the main male protagonist, he projects his look onto that of his like, his screen surrogate, so that the power of the male protagonist as he controls events coincides with the active power of the erotic look, both giving a satisfying sense of omnipotence. (838)

Pluto gazes into the cage at the glowing images of women and exults in his power over them—a power of looking that is also the power of narrative (he controls what will happen to them next) and the power of rape.

As I suggested earlier, rape-revenge films tend to undo or complicate this identification and omnipotence. Men may have the power of the look and of rape in the first part of *I Spit on Your Grave*, but the second half decisively reroutes that omnipotence to the former victim—top becomes bottom, and the viewer must either switch identification or identify directly with the disempowered. For that matter, Carol Clover argues that all viewers are intended to identify with the female victim *throughout* the film, experiencing first her disempowerment, then her empowerment: "A film like *I Spit on Your Grave* is literally predicated on the assumption that *all* viewers, male and female alike, will take Jennifer's part, and via whatever set of psychosexual translations, 'feel' her violation. Without that identification, the revenge phase of the drama makes no sense" (159). Rape-revenge films, then, don't seem to support Mulvey. The viewer is not placed in the position of the male rapist, and the male rapist does not (at least ultimately) control the narrative.

Nonetheless, these films are, emphatically, even obsessively, narrative based. It is true that *I Spit on Your Grave* dwells interminably (for more than half an hour) on the rape, frozen in fetishistic contemplation. And yet even that extended intermission of trauma doesn't so much derail the film's grim, linear economy as validate and enforce it. Rape-revenge is a ritualized narrative, and the ritual sacralizes and validates that narrative, not the other way around. Violence and trauma lead to violence and trauma—an eye for an eye, a castration for a rape. The film's pleasures—and they are pleasures—are in the satisfying fulfillment of a prophecy. Thus, though rape-revenge does not validate a single male protagonist, and though it often puts the viewer in the position of the disempowered, it in many ways confirms Mulvey's connection between narrative and omnipotence. The viewer knows what will happen, is there to see it happen, and is, therefore, in a real sense, the cause of its happening. The rape-revenge viewer does not get to be a man, acting; instead, he gets to be a just god, knowing. And what the god knows is the rush of narrative: the violent, linear thrust of desire, climax, and satiation.

Wonder Woman #16 does have some of the hallmarks of rape-revenge. It opens with a rape (Lorrie being taken from her bed), and it closes with a symbolic antirape or castration (Wonder Woman using

Pluto's trident to break open his "ice"). But the path from *a* to *b*, rape to revenge, is far from linear. Instead, the plot goes like this: Lorrie wakes up screaming in her room at Holliday College because she has seen a man in her room. The other girls don't believe her. In the morning, Lorrie is gone, a trident left behind. The girls call Wonder Woman, who takes the trident to show to Aphrodite. Aphrodite tells the story of Pluto's rape of Persephone. Hippolyte and Wonder Woman use a magic sphere to watch Pluto capture Lorrie. Wonder Woman determines to go after Pluto to the planet Pluto. Meanwhile, Steve shows the Holliday girls a new army rocket. Etta accidentally sets the rocket off, and she and the Holliday girls are carried toward Pluto. Wonder Woman happens to be flying past in her invisible plane when the rocket takes off. She lassoes it and is dragged along behind. Wonder Woman and the Holliday girls eventually land on Pluto, along with Pluto's trident, which Wonder Woman still carries. Wonder Woman tosses the trident aside, it splits the ice, and Wonder Woman and her companions fall into a crevice, where black hands grab them and spin them around, separating their light bodies from their physical shadow bodies. The Holliday girls as light bodies are then hypnotically summoned to Pluto's castle. Wonder Woman resists but is captured and put in a Bunsen burner with Lorrie to be dissolved. Wonder Woman rescues Lorrie, and then she and the Holliday girls defeat Pluto's guards. Pluto runs away.

And that's just part one of three! We haven't even gotten to the defeat of Pluto, the reintegration of the Holliday girls, Pluto's return to Earth to abduct Steve, Wonder Woman's return to Earth, her discovery of Steve's abduction, and her return to Pluto, where she rescues Steve and all the other light bodies, defeating Pluto again once and for all. Whew!

Clearly, this is not a linear story. Instead, the narrative repeats, vacillates, reverses, moves off to the side, skips across interstellar reaches, and then does it all again. The power shifts of rape-revenge are definitely present, but they're run through in cyclical variations and are so embroidered with extraneous detail that they lose their sense of savage, inexorable necessity. You have time, and are encouraged, to stop and look at the flowers—literally, whether they be the red, labial blooms in the image in which Persephone is abducted or the frozen

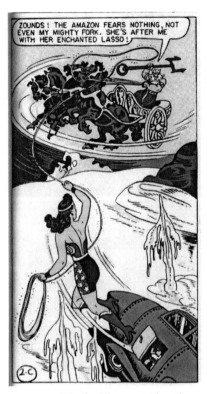

FIGURE 9. *Wonder Woman #16* (1946)

flowers on Pluto. "How they sparkle!" one of the Holliday girls exclaims (8A).

Sharon Marcus, in a remarkable essay at the *Hooded Utilitarian* on the Marston/Peter comics, describes the experience of reading *Wonder Woman* as one of constant distraction from the plot, so that the reader is watching feet and shadows and expressions and colors rather than paying attention to who is doing what to whom. Marcus concludes that as a result, the violence and power disparities become stylized and immobilized: "It's as if the *scene* of sadism were more important here than the *story*—as if sadism has itself become subject to the loopy visual tempo of the fetish. What matters most is not generating anxious suspense about what will happen next, but a feeling of secure suspension in a continuous series of images of women tying up women" ("Wonder Woman"; italics in original). Narrative becomes a tableau; the hurtling urgency of rape-revenge is turned into a leisurely, comfortable stroll. *Wonder Woman*, Marcus concludes, "gently thwarts sadism, because while reading it, I find it difficult to sort out who is active and who is passive, who is subject and who is object. You're dominant if you hold the lasso, submissive if it holds you." *Wonder Woman #16*, then, takes rape seriously—but that seriousness does not allow rape to control the whole course of a story or a life. Trauma recurs, and violence repeats, but that doesn't mean the traumatized should only be allowed to be submissive victims—or that they should only be allowed to be empowered angels of vengeance. Rather, Marston seems to believe, once the power of rape is broken, the world will be safe for rape fantasies and for dominance and submission—the normal emotions.

In one panel in the story's last chapter, the Holliday girls are attempting to escape from the planet Pluto in their rocket (2C; see figure 9). King Pluto comes to stop them in his chariot, drawn by four black horses. Wonder Woman leaps from the rocket, swinging her lasso; the horses rear and buck, Pluto swings his trident. There is no shortage of action, but I find myself looking just as much at the frozen, treelike growths, each one with two major ice-laden branches, each ending in a tapering point. The trees look a little like swans readying to take off, a little like human figures robed in gowns rooted to the spot. They seem both plaintive and hopeful, frozen but ready to ascend. They're not especially important to the comic, and it's possible that Peter didn't even draw them—assistants would occasionally help him with backgrounds. But there they are, eloquent, beautiful, and not a little goofy, neither defined by the narrative nor entirely separate from it, looking for all the world as if somebody has taken the time to care about them.

CHAPTER TWO

CASTRATION IN PARADISE

For Marston and Peter, Wonder Woman was both a mighty, battling Amazon and an avatar of peace. This chapter explores the logic and paradoxes of a hero who literally fights for pacifism. It is split into four parts. In the first part, "Just Warriors," I examine the way in which superhero comics typically handle pacifism and violence, looking specifically at the use of the Amish in *The Nail* and at the conflation of gender and violence in Spider-Man's origin story to create an iconic male Just Warrior, in whom the good and the powerful are one.

In the second part, "Education Mothers," I look at the way in which Marston and Peter both embrace the idea of a female Just Warrior and replace it with the alternate idea of heroine as love leader or education mother. I use the work of Anne Allison on the mother-centered pop culture of Japan to discuss the extent to which the education mother does not so much separate the good and the powerful as she provides a better good through a more effective technology of power.

In the third part, "Wounded Soldiers," I look at Marston and Peter's comics in the context of World War II and suggest that they use the idea of the wounded soldier to undermine or balance the idea of the Just Warrior. I link this discussion to the literature on the erotic and political potential of masochism and contrast Marston and Peter with Leopold von Sacher-Masoch's *Venus in Furs*.

In the fourth part, "Empowered Servants," I argue that Marston and Peter challenge the link between the good and the powerful by appealing to an ethic of submission and love analogous to Christian pacifism. Goodness is in giving up control, not retaining it—an ethic that challenges the norms of superhero comics and of the society of which those comics are still a part.

Wonder Woman will "weave her spell of love and beauty and peace over throbbing human hearts!" Marston exulted in a typically over-heated introduction to Sensation Comics #4, April 1942 (1). In Wonder Woman #12 from spring 1945, he went even further, insisting that Wonder Woman had learned "a way to change the warlike natures of Earth men and start a new era of world peace and happiness!" (1A). Weaving a spell of peace over human hearts and transforming humans' warlike nature is quite a feat—especially if you're a superhero. Superheroes, after all, don't usually resolve conflict through negotiation or passive resistance. They usually solve problems by hitting things.

That's an oversimplification, of course. Sometimes superheroes solve problems by shooting them with a blast of cosmic energy or by whacking them with a mighty hammer. The less pugnacious superheroes sometimes may even resolve conflict by throwing a lasso over it. And then hitting it. But whether by fist or blast, whether by hammer or lasso, the fact remains that superheroes as a genre are built on violence—not, perhaps, exclusively but not incidentally either. Why read about the strongest man in the universe, after all, if you're just going to watch him shuffle paper? Why purchase a comic about a hero with foot-long claws in order to watch him slice bread?[1] A superhero can spend an issue chatting with teammates in the pursuit of character development rather than villains. Superheroes such as Wonder Woman or Grant Morrison's Animal Man[2] may prefer to settle conflicts without bloodshed when they can. But a superhero who eschews violence in every case is in serious danger of ceasing to be a superhero—either diegetically or through the extranarrative doom of cancellation.

The bulk of this chapter is devoted to showing how Marston and Peter tried to undo the connection between superheroes and violence. Before examining Marston/Peter, though, I think it's important to look in some detail at the precise ways in which violence is central to super-heroics—and, perhaps, vice versa. In order to understand the oddity and difficulty of the pacifist superhero, in other words, we need a better understanding of the nonpacifist superhero. For that reason, I start with an extended discussion of two non–*Wonder Woman* comics—writer/artist Alan Davis's 1998 DC-universe alternate-history graphic novel *JLA: The Nail* and Stan Lee and Steve Ditko's first Spider-Man story.[3] To be sure, neither of these comics is particularly violent as superhero stories go. They are, however, both ideologically committed to violence—not as excessive, gratuitous spectacle but as the essence of heroism. In these narratives, a hero must be violent. As such, they provide insight into what conditions must obtain for Marston and Peter to create a hero who is not.

The Amish Plot to Destroy the Superheroes

Alan Davis's *JLA: The Nail* is a what-if story involving an alternate DC universe. Davis's high concept is that John and Martha Kent ran over a nail on the day that baby Superman's rocket ship landed on Earth. As a result, the Kents didn't find the ship. Instead (as we learn toward the end of the book), an Amish family found it. Since the Amish won't interact with the rest of the world, and since the Amish are pacifist, the fact that this family discovered Superman meant that he never became a superhero; he just stayed on the farm. Without Superman's iconic presence, superheroes (and especially aliens) are distrusted, Lex Luthor gains legitimate political power to further his nefarious ends, and no one is tough enough to stand up to various uber-powerful Kryptonian villains. In short, things go to the bad, and it's all because of the stupid Amish.

The Nail is an exercise in bottom-drawer fanscruff, a chance to banally reimagine a universe of characters who were plenty banal to start with (What if Green Lantern were the most powerful hero in the universe?! Great Scott, that would change *everything!*) Still, while no one would call *The Nail* an even marginally intelligent comic, there is something of the idiot savant about it. Davis was looking for a way to neutralize Superman and, by extension, all of superdom. So what is the opposite of the superhero? The obvious answer is a supervillain. Too obvious—and, incidentally, untrue. Superheroes and supervillains are part of the same world and the same milieu. Indeed, since the grim-and-gritty turn of the 1980s, many heroes (such as Ghost Rider, the Punisher, and Spawn) have become virtually indistinguishable from villains (Klock 80). If Superman were a supervillain, it would not remove or negate him; it would simply put him front and center in a different role.

So making Superman a supervillain does not cancel him. But what if you make him a pacifist? Then he's ineffectual, irrelevant—he's nothing. That is to say, it's not supervillainy that's the opposite of superheroics but pacifism. Thus, *The Nail* confirms the greatness of superheroics by having the greatest superhero of all explicitly repudiate nonviolence. This repudiation is sealed by the gratuitous and gruesome obliteration of Superman's Amish parents, who barely get a panel or two to express their misguided philosophy before Davis reduces them to ash. You can almost hear the creators cackling gleefully, "That's what you get for keeping Superman down, you religious weirdos!"

Following this sequence in which Superman sees his (Amish) parents killed and then attacks the superpowered evil Jimmy Olsen (don't ask), Superman and Jimmy battle. Unfortunately, Superman (being Amish and not good at fighting) can't beat the villain. Luckily, though, Olsen spontaneously disintegrates because his powers are unstable. In the aftermath, Superman decides to become a standard-issue superhero, and the implication is that his innate awesomeness will defuse the antialien hysteria that has swept the world.

So parents killed, check. Vengeance inflicted, check. Dedicate life to superheroics to honor parents, check—except that, from the point of view of both the drama and the plot, Superman's repudiation of nonviolence is completely superfluous and even, arguably, detrimental. After all, Superman could have just as easily handled Olsen through nonviolent means—by getting in his way or holding on to him or chatting with him about the weather. Since Olsen essentially disintegrated on his own, the outcome would have been the same. The only difference is that Superman would have actually kept faith with his parents rather than betraying their beliefs for nothing. Similarly, if the world is terrified of malevolent aliens, the sudden revelation of an even more powerful violent alien in their midst seems unlikely to calm things down. Instead, couldn't Superman have revealed himself to the world as a superpowerful alien who embraced nonviolence and noninterference in the affairs of the world? Wouldn't that have been a more effective statement? The logic of the story that Davis has constructed—with Superman as Amish—seems to lead naturally to a parable about the triumph of nonviolence. If the greatest hero in the world is a pacifist, it makes sense that you'd end up with a story in which pacifism is heroic. Unless, of course, you see pacifism and heroism as mutually exclusive, in which case the heroism comes not from the pacifist witness but from repudiating your entire past in order to embrace violence in the name of your dead parents, who would, undoubtedly, be appalled.

Ben Saunders in his book *Do the Gods Wear Capes?* argues that Superman is defined not by his powers but by his "moral beauty" and by his "absolute *a priori* commitment to a finally unverifiable and unknowable good" (32). *The Nail* puts a good deal of pressure on that argument. The goodness of Superman, and of superheroes in general, the *Nail* suggests, is a goodness that relies on, and is inseparable from, power and violence. If Superman does not use violence, he is not Superman and cannot do good. Q.E.D. In superhero comics, then, power is something you must live up to—it is something that elevates you, something that makes you good. This fits with Robert Jewett and John Shelton Lawrence's characterization of the superhero as one who "couples transcendent moral perfection with an extraordinary capability for effective acts"—those acts intrinsically involving, as Jewett and Lawrence argue, vigilante violence (29). To be that transcendentally moral superhero, you need to do those extraordinary acts, which means that Amish Superman is a better person when he embraces his power and starts hitting villains. Superheroes are ideal heroes because they are stronger than the rest of us, and being good is predicated, in no small part, on being strong.

Peter Parker, the Spectacular Spider-Finger

The phrase "being good depends on being strong" echoes in spirit, if not precisely in meaning, Stan Lee's famous dictum, "with great power comes great responsibility." That phrase was coined in Spider-Man's first appearance in *Amazing Fantasy #15*, with a cover date of 1962, written by Lee and drawn by Steve Ditko. As most comics readers know, Spidey's origin hinges on a moment of moral turpitude. Nerdy, put-upon Peter Parker, having been bitten by that pesky radioactive spider, gains superpowers and starts a successful career as a television variety act. Basking in his newfound fame and bucks, Peter (in Spidey costume) is standing in a corridor when he sees some schmo fleeing from a cop. Cop yells to Peter to stop schmo, but Peter refuses; schmo gets onto a high-speed elevator and escapes (8). The cop chews Peter out: "All you hadda do was trip him!" Peter, though, is unrepentant: "Sorry, Pal! That's your job! I'm through being pushed around!" Peter walks off, and then on the next page, his uncle is murdered! And two pages later, Peter learns that the guy who shot his uncle is the same guy he allowed to escape! Oh, the irony!

So that's the story, in all its melodramatic improbability. But now, for a moment, let's imagine a what-if version of this tale. Everything is the same, except that Peter is a girl named (to keep things alliterative) Patricia. Like Peter, Patricia is a nerdy kid with few friends and parents who can't pay their bills. Like Peter, Patricia is bitten by a radioactive spider; like Peter, she decides to become a television performer to make a little money. And like Peter, she is standing in a corridor when some random schmo runs past. And like Peter, the cop sees her and shouts . . . and shouts what?

It strains credulity a little to imagine that a cop would demand that a random *male* bystander apprehend a fleeing and dangerous felon. But it's substantially more difficult to believe that a cop would demand that a woman put herself at risk. This is especially so in the early 1960s. But even, still, today, despite many images of female action heroes from Ripley to Buffy to Xena, gendered expectations remain quite different for men and women. Certainly, women *can* be heroes, but they are very rarely *obligated* to be heroes. If a male cop saw a woman in the path of a fleeing perp, he wouldn't tell her to trip the perp or to hit the perp. On the contrary, he'd probably tell her to get out of the way.

In considering Wonder Woman, this connection between heroism, maleness, and violence is suggestive. It reminds us that, as Jean Bethke Elshtain writes in *Women and War*, "We in the West are the heirs of a tradition that assumes an affinity between women and peace, men and war." Elshtain goes on: "Thus in times of war, real men and women—locked in a dense symbiosis, perceived as beings who have complementary needs and exemplify gender-specific virtues—take on, in cultural memory and narrative, the personas of Just Warriors and Beautiful Souls" (4). Those men who refuse to be Just Warriors are subject to ridicule, abuse, and other forms of coercion (203). Thus, Elaine Showalter describes how during World War I, the poet and officer Siegfried

Sassoon was placed in a mental hospital for speaking out against the war. There he was treated by psychiatrist William H. R. Rivers, who, Showalter says, deliberately attempted "the reinscription of male gender anxieties in someone who had spoken against the war" (67).

> In lengthy conversations three times a week, Rivers and Sassoon talked not only about Sassoon's life and war experiences but also about European politics, German military history, and the dangers of a premature peace. This talking cure was intended to make Sassoon feel uneasy about the gaps in his information and to emphasize the contrast between his emotional, and thus feminine, attitude toward the war and Rivers' rational, masculine, Cambridge don's view. At the same time, Sassoon found himself in the company of "nurses and nervous wrecks" and men who had "done their bit in France" crying like children. He was anxious to assert his superiority to his fellow officers. (66)

Similarly, some World War II conscientious objectors were so eager to prove that they were not yellowbellies that they volunteered for medical experimentations. They allowed themselves to be put on starvation diets or to be injected with typhus or hepatitis. A number of them died, martyrs to pacifist machismo (*Good War*).

Like Siegfried Sassoon's, Peter's moral turpitude is, then, a *gendered* moral turpitude. His failure is a failure not merely to be a good person but to be a Just Warrior—to be a man. The Lee/Ditko story is constructed around, and even obsessed with, the demand that Peter assume his normative, Just Warrior role. The opening page of the story, for example, shows the awkward, bespectacled Peter standing against a wall. His shadow is a silhouetted, giant Spider-Man shadow, which takes a virile, legs-spread pose. Meanwhile, below, the real Peter is crouched in an unmanly hunch. A shadow-web stands behind the shadow-man, and that shadow-web is topped by a giant, ominous silhouette spider. Peter is, effectively menaced by his own heroism; he is about to be trapped (and eaten) by the masculine Just Warrior that he is to become.

More subtly, in the panel in which Peter is scolded by the cop, the policeman is shown leaning over; the perspective makes it look as if he would tower above Peter if he stood straight up. The guard, then, becomes a kind of adult father-figure. His hands, meanwhile, gesture eloquently—one of them points over his shoulder at the vanished perp; the other, with one finger stuck out, almost touches Peter's chest. Craig Fischer has noted that Ditko's stories are replete with the "fear of being touched"; here that anxiety recalls and is enmeshed with paternal chastisement. And just as the guard would not have shouted to *Patricia* Parker to stop a felon, so he surely would not have pointed at her in that intimate, threatening way—at least not if Lee and Ditko wanted him to appear as a moral authority rather than as a big, blustering bully. The patriarchal finger, both threatening violence and summoning to violence, is not to be deployed against women. It is shared between men.

Superheroes are, then, a kind of Just Warrior—and the Just Warrior is, Elshtain argues, a specifically masculine role. For the superhero, it is not just the good and the powerful that are bound together but the good, the powerful, and the male. In Spider-Man's origin, gender is the lever—or the finger—that pushes Peter to fulfill the genre expectations of violence. Since Wonder Woman is a different gender, her genre expectations, and her relation to violence, might be different too.

This raises some thorny questions. A basic feminist tenet is equality for men and women—especially intellectual and moral equality. "My doctrine," the early feminist Angelina Grimké wrote in 1837, "is, that whatever it is morally right for man to do, it is morally right for woman to do" (93). But, as Elshtain notes, feminists have been torn in applying this doctrine of moral equality to issues of violence and war (231). If it is morally right for women to do what men do, then should Wonder Woman, like Peter, be expected to stop the robber with violence? Or is the expectation of violence, for Peter as for Wonder Woman, a bullying imposition? Should women be heroes, or should men not be? And where exactly does that leave Wonder Woman?

One way to approach these questions is to see women's different experience in relation to heroism and violence not only as an example of discrimination and sexism (which it certainly is) but also as a resource. Stanley Hauerwas, a Christian theologian and pacifist, relates one example of how women's experiences can challenge thinking about war:

I once remarked that, as a pacifist, I represent the minority tradition in Christian history; but I was challenged by one of my feminist graduate students. She observed that most Christians through most of Christian history were nonviolent, since most Christians have been women who have been prohibited from warfare. That they had no choice . . . makes the nonviolence that characterized their lives no less significant. Such observations require a much greater framework of support to be compelling, but they at least remind us that the church has never been devoid of nonviolent witness. (122)

Hauerwas's student suggests that instead of seeing Peter's position as the baseline, we might instead switch to Patricia's perspective. Violence could be seen as an aberration rather than as normative. Instead of the powerful being tied to the good, one could instead see power, especially the power of violence, as diminishing or corrupting.

This is the tack Simone Weil takes in her discussion of the *Iliad*. Violence in this poem about heroism, she argues, "obliterates anybody who feels its touch," whether victim or perpetrator (20). And again: "The wantonness of the conqueror that knows no respect for any creature or thing that is at its mercy or is imagined to be so, the despair of the soldier that drives him on to destruction, the obliteration of the slave or the conquered man, the wholesale slaughter—all these elements combine in the *Iliad* to make a picture of uniform horror, of which force is the sole hero" (27). For Weil, the use of violence and power makes you less good and, indeed, less human. When you use violence, you become an object, and the only "hero" is force itself—the only protagonist, death. As Marston says in *Emotions of Normal People*, "Hatred is the abnormal emotion that accompanies destruction of *human things* by *human things*" (378–379).

Weil's gender makes her, historically, an unusual figure to speak on violence. Elshtain notes that men are usually seen as the ones empowered to talk about war; they are the ones who have "been there" and who know what it "must be like" (212). One thing men don't know, though, is what heroism, violence, and power look like to a woman. For Peter Parker, just war means obligation, guilt, and an index finger—but it might mean something different to Patricia. Just because the Amish are the opposite of Superman, that doesn't necessarily mean they are the opposite of Wonder Woman. Looking at Spider-Man's origin makes it clear, I think, that superhero violence is built on, and reliant on, masculinity. Thus, female heroes are, in the words of Frances H. Early and Kathleen Kennedy, "capable of disrupting the narrative tradition of the male just warrior, notably its reliance on violence and its concomitant objectification and exploitation of women" (3). In theory, then, Wonder Woman's gender could open up a space between violence and heroism that might not be available to Peter—or, for that matter, to Amish Superman. But what about in practice? Do Marston and Peter show Wonder Woman in their comics as having a different relationship to violence than other superheroes do?

It is certainly true that, in Marston and Peter's initial conception, Wonder Woman, like other heroes, often solves problems in the quintessentially superhero manner. That is, she hits things. Even beyond her enjoyment of fisticuffs, though, the Marston/Peter Wonder Woman was defined by violence—specifically by her participation in World War II. It's true that she came from an isolated island populated by ancient Greeks, but that didn't stop her from donning a star-spangled swimsuit. Patriotic bombast, in this case, thoroughly trounced diegetic probability. Wonder Woman's first adventure had a cover date of December 1941, and she leaped enthusiastically into the war effort, fighting Nazis, Japanese, spies, and, in *Wonder Woman #2*, a slobbering, literally rug-chewing Hitler himself (3B).

In this, again, Wonder Woman was in line with her fellow male superheroes. According to Bradford Wright, sales of comic books skyrocketed following America's entry into World War II. In early 1942, shortly after Pearl Harbor, comic-book sales were around fifteen million copies sold a month. By December 1943, they had leapt to more than twenty-five million copies a month (Wright 31). "Publishers . . . sought to boost their image by linking their products to patriotism and the war effort"—so heroes encouraged the public to buy war bonds, chastised noninterventionists, and, of course, fought the Axis in nearly every issue (Wright 36–45). It was natural that Wonder Woman's alter-ego, Diana Prince, worked as a secretary for army intelligence, just as it was natural for Wonder Woman herself to foil spy rings and Nazi plots. Superheroes and the war went together as surely as did goodness and power. But while Marston was committed to having Wonder Woman fight in the war effort, he also saw her, contradictorily, as a force for peace. Other super male do-gooders could simply fight the good fight. Wonder Woman had to be a supersoldier *and* an icon for peace—which is sort of like having to do everything Captain America does but backward and in heels.

So how can an Amazon warrior be a fighter for peace? Marston and Peter had several overlapping answers to that question. Some of these answers are surprisingly pragmatic. For example, in a panel in *Wonder Woman #1*, we see two gods debating the future of the Earth. On the left sits Mars, who is so overmuscled that his limbs have the bloated, unformed look of a child's. He points one fat digit and chortles with four-year-old glee, "Ho! Ho! The whole world's at war—I rule the earth!" Across from him, Aphrodite sits stretched out on a cot, her gown draped gracefully around her, one arm raised in a gesture of matriarchal admonishment. "Your rule will end when America wins! And America will win! I'll send an Amazon to help her!" (8A).

Or again, in an introductory text page to *Wonder Woman #2*, fall 1942, Marston declares,

> Mars and Aphrodite, Goddess of love and beauty, have been rivals for control of this earth ever since life began. At present, Mars is far ahead in the struggle against his beautiful opponent. More than four-fifths of the entire world is at war! More than two billion people are involved in the present colossal conflict! Mars is triumphant!
>
> But one Amazon girl is more than a match for all Mars' cohorts! Wonder Woman is helping America win the War and if America wins, peace will return—the world will be ruled happily by the love and beauty of Aphrodite!

And that is the basic algorithm. The Nazis embody war; therefore, fighting the Nazis is fighting on behalf of peace. Or, more broadly, masculinity embodies war; therefore, fighting on behalf of an America that Marston sees as feminine means fighting on behalf of peace.

The form in which Marston puts the argument is crude, but what he is saying is not absurd on its face. Reinhold Niebuhr, in his famous

1940 essay "Why the Christian Church Is Not Pacifist," argued that Christians judging the rightness of wars needed to make "discriminate criticisms" based on the "law of love" (116–117). Niebuhr was, perhaps, not specifically arguing that the goddess of love should back America in the interest of peace, but I think he would nonetheless appreciate Marston's general sentiment.[4] Along the same line, when Barack Obama declared in his Nobel Prize speech that "the instruments of war do have a role to play in preserving the peace," he wasn't thinking about invisible planes and magic lassos, but there's no reason to think he would rule them out if they were available. This kind of pragmatic balancing of war and peace fits easily enough into conventional gendered narratives of goodness, heroism, and power. When Obama says, "Peace requires responsibility," you can hear the echo of Stan Lee letting Peter Parker know how to be a man (perhaps even an intentional echo, given the president's avowed fondness for comics).[5] When Niebuhr says that those who oppose the war harbor "sentimental illusions" (118), he might as well be Rivers admonishing Sassoon for his irrational, unrealistic, unmanly pacifism.

In *Wonder Woman*, the warrior who is actuated by pragmatic, manly motives is not a man but a woman. Thus, in *Wonder Woman #1*, Diana begs her mother, Hippolyte, to be allowed to go fight in man's world, using an appeal to reason: "But Mother! *Some* girl must do it!" In the next panel, Diana has donned a mysterious mask; two panels later, she's performing gladiatorial feats atop Peter's gorgeously scribbly fighting Amazonian battle kangaroos (9A–10A). The quick leap from pragmatic reasoning to kangaroo battle suggests that the pragmatism may not be quite so pragmatic after all. Instead, reasoned duty is the prerequisite—the pretext?—for mystery, excitement, adventure. Peter Parker and Reinhold Niebuhr whine about the difficult burdens of duty—but would they really rather be stuck at home with mother than out there in the world battling evil (whether supervillains or pacifists) and righting wrongs? Similarly, from Marston and Peter's perspective, Virginia Woolf seems to be protesting too much when she insists in *Three Guineas*, "Though many instincts are held more or less in common by both sexes, to fight has always been the man's habit, not the woman's. . . . Obviously there is for you [men] some glory, some necessity, some satisfaction in fighting which we have never felt or enjoyed" (6). Everything Diana does is in contradiction to Woolf's idea that women do not understand the satisfactions of glory or of fighting. It's true that in her origin story, Diana is said to want to go to man's world because she's in love with Steve Trevor. But it seems just as true to say that she's in love with Steve Trevor (whom she's barely met, after all) because she wants to go to man's world and, indeed, to take her place in the traditionally male narrative of duty, violence, and adventure. Just as in George Eliot's *Middlemarch* Casaubon appeals to Dorothea because he seems to offer her a wider world for her ambitions and skill, so Steve appeals to Diana because he gets her (first) onto that kangaroo and (later) off the island and into battle.

A big part of Wonder Woman's attraction, then, is not that she comes from a female-only island but that she embraces man's world and makes it hers. As Lillian Robinson notes, Wonder Woman is in many ways a tomboy who "challenged traditional feminine roles" (48)—she's physical, competitive, and even mischievous. In *Wonder Woman #1*, when she receives the magic lasso that compels obedience, the first thing she does with it is to throw the rope around a nearby Amazon doctor and force her to stand on her head.[6] In Peter's drawing, Wonder Woman holds the lasso like a pair of reins while the doctor, head down, legs up, ends up looking like a rearing pony (12A). Power may corrupt, but corruption, as it turns out, is pretty fun. The narrative of the Just Warrior creates a space not only for adventure, and violence, but also for high spirits—and, not incidentally, for sexualized fantasies of dominance and control.

As I touched on in chapter 1, one feminist who articulates the strong feminist appeal of a female Just Warrior is Susan Brownmiller. In her classic study of rape, *Against Our Will*, Brownmiller argues that it is of vital importance for feminists to break the female tradition of nonviolence. "We have been trained to cry, to wheedle, to plead, to look for a male protector, but we have never been trained to fight and win," Brownmiller says (402). She then goes on to a gleeful description of her own brief exposure to martial arts training and her recognition that she could "inspire fear in the men" in the class—especially by threatening to kick them in the crotch. Brownmiller concluded that "fighting back"—physically, politically, literally and figuratively— is vital for women to end patriarchy and to end what she calls the "ideology of rape," in which men are always figured as attackers and women are always figured as victims (403–404).

Thus, if the Just Warrior for men can be a trap and a weight, for women it can be a release and a joy. When a woman fights on kangaroo-back or kicks an attacker in the crotch, it's an adrenalin rush of good, violent fun. And if it's fun for women, that suggests strongly that—despite a certain amount of Spider whining—it's fun for men as well. Virginia Woolf was certainly right when she argued that men get pleasure from violence. But she was just as certainly wrong when she argued that women don't. Rather, if genre narratives tell us anything, it's that both men and women, civilians and warriors, misogynists and feminists, presidents and theologians, find a powerful appeal in the idea of righteous combat. Marston and Peter were among the first to package the Just Warrior for women, but—as Susan Brownmiller, Buffy the Vampire Slayer, Katniss Everdeen, and many other examples show—they weren't the last.

In one sense, then, Marston and Peter did not use gender to undermine the connection between the good and the powerful. Instead, they pried gender loose from the narrative while leaving the basic superhero structure intact, so that a woman could occupy the position normally taken by a man. Instead of a Just Male Warrior, Marston and Peter created a Just Amazon. Wonder Woman, from this pragmatic perspective, is simply Superman in a bustier.

However, the Amazon Just Warrior was not Marston and Peter's only take on violence. They and their audience definitely enjoyed allowing women to hit villains in the jaw. But they also, at times, were willing to approach the relationship between the good and the powerful in different ways.

EDUCATION MOTHERS

Again, for men, the role of Just Warrior is often a duty. Spider-Man and Amish Superman have to be heroes, whether they will or no. Wonder Woman, in contrast, almost never has to be coerced into heroism. Whether it's nonchalantly sending her astral body off to Mars in *Wonder Woman #2* ("Bye Etta—I'll be back—don't worry if I seem dead"; 4C) or bursting her bonds for the billionth time ("Why did they bind me with such small chains? It's an insult!"; *Sensation Comics #21* 11), she is always game for a rollicking adventure.[7]

But while Wonder Woman is cheerful about leaping into peril, she is less enthusiastic when called on to perform other duties. In particular, she doesn't want to be a schoolmarm. You wouldn't think there would be much call for a superhero to be a schoolmarm in the first place. But Marston had other ideas. In his psychological treatise, *Emotions of Normal People*, Marston argues that society and culture are too competitive—or, in his terminology, too appetitive, or based on appetites. He says that society must be transformed so that it is based on love rather than competition. To bring this about, individuals must be emotionally reeducated by a group of super schoolmarms—or, in Marston's terminology, "love leaders" (392). He then asks the obvious question: "Where can the emotional re-educator look for persons capable of being trained toward ultimate love leadership? We have already seen that males cannot be counted on, unless the male organism changes radically. The only possible candidates for love leader training, therefore, are women" (394). Marston argues that women are unfortunately not yet assertive enough to grasp the role of love leader. But, he says optimistically, there is hope: "women are beginning to develop both the power and willingness to support themselves" (394). Once women have developed this capacity by "three or four times," they will be in a position to become love leaders, to command men, and to transform the world. For Marston, then, Wonder Woman is not, or not only, a Just Warrior. She is also a love leader—a superpowerful reeducator, strong and independent enough to lead the world in the ways of love.

You may well think that Marston's vision of superhero as instructress is a bit . . . cranky, shall we say? If so, you would be in good company. Even Wonder Woman herself is not entirely on board. Her doubts are expressed most clearly in *Wonder Woman #4*. In that issue, she encounters a bunch of male tycoons who have been deliberately impeding the war effort because they are selfish and greedy and (though this is probably redundant for Marston) male. Paula, Wonder Woman's superscientist ally, decides to take the tycoons in hand. She straps them into a special chair, puts electrodes on their heads, and then . . . shows them pictures of Wonder Woman. Or, as Paula's assistant tells a helpless industrialist, "We're printing a picture of Wonder Woman on your brain!" (12C).

The process suggests both mother-child imprinting and the sort of media-sensitization paranoia that Stanley Kubrick later made famous in *A Clockwork Orange* (1971). In one goofily disturbing panel, Peter draws Wonder Woman's enlarged head staring out at the tycoon, her skin perfectly smooth, her mouth set, her eyes looking almost cruelly into the distance. In contrast, the tycoon seems shrunken and dwarfed. As Derik Badman notes, the men in Wonder Woman always look "a bit grotesque," but in this instance, Peter goes even further than usual. The series of lines on the industrialist's face are probably meant to indicate sags and folds, but they also look like motion lines, so that his skin seems to be quivering atop his skull. "I-submit-to Wonder Woman!" the industrialist gasps. "She is my commandress—I must obey Wonder Woman always!" (12C).

FIGURE 10. *Wonder Woman #4* (1943)

Paula works with a will, and soon there is a whole phalanx of tycoons with Wonder Woman's image stamped on their brains. Alas, though, and understandably, Wonder Woman is not entirely pleased to have a bunch of aging assholes in her thrall. Just as Peter Parker was reluctant to be a hero and catch the villain, so Wonder Woman is reluctant to be a love leader and reform him. "But I don't want to be commandress over a lot of men—why don't you do it?" she asks Paula. However, Paula explains that she is not yet an initiate in Aphrodite's service, and so the emotional reeducation program is up to Wonder Woman (12C).

As I've already suggested, Paula's indoctrination machine bears more than a passing resemblance to a movie projector. This is no coincidence. Before Marston began writing comics, he worked as a consulting psychologist with the Hollywood studios, using his work with lie-detector technology to measure the emotional effect of motion pictures. He then went on to do similar consulting work for a number of advertising agencies. No doubt Paula's experiments are based in part on that experience and on Marston's certainty that "motion pictures are emotion pictures"—that films can directly influence human biopsychology (qtd. in Alder 186; Valcour 61). While there's definitely a link to Marston's film-industry work, though, it's also hard to miss the comics-centered self-reflexivity of Paula's hypno–Wonder Woman treatment. The men are strapped into a chair and forced to stare at images of Wonder Woman—the same images of Wonder Woman that are, in all their frozen, repetitive glory, being implanted on the brain stems of willing comic-book readers. Wonder Woman commands the tycoons to support the war effort—and, in parallel, Wonder Woman is telling her readers to support the war effort. In a letter written to the comics historian Coulton Waugh, Marston referred to Wonder Woman as "psychological propaganda" (qtd. in Daniels 22). In *Wonder Woman #4*, he shows explicitly how that propaganda is supposed to work. Eroticized images of our heroine are repeated and repeated until, as Paula says, "You shall see her picture always stamped on your brain." Legions of comic-book readers, all of them following Wonder Woman as their matriarch/commandress—you can almost see Marston rubbing his hands together and trembling with delight. What a brave new world that has such media delivery systems in it.

So Paula's brain-stamping technique is like movies and it's like comics. But it is also, more generally, like any kind of education—or, less kindly, indoctrination. The educational endeavor is, moreover, eroticized. After Wonder Woman agrees to command the tycoons, for example, she's shown in a panel checking her men over as they all stand rigidly at attention in an oddly empty room. Their stiffness and Peter's haphazard anatomy make them look less like humans than like some sort of toy soldiers (see figure 11). Wonder Woman even gives them the pet, Transformer-esque appellation of "Reformandos" (13C).

The men and the educational endeavor itself are, for Marston, fetishized. The industrialists are both Wonder Woman's imprinted children and her playthings—which means that the relationship between them and mother/lover Wonder Woman is incestuous. This eroticization of mother-child bonds runs throughout Marston's work, more or less openly. For example, in his book *Integrative Psychology*, Marston talks about women's power of "captivation"—a term he uses to describe both the way that women control their lovers and the way

FIGURE 11. *Wonder Woman #4* (1943)

that mothers control their children (Marston, King, and Marston 197, 215). In *Sensation Comics #28*, Marston has a gangster declare after Wonder Woman has knocked him around, "You handled me like a kid, Wonder Woman, and danged if I don't like it!" (6). And in *Emotions of Normal People*, Marston suggests that male failure to form loving attachments later in life "might, of course, be prevented by social sanction of genital organ stimulation [of infants] by the mother" (314).[8]

Mother Power

Men, for Marston, can be made more loving, and presumably less violent, if only their mothers would play with their genitals. Love leaders can socialize their children by seducing them. With great power comes great responsibility—but the great responsibility is not violence, as for male Just Warriors. Rather, the great responsibility is a specifically incestuous love. Spider-Man has to punch the bad guy in the face; Wonder Woman has to give him some very special care. Marston and Peter, then, appear to have used gender to cut the knot that ties superheroes and violence. Instead of the father's thrusting finger, we have the mother's gentle hand. Wonder Woman does not win by bashing people but by seducing them.

The question, though, is whether seduction can be itself a kind of violence. What does it mean, in terms of violence, to have Wonder

Woman burned into your brain? Is the rule of the mother really less coercive than the rule of the father? To answer that question, you need to have an example of mother's rule. Since most societies have historically been patriarchal, this is trickier than it might at first appear. However, there is at least one excellent anthropological study of a society organized to at least a limited degree around maternal authority: Anne Allison's *Permitted and Prohibited Desires: Mothers, Comics, and Censorship in Japan.* While 1980s Japan is obviously very different from 1940s America, Marston's fantasy matriarchies eerily anticipate in many respects the mother-centered, middle-class Japanese community that Allison describes. Allison's book, in turn, provides numerous insights into Marston's obsessions with incest, mothers, reeducation, and violence.

Allison's study examines how images of motherhood interacted with systems of social control and sexual fantasies in late-capitalist Japan. One of the most striking cultural phenomena she looked at were urban legends about mother-son incest:

> In the 1980s a number of stories about mother-son incest were reported in the popular press in Japan. The elements of each were remarkably consistent: An adolescent male entering the period of intense study leading up to entrance exams is distracted by sexual desire. His mother, who has assumed the role of a *kyōiku mama* [education mother], notices the distraction and worries that it will obstruct the boy's work. To prevent this, she offers to become her son's lover and thereby satisfy his pressing need. The boy complies and the two commence an affair. The sexual relationship, found deeply pleasurable by both partners, quickly turns the boy into a model student. In the end the boy typically passes his exams and is appreciative to his mother for her help. The incest, however, does not end. Rather, the confusing relationship between man-woman and mother-son is left unresolved at the story's close. (123)

The *kyōiku mam,* as indicated in the quote, is the Japanese term for an education mother—or, if you will, for a love leader. An education mother in Japan is devoted, even consumed, with helping her son through the challenging Japanese school system, in which scores on high-stakes exams can determine a child's entire career. In these urban legends, then, an education mother has sex with her son in order to help him do better on his exams. Erotic energy here does not undermine or compromise social order; it is used in the interest of social order. Instead of repressing the Oedipal complex for the greater good of society, these stories suggest that Oedipal frolicking will lead to better socialization and higher test scores—just as motherly manipulation of infant genitals will, in Marston's view, result in better-adjusted adults.[9] In the same way (if less explicitly), Wonder Woman uses her maternal/erotic love to make the wayward children/industrialists into useful citizens. Thus, Oedipal love is seen as central to the act of education and, by extension, of socialization. For both Wonder Woman and the education mother, the child figure becomes erotically invested in the mother, and that erotic investment is what allows him to succeed (at exams or industrial production, as the case may be).

As Allison points out, this is definitely *not* the way things are supposed to work, either from a strict Freudian perspective or from a looser, rule-of-thumb Western perspective. In the West, a child with a major erotic investment in his mother is a child that has *failed* at socialization. A man tied to his mother's apron strings as the tycoons are bonded to Wonder Woman is characteristically infantilized; he is not mature. To understate the point wildly, incest in the West is not supposed to be a path to career success. In Japan, however, things are somewhat different. The education-mother incest stories were seen as deviant and even horrific in Japan, just as they would have been in the United States. And there's no evidence that incest is any more prevalent, or any more acceptable, in Japan than it is in America. And yet, clearly, there was an appeal to these stories of mother-son incest. This appeal, Allison argues, was based in part on the fact that such stories were *not* deviant. Rather, in the Japanese context, the stories fit into normal, and even normative, cultural mores.

To make this argument, Allison relies in part on the work of Kosawa Heisaku, the pioneer of Japanese psychoanalysis. Kosawa argued that child development and psychoanalytic categories were different in Japan than they were in the West. In particular, Kosawa maintained that in Japan, socialization is mother centered rather than father centered (Allison 136). Allison applied this insight to late-capitalist Japanese society. In the 1980s, when Allison was doing her anthropological fieldwork, middle-class Japanese fathers were very marginal to family life. Spending long hours commuting and even longer hours in the office, Japanese men barely had time to wave to their children, much less threaten them with castration in the Freudian tradition. Indeed, Allison says, in Japan maturation "barely involves the father" (3). With the father gone, and the threat of castration with him, there is, from a Freudian perspective, no incentive for the son to stop loving the mother or to seek a relationship outside the family. Thus, Japanese sons remain bonded to their mothers even while moving into the world of work and society. Maturation, Allison concludes, is accomplished not by the father's rod (or finger) but by the mother's love.

Obviously, William Marston was not aware of late-capitalist Japanese family structures when he began writing *Wonder Woman* in the 1940s. Still, Marston was trying to imagine a world ruled by mothers rather than fathers—and what he arrived at was similar in important ways to the mother-centered world of 1990s middle-class Japan as described by Allison. Marston's superhero, therefore, is not (or not only) a male Just Warrior—she is (or is also) a love leader. And love leaders look surprisingly similar to Japanese education mothers.

The Force of Love

As we've already seen, violence—characteristically male-gendered violence—is central to the identity of the Just Warrior. The education mother, on the other hand, seems like a model that can pry apart maleness from heroism and (not coincidentally) also pry apart the good and the powerful. The education mother does not bludgeon her foes and toss their battered bodies in the hoosegow. Instead, she fascinates them and cajoles them into the hoosegow through a bond of affection.

In an introduction to a 1972 *Ms.* collection of Wonder Woman stories, Gloria Steinem talks about how much she appreciated the nonviolent methods adopted by both Marston and Wonder Woman:

[Wonder Woman's] creator had . . . seen straight into my heart and understood the secret fears of violence hidden there. No longer did I have to pretend to like the "Pow!" and "Crunch!" style of Captain Marvel or the Green Hornet. No longer did I have nightmares after reading ghoulish comics filled with torture and mayhem, comics made all the more horrifying by their real-life setting in World War II. . . . Here was a heroic person who might conquer with force, but only a force that was tempered by love and justice. (Introduction to *Wonder Woman* [1972] n.p.)

Thus, Wonder Woman's weapon is the magic lasso; she wraps her enemies in its golden strands, and they are compelled to obey her. As Marston said in an interview in the *Family Circle*, the lasso is "a symbol of female charm, allure, oomph, attraction," of the power that "every woman has . . . over people of both sexes whom she wishes to influence or control in any way" (Richard 17). Wonder Woman does not punish her enemies but reforms them. The superscientist Paula—she who imprinted Wonder Woman on the brains of industrialists—was herself initially one of Wonder Woman's deadliest foes. But then Wonder Woman, in her role as educator, saved Paula's child and turned the villainous Nazi mother to the good (in *Wonder Woman #3*). Similarly in *Wonder Woman #12*, evil, warmongering weapons manufacturers determined to start World War III are teleported to the planet Venus. There they are fitted with golden girdles of loving submission and thereby transformed into peaceful (and oddly Edwardian) upstanding citizens. Again, if Wonder Woman were Peter Parker, she would not bash the baddy as he ran past but would convert him to the right through the power of love. (Presumably she would convert the cop too.)

So the love leader, the supermarm, has taken the violence out of superheroing once and for all? Well, not quite. Despite the success of the education mother in converting mad scientists and weapons manufacturers, she is not quite as pacifist as she seems. Consider, for instance, this revealing anecdote about mother love and violence from the beginning of Marston's psychological treatise, *Emotions of Normal People*:

I can still remember vividly the fear I once experienced, as a child, when threatened, on my way to school, by a half-witted boy with an air-gun. I had been taught by my father never to fight; so I ran home in an agony of fear. My mother told me, "Go straight by F——. Don't attack him unless he shoots at you, but if he does, then go after him." I was an obedient child, and followed orders explicitly. I marched up to F—— and his gun with my face set and my stomach sick with dread. F—— did not shoot. I have known, ever since that well-remembered occasion, that fear does *not* give strength in times of stress. Part of the strength with which I faced F——'s air gun came from my own underlying *dominance*, newly released from artificial control. But most of it belonged to my mother, and she was able to use it in my behalf because I *submitted* to her. (2–3)

Marston's mother influenced him through love, but her influence was not in the interest of pacifism. Rather, mother love here functions much as did the father finger—it urges reluctant peaceful boys to become manly Just Warriors, smiting criminals or bullies as the case may be. From this anecdote it's clear that submitting to the mother does not necessarily mean a submission to peace. On the contrary, for the young Marston, submission meant that he was more, not less, capable of violence. Through mother love he became weaponized.

Similarly, as commandress in *Wonder Woman #4*, Wonder Woman instructs her Reformandos to redouble their efforts to produce goods for the war effort. In one panel, a short industrialist with a massive pipe spreads his arms out, almost as if he's going to embrace Wonder Woman. He boasts about how much progress he's making in growing cryptostegia for high-grade rubber. Before him, men move about stooping in a yellow field (13C). Clearly, Wonder Woman's maternal eroticized education is not opposed to war, nor is it opposed to hierarchy. A rule by mothers is not in opposition to the traditional rule of fathers. On the contrary, motherly persuasion is preferable to fatherly force because the motherly persuasion is a *superior* means to win war and encourage capitalist production.

Or again, as one final example, the mother-centered Japanese home is organized around mother love rather than father fear not because mother love is more humanitarian but because it is more *efficient*. The Just Warrior can puff out his chest and hit robbers in the face till his knuckles swell up, but if he ever tussles with an education mother, he is going to find himself with his legs under the desk sweating over his homework while glancing surreptitiously at her bits. To mangle a James Brown lyric, Dad won't change you, but Mom will take you on.[10]

Anne Allison describes in some detail just how Mom takes you on—and for that matter, how the role of Mom takes on mothers themselves. In Japanese nursery schools, mothers are expected to make elaborate *obentos*, or stylized lunches, for their children. The *obentos* are meant to be visually pleasing, nutritionally balanced, and flavorful, and they can take "twenty-five to forty-five minutes" every morning for one child (Allison 89). Let me repeat that: "twenty-five to forty-five minutes" every morning for one child. If you are a parent, those words should send a thrill of terror through your bowels. Furthermore, at school, the child is expected to sit still and eat the entire *obento* quickly and efficiently. If he or she does not, the class is kept inside, and other students will reprimand the child. For that matter, if the child does not eat the *obento*, the mother herself is often reprimanded. (Bad mother! More time preparing *obentos* for you!) Thus, mother love, as externalized in the *obento*, is supposed to integrate the child into the workings of the school and of the school community. As Allison says, "a feeling of coerciveness is rarely experienced" (92)—which is precisely why the coercion is so effective. And this coercion is directed not only at the child but also at the mother, who is inscribed in her gendered role of educator and *obento* maker as surely as the Just Warrior is inscribed in his gendered role of heroic enforcer.

Wonder Woman herself feels the coercion of love in *Wonder Woman #4*. In part because she hesitated to become the commandress of a bunch of loser tycoons, she is hauled before Aphrodite and chastised for failing to shoulder her responsibilities. In one panel, instead of Wonder Woman appearing as an enormous head, she is

FIGURE 12. *Wonder Woman #4* (1943)

drawn miniaturized before the goddess's throne, her face in her hands
and her body doubled over (5D; see figure 12). By not taking on her
proper role as mother and teacher, she has become herself an infant
to be punished. She might, indeed, be a Japanese mother, being reprimanded by the teacher for failure to produce a sufficiently charming
obento.

If the regime for the mother is harsh, the regime for the children is
even more so. In *Wonder Woman #7*, we get to see how kids are treated
on Paradise Island, and it is not especially pleasant. "At the school of
Athena, Amazon children are taught to concentrate on their studies
by kneeling before their books at rigid attention. They are permitted
to move only one hand to turn a page" (1D). And sure enough, Peter
draws a panel of girl children kneeling with their hands tied behind
their backs, their rigid posture and flowing gowns connoting what
rigid postures and flowing gowns generally connote for Peter—that
is, fetishized, eroticized discipline (1D; see figure 13). Thus, Marston
and Peter are subjecting their imaginary students to an unnecessarily
elaborate and arguably cruel school regime, apparently in part because
they find that school regime sexy—which, it seems to me, is a little
nauseating.

FIGURE 13. *Wonder Woman #7* (1943)

Things only get worse as the narrative progresses. Gerta, Paula's child, very reasonably resents having to sit rigidly in place for hours at a stretch just because Marston finds it exciting—I mean, just because her teacher tells her to—and she kicks up a fuss. Most of us would consider said fuss a natural reaction, but Marston does not see it that way. Instead, he interprets it as a sign that Gerta lacks discipline. Using superscientific Amazon technology, Hippolyte looks into the future and sees that not only will Gerta not pass her exams but she will become a world-class supervillain, spreading terror and evil unless she is reprimanded and made to see that it is wrong, wrong, wrong for children to want to move around when they've clearly been told to sit still (2D). Wonder Woman prevents Gerta from choosing the dark side through a plan that involves (improbably) a gorgeously rendered Peter octopus and (more predictably) Gerta's love for her mom. Only mother Paula, Wonder Woman says, can teach Gerta "love and obedience" and lead the child on to a "happy, successful life" without supervillainy (6D).

The point here is that, in raising children, loving submission can actually be seen as more, not less, repressive than an arbitrary, rule-based father law. The father only cares what you do and how you behave. As long as you don't break the law, you can think and feel what you wish. Sometimes it's impossible not to break the law, and, indeed, the point of even having the law is to get people to break it so they can be punished—but, still, you're dealing with externals. Mother love, on the other hand, requires internal acquiescence. It uses love as a lever to break the will. As Sharon Marcus says in her discussion of the Marston/Peter stories at the *Hooded Utilitarian*, "Isn't moral reform the ultimate invasion? What's left of a person if she lacks even the desire to do evil? Is the problem with Wonder Woman that she is too sadistic, rather than not sadistic enough?" ("Wonder Woman").

If this kind of ultimate invasion is disturbing when practiced between consenting adults, it's even more so when deployed against kids—not least because such techniques actually are often at the basis of our school system and have been for a long time. Here, for example, are some hints for psychological discipline for ushers at the Jesuit school at Port-Royal in 1615: "A close watch must be kept on the children, and they must never be left alone anywhere, whether they are in ill or good health. . . . This constant supervision should be exercised gently and with a certain trustfulness calculated to make them think that one loves them, and that it is only to enjoy their company that one is with them. This will make them love their supervision rather than fear it" (qtd. in Ariès 112). "Calculated to make them think that one loves them"—that pretty much says it all.

The education mother, then, cannot really be said to break the link between the powerful and the good. If the father's law and the father's violence is deprecated, it is not because the good wins out over the powerful but precisely because the father's law is neither good nor powerful *enough*. Love, from this perspective, is a better way to run the world not because it is the opposite of force but rather because it is the quintessence of force—because it is more coercive than coercion. Love turns people into superior, more erotically invested state cogs, who will socialize better, produce better, and if need be, fight better than their less submissive Just Warrior peers. Thus, whether Just Warrior or education mother, superheroes are still defined by the duty to exercise force. Superheroes are good to the extent that they are powerful and are not good to the extent that they fail to deploy their powers, whether that means refusing to stop a bank robber or failing to take a recalcitrant tycoon in hand.

We're left again with the question, then, is there any way in which heroism and coercion can be separated? Or, for superheroes, must the powerful and the good always go together? To try again to answer that question, we'll look at the very first Wonder Woman comics and turn from Wonder Woman herself to that other Marston hero, Steve Trevor.

WOUNDED SOLDIERS

The first Wonder Woman story, published in *All-Star Comics #8* with a cover date of December 1941, begins with a scene from the war. In the first narrative panel, we see the plane of army intelligence officer Steve Trevor heading down for a crash landing on a mysterious island. The island is Paradise Island, and two Amazons—Princess Diana (not yet Wonder Woman) and her friend Mala—race to pull Trevor free. "A Man! A Man on Paradise Island!" Diana announces in all-bold script as Trevor's head rests on her bikini-clad bosom (1).

Trevor's role here is gendered masculine in a number of ways. First, he is an invader or outsider, his plane penetrating into the feminine, undiscovered island. Second, he's a soldier—and as we've already seen in Elshtain's discussion, war and violence are iconically masculine.[11] It's no wonder, then, that the dashing, adventurous man in uniform sets Diana's heart aflutter. Even out cold, the warrior conquers.

If Trevor's centrality and Diana's instant infatuation suggest a reification of martial masculinity, however, the rest of the tale noticeably fails to follow through. Steve does not rally and take his place as the bold conqueror. On the contrary, he remains unconscious, mostly in a hospital bed with his head bandaged, throughout the entire nine-page story (though he does get a few panels of lucidity in flashback; 5–6). Nor does Steve's convalescence end with that first tale. In the January 1942 *Sensation Comics #1*, Wonder Woman's first full-length adventure, Steve is *still* comatose. In this story, he first appears lying bandaged on a cot in Wonder Woman's invisible plane as she flies him back to man's world. When she lands, she carries him like a child, head slumped on her shoulder, to a hospital (1–2). Partway through, Steve does finally get to sneak out of his room to help foil some dastardly Nazi plot (8–12). He quickly gets reinjured, though, and by the end of the comic, he's right back to convalescing, with his nurse, Diana Prince (Wonder Woman in her secret identity), at his side (13).

And so it continues. In *Sensation Comics #2* (February 1942), Trevor is out of his hospital bed—but still confined to a wheelchair. ("I can't stand it! Wheeling me like a child!" he protests to Diana, who admonishes him, "Don't be a crybaby!"; 1.) It is only at the beginning of *Sensation Comics #3* (March 1942) that Steve finally gets to return to duty (1–2). In short, the ur–Steve Trevor, the first vision of male masculinity in *Wonder Woman*, is not a fighter nor a lover, not a Just Warrior nor an education mother. Instead, he's a patient. The true, original Steve Trevor is the wounded Steve Trevor, an infantilized baby-man who is carried about by his Wonder Mother and chastised by his Wonder Nurse. Whether flat on his back or waiting to be rescued by his girlfriend, what kind of manly hero is Steve Trevor supposed to be, anyway?

It's true that the supine Steve does not necessarily embody martial manliness. However, he does embody a different, less acknowledged, but in some respects even more powerful image of modern military masculinity—that of emasculation. For many soldiers, the experience of modern warfare was anything but stereotypically masculine. Trapped in trenches or huddling to escape from bombs, the twentieth-century warrior was less a valiant knight defending freedom than a convalescent waiting to happen. This sense of enforced powerlessness was directly related to the sudden emergence of shell shock as a serious problem during World War I. According to Eric J. Leed, "The dominance of long-ranged artillery, the machinegun, and barbed wire had immobilized combat, and immobility necessitated a passive stance of the soldier before the forces of mechanized slaughter. The cause of neurosis lay in the dominance of material over the possibilities of human movement" (164). Shell shock was not caused by fear per se but by immobility. The Just Warrior in World War I was not an empowered knight fighting villainy on horseback; he was a disempowered victim cowering womanlike in a ditch. Driving home this point, Elaine Showalter has argued that shell shock was "the first large-scale epidemic of male hysteria" (63). Forced at gunpoint to adopt the passivity that Victorian society had demanded of women, males retreated, as their sisters had, into neurotic incapacity. Soldiers were literally unmanned.

World War II did not involve trench warfare, but that didn't mean it was an empowering, masculine experience. On the contrary, Susan Gubar argues that male authors of World War II "record a hopeless sense of emasculation." She adds that "male characters are made to realize that the gun always wins in its competition with the penis" (251). Thus, in Randall Jarrell's poem "Death of a Ball Turret Gunner," war makes of the narrator not a man but an infant (Gubar 247–248). The turret gunner's station is a kind of womb ("From my mother's sleep I fell into the State") and his death an abortion ("When I died they washed me out of the turret with a hose"). In the same vein, British World War II soldier Vernon Scannell referred to shelling as "emasculating" because of "the pure physical terror that savages you when loud and violent death is screaming down from the sky and pounding the earth around you, smashing and pulping everything in the search for you" (qtd. in Fussell 278). Obviously, no one wants to be turned to jelly, but it may seem odd that such a fate should be seen as gendered.

After all, a shell burst doesn't discriminate in its effects on the basis of whether you're a man or a woman. But that is, perhaps, precisely the point. Shells treat men as if they were women. It is the female body that is supposed to be penetrated; it is the female body that is supposed to leak fluids. The "phallicized male body," on the other hand, "has been constructed as self-contained, impermeable, and sealed up" (Jarvis 89). When men in combat lost control of their bowels or were torn open by shrapnel, they were not only humiliated or harmed—they also symbolically became less-than-men.

There is an analogy here, I think, with John Carpenter's 1981 film *The Thing*, in which an all-male cast is hunted by a seething, orifice-laden alien slime. The slime devours and replicates its victims, turning them into its gelatinous self. In the economy of the film, there are male bodies and there are not-male bodies, and the first are constantly in danger of dissolving into the second. Men in *The Thing*, like Randall Jarrell's turret gunner, exchange coherent maleness for soft, oozing mess. Masculine heroes are constantly on the verge of transforming into a castrated and genderless pudding.[12] In *The Thing*, this fear of losing purchase on the rigid integrity of maleness is expressed characteristically through paranoia. The threat of not-male Thingness comes from everywhere—"Trust is a hard thing to come by these days," as the protagonist says. Gendered panic leads not merely to ducking and covering but to corrosive mistrust and violence.

During World War II, this mistrust and violence was often aimed at the nearest symbol of not-men available—which was women. Susan Gubar refers to this wave of misogyny as "the Blitz on women" and goes on to provide a catalogue. She points, for example, to propaganda posters warning that women's loose lips would sink men, as well as to C. D. Batchelor's famous 1937 cartoon portraying the coming war as a "syphilitic whore." She also discusses Melvin Tolson's poem "The Furlough," with its lurid fantasy of a soldier coming home to kill his girl. And there is that evergreen sexist standby Norman Mailer, who insists in *The Naked and the Dead* that women are simply, in Gubar's words, a "gauge" by which men "measure superiority" (240–255). Christina Jarvis adds further examples, pointing especially to Monte Sohn's 1948 *The Flesh and Mary Duncan*, in which the emotionally wounded veteran George regains his masculinity and virility by hitting his fiancée in the face before tearing her clothes off and fucking her (Jarvis 161). Nothing cures castration like a little rape.

Even more depressing than such literary violence are the incidents of actual sexist attacks on women service members by their male counterparts. As Gubar reports,

> [W]omen in the military . . . continually confronted . . . sexual assaults from men who jokingly translated WAAF as "Women All Fuck." . . . WASP (Women's Air Service Pilots Association) pilots . . . were physically endangered by their male colleagues. . . . [W]hen they tested planes for faults or damage, their safety was threatened by mechanical failures which were the result of sabotage, or so they suspected when traces of sugar (sure to stop an engine in seconds) were found in the gas tank of one WASP plane. (255)

There is no doubt that the gender turmoil attendant on war made room for some feminist images of women, such as Rosie the Riveter and, indeed, Wonder Woman herself. But there's also little doubt that those same gender uncertainties created a violent misogynist backlash, not just after the war concluded but while it was going on.[13]

Given the reaction of so many of Steve Trevor's peers, you would expect a wounded, emasculated Trevor to respond to his incapacity with anxiety, violence, and most of all, misogyny. But his reaction is just the opposite. As mentioned earlier, the first time he awakes from his coma (in *Sensation Comics #1*), he's lying in Wonder Woman's invisible plane, positioned on a white cot and covered with a white blanket. The wall of the invisible plane is also colored white, with blue-black streaks suggesting a reflective surface. The effect (as seen in figure 14) is unearthly, an impression only heightened by Peter's stiff figures and graceful line work. Wonder Woman, sitting in her seat, is poised with one arm out like a statue, holding Steve's bandages almost as if she intends to bless him with them. Her lashes are lowered as she looks down at her patient, and she appears both distant and affectionate, loving and unattainable.

Steve, understandably, can't figure out where he is or what's happened to him and leaps to the obvious conclusion. "Where—? I'm in

FIGURE 14. *Sensation Comics #1* (1942)

heaven! There's an angel smiling at me—a beautiful angel!" Overcome, he then further impugns his manly cred by fainting, while Wonder Woman leans over him musing, "That's the first time a man ever called me—beautiful!" (2) Even more telling, perhaps, is a scene from the end of the same issue. Steve (briefly ambulatory) and Wonder Woman are caught in a bomb blast. Wonder Woman jumps clear, but the less competent Steve is wounded. Wonder Woman supports Steve, one hand clutching the wrist of his right arm, which is draped over her shoulder, while he half leans, half sits on her left knee. Steve's broken right leg, though, is what makes the picture (see figure 15). Peter, whose anatomy is always delightfully hit and miss, draws the flaccid limb with a disturbing, fluid verve (13). It's hard to imagine how the castration imagery could be any clearer without actually showing Wonder Woman hacking the thing off with a battle axe.

As arresting as Steve's injury is to contemporary eyes, it would have been even more striking at the time the comic

FIGURE 15. *Sensation Comics #1* (1942)

appeared, in January 1942. During the first year of the war, censors ensured that the U.S. public viewed almost no images of wounded servicemen (Jarvis 97). For some readers, Steve may have been the most dramatic image of a wounded World War II soldier they had ever seen.

Marston and Peter, then, have taken unusual pains to show us that Steve is badly injured. He has barely gotten off his sick cot, and it looks as if he's going to immediately return there. For most people, even setting aside the considerable pain of the wound, this would be upsetting. One could hardly blame our hero if he uttered a mild epithet ("Suffering Sappho!" perhaps) or cursed the luck that has him shuttling back to his hospital bed almost before he left it. And yet Steve seems utterly unfazed. This is not because he's courageous but because—well, let him speak for himself: "My leg does seem bent a bit—but I'm glad of it. At least it shows you care!" Other men might fear emasculation, but not Steve. On the contrary, he eroticizes his wound. His damaged leg, in all its soft, boneless glory, is the mark of helplessness that touches the heart of the goddess/mother. And so "he actually relegates castration to the status of foreplay" (Silverman 208).

Venus in Swimsuits

That last quote about castration and foreplay is from Kaja Silverman's *Male Subjectivity at the Margins*. Silverman uses the phrase in reference to an elaborate masochistic fantasy related by a patient of Theodor Reik's:

> To an ancient barbaric idol, somewhat like the Phoenician Moloch, a number of vigorous young men are to be sacrificed at certain not too frequent intervals. They are undressed and laid on the altar one by one. The rumble of drums is joined by the songs of the approaching temple choirs. The high priest followed by his suite approaches the altar and scrutinizes each of the victims with a critical eye. They must satisfy certain requirements of beauty and athletic appearance. The high priest takes the genital of each prospective victim in his hand and carefully tests its weight and form. If he does not approve of the genital, the young man will be rejected as obnoxious to the god and unworthy of being sacrificed. The high priest gives the order for the execution and the ceremony

continues. With a sharp cut the young men's genitals and the surrounding parts are cut away. (Qtd. in Silverman 206)

While this Moloch scenario may seem a far distance from *Wonder
Woman*, it is worth noting that, in both cases, the setting is ostenta-
tiously fantastic. The masochist, whether Steve or Reich's patient, has
gone off the map, to Paradise or barbarism, as if only by becoming lost
can he lose what he has to lose.

In addition, Silverman argues that in the Moloch scenario, the
masochist "loudly proclaims that his meaning comes to him from the
Other, prostrates himself before the gaze even as he solicits it, exhibits
his castration for all to see, and revels in the sacrificial basis of the
social contract" (206). This description surely applies to Steve Trevor
in *Wonder Woman* as well. He exhibits his wounded leg, soliciting the
gaze. He revels in the fact that his bodily sacrifice can be exchanged
for love and, in doing so, suggests that his meaning comes to him
not from his own bravery and strength but from Wonder Woman's
acknowledgment of his weakness.

There are a number of other ways in which Silverman's account of
masochism, based in part on that of Gilles Deleuze, seems to fit Marston
and Peter's *Wonder Woman*. Consider this passage, for example: "the
masochism [Deleuze] celebrates is a pact between mother and son to
write the father out of his dominant position within both culture and
masochism, and to install the mother in his place" (211). For Silverman
and Deleuze, then, male masochism is a matriarchal utopia. It looks to
the power of mothers to end the power of fathers. Compare that to a
letter Marston wrote describing his goals in creating Wonder Woman:

Frankly, Wonder Woman is psychological propaganda for the
new type of woman who should, I believe, rule the world. There
isn't love enough in the male organism to run this planet peacefully. Woman's body contains twice as many love generating
organs and endocrine mechanisms as the male. What woman
lacks is the dominance or self-assertive power to put over and
enforce her love desires. I have given Wonder Woman this dominant force but have kept her loving, tender, maternal and feminine in every other way. (Qtd. in Daniels 22–23)

Like Silverman, Marston sees utopian transformation as predicated on the overthrow of patriarchy. Mothers will displace fathers; women will displace men. The phallus must diminish that the world may increase. (Double the love organs!)

There are also some ways in which Marston diverges from Silverman/Deleuze, however. Deleuze's ideal mother figure is, according to Silverman, a "cold, maternal, and severe woman (211). That does not describe Wonder Woman at all. Instead, Wonder Woman is, as Marston says, "loving, tender, maternal and feminine." Both Deleuze and Marston want their masochistic ideal to be "maternal"—but the kind of "maternal" they are talking about is very different. This contrast becomes even more dramatic when you return to the text that forms the basis of Deleuze's theories—Leopold von Sacher-Masoch's *Venus in Furs*. *Venus in Furs* is (in)famously filled with images of male submission. The novel's hero, Severin, is repeatedly humiliated, whipped, and cuckolded. Finally, in a transcendence of degradation, he is beaten by his mistress's lover ("The sensation of being whipped before the eyes of a woman one adores by a successful rival is quite indescribable: I was dying of shame and despair"; 268).

Such degradation, shame, and despair is presented by Sacher-Masoch as, and meant to be experienced by the reader as, sexually and emotionally stimulating. But this is a guilty pleasure, and at the end of the novel, Sacher-Masoch emphatically repudiates his fantasy of submission. Wanda, his cruel mistress, abandons Severin, because she cannot respect a man who allows her to dominate him. Or, as she tells him, "From the moment that you became my slave, I felt that it would be impossible for you ever to be my husband" (270). Severin himself spurns his former pleasures; he returns to his home and takes up his proper role on his father's estate ("with great power comes . . ."). When the old man dies, Severin takes his place, performing his duties as if his father were still standing behind him: "watching over my shoulder with his great wise eyes" (270). The last paragraph couldn't be much more explicit in its embrace of patriarchy:

The moral is that woman, as Nature created her and as man up to now has found her attractive, is man's enemy; she can be his slave or his mistress but never his companion. This she can only

be when she has the same rights as he and is his equal in education and work. For the time being there is only one alternative:
to be the hammer or the anvil. I was fool enough to let a woman make a slave of me, do you understand? Hence the moral of
the tale: whoever allows himself to be whipped deserves to be
whipped. But as you see, I have taken the blows well; the rosy
mist of supersensuality has lifted, and no one will ever make me
believe that the sacred wenches of Benares or Plato's rooster are
the images of God. (271)

Deleuze, who is determined to separate sadism from masochism, is
insistent in arguing that the end of *Venus in Furs*—the decision to become the hammer rather than the anvil—is not an embrace of sadism.
Specifically, Deleuze argues that Severin's decision to become dominant is not a sadistic fantasy. Instead, he insists, it is the disintegration of the masochistic fantasy in the face of reality (65). The contrast,
then, is not between masochism (bad) and sadism (good) but rather
between the beautiful illusion of masochism (good) and dull quotid-
ian reality (bad).

Whether or not that is convincing (and I would say not), the fact
remains that, even if Deleuze is correct, sadism is figured in the novel
precisely as normative and realistic. Submissive men and powerful
women—for Deleuze, these are childlike fantasies, and any value they
have is precisely in their unreality. Sacher-Masoch raises the possibility of feminist change and equal rights for women—but only to wave
them away as a vague future possibility with no real implications for
the present.[14] The facts are the facts, and the real man in the real world
must take up the rod and beat women with it. As Amish Superman
must leave the farm and fight, as Peter Parker must follow the finger
and fight, so Severin must accept the violence and power that is his
masculine destiny.

Submission Makes the Man

William Marston's vision of masochism, and, indeed, of reality, is very
different from Sacher-Masoch's and Deleuze's. For him, heroism, manliness, and violence are split apart. The ideal hero is not the Just Warrior
wielding phallic power but the submissive object of (characteristically

maternal) power. As an example, consider another of the stories in *Wonder Woman #4* (April–May 1943). Here, Wonder Woman captures Ivar Torgson, a villainous industrialist. She encourages Torgson's lover, Elva, to take command of the wicked man and lead him to the good. To this end, Wonder Woman dresses Elva in finery ("You must make him think of you as his Queen in his subconscious mind instead of his slave!"; 9C) and gives Elva the magic lasso of obedience. Wonder Woman then leaves Elva in a secret, lavishly furnished subterranean suite with Torgson, now her slave (9C). The queen sits in a throne with voluptuously curving lines; her slave crouches before her. His head is stiff and awkwardly tilted while he exclaims, "This is absurd—ridiculous! What a fool you're making of me!" Elva responds, "I'm making a man of you! Learning to submit is the final test of manhood!" (9C). And, as if in agreement, Peter's art definitively and enthusiastically sexualizes Torgson. Earlier in the comic, the industrialist was drawn as a standard-issue thuggish criminal. Here, though, his shirt has been stripped off, and his physique bulges improbably. In one panel, Peter's wavering perspective makes Thorgson appear at least a head shorter than Elva, while his outthrust arms and whiny speech bubble ("Oh please keep me with you—"; 9C) contrast bizarrely with his hypertrophic muscles. He is both infantilized and masculinized, and the suggestion is that the first is a prerequisite for the second.

As Wonder Woman predicted, Torgson quickly learns to love his newfound manliness *and* his newfound submission. Like Wanda in *Venus in Furs*, however, Elva eventually grows sick of being in control, declaring, "I'm tired of this game—I just want to be your adoring wife!" (10C). No sooner does she free him from the lasso of submission, though, than he goes back to being a bully and a villain. He knocks her across the room, captures Wonder Woman in her own rope, and rigs a death trap to kill both women. Wonder Woman escapes, of course, and Torgson is eventually exposed to that hypnotic machine that makes him submit to Wonder Woman. Elva, as punishment for her failure, is willingly bound in chains and sent to Paradise Island, where she will undergo strict training in "ruling men" (13C). Sacher-Masoch and Marston agree, then, that submission of men to women is unstable and that women do not want to rule. But whereas Sacher-Masoch concludes from this that men need to become manly hammers, Marston, as we've seen, insists that both women and men simply need more and better training in submission.

This training must be provided by a female community. The scene in which Elva pledges herself to the Amazons at the book's end is set, for no discernible diegetic reason, in what appears to be a female dorm room at Holliday College. Wonder Woman and her friend the scientist Paula stand over Elva, who kneels before them with her hands up. In the background, there's a bed with pillows that are as suggestively curvy as Elva's former throne. "Oh yes! Chain me like Paula's slave girls!" Elva begs (13C). In *Venus in Furs*, the humiliation of the eroticized male-male whipping makes Severin finally cast off childish things and become a man. In Marston and Peter, on the other hand, an eroticized female-female community is the prerequisite for a successful male-female relationship. For Sacher-Masoch, authority flows from patriarchy. In Marston/Peter, it emphatically does not.

Masochism and Matriarchy

Sacher-Masoch/Deleuze and Marston/Peter are both flamboyantly masochistic in their imagery and their obsessions, and both have a great deal in common. Yet, as we have seen, in their relationship to patriarchy, to gender, to women, to mothers—in short, to all their major themes—their attitudes are in many ways directly opposed. Severin flirts with other identities but ends by embracing the Just Warrior. Wonder Woman flirts with the Just Warrior, but the comic ends up endorsing other possibilities—which raises the question, why? If Sacher-Masoch/Deleuze and Marston/Peter both are masochistic, if they both want to be symbolically castrated, why do they disagree so vehemently on how, and by whom, the knife is held?

Tania Modleski suggests one answer in *Feminism without Women* when she observes that Deleuze is, "to be sure, unconcerned about feminism" (69–70). Modleski elaborates by arguing that for Deleuze, "the equation of woman with the law has the effect not of empowering women, but of throwing the law itself into question and crisis, by deriding it" (69–70). The issue for Deleuze, then, is not gender but hierarchy. Mothers are not valuable in themselves; they matter only insofar as they allow the son to score points against the law that is the father. Far from respecting or elevating the mother, Modleski argues,

Deleuze relies on her degradation—the mother-as-father is so obviously ludicrous, so wrong, that it functions as parody.[15]

The Deleuzian masochist, then, is playing a game in which the father is trivialized, on behalf not of women but of the game-playing masochist. Though Deleuze's masochist appears weak, that weakness is the phallic lever by which he controls the world—or at least the woman. Masochism is just another move in the eternal psychodrama between father and son. Through masochism, the father is ridiculed and the son becomes, in Deleuze's words, a "new man" (99–100). Masochism in this sense is a perverse Bildungsroman.

Deleuze denies that this new-minted "new man," with his new authority in pleasure and pain, has anything to do with the lawgiving, punishing father and his phallus. But as Silverman points out, this disavowal is itself simply part of the masochistic Oedipal drama, whereby the son (in this case Deleuze) repudiates his forebear (in this case Freud) (211). Deleuze's castration is a secret ritual of power; he feeds his genitals to Moloch so that he can enter and embody the Ogre-God. Like Siegel and Shuster's Superman, whose emasculated Lois Lane–dominated Clark Kent is just a disguise for the Lois-dominating Superfather, Deleuze cuts his penis off not to destroy it but rather to let it go forth and triumph.[16]

Marston, in contrast, doesn't want the penis to triumph, surreptitiously or otherwise. Instead, he believes, as noted earlier, that "there isn't love enough in the male organism to run this planet peacefully." Marston does not want to replace the phallus with another phallus. Rather, he wants to replace it with "woman's body," which "contains twice as many love generating organs and endocrine mechanisms as the male." The phrase "twice as many love generating organs" evokes (not least in its awkwardness) Luce Irigaray's essay "This Sex Which Is Not One": "Woman 'touches herself' all the time," Irigaray says, "and moreover no one can forbid her to do so, for her genitals are formed of two lips in continuous contact. Thus, within herself, she is already two—but not divisible into one(s)—that caress each other" (24). For Irigaray and for Marston, women embody love through a multiplicity that overwhelms man's bloated unitary power. Marston doesn't see female power as a parody of the law; rather, the law is a parody of itself. Thus, in *Wonder Woman #1* (summer 1942) Peter draws the mighty Hercules, the epitome of masculinity, as a cartoonish joke. In one particularly preposterous panel, Hercules is depicted with such weird foreshortening that his legs appear shriveled, barely able to hold up his massive chest. The Greek hero of song and story ends up looking like a child trying to fill out his own disproportioned body (see figure 16). And, oh yes, did I mention the suggestive, ludicrously massive stick he carries in his right hand? (3A).

Despite Hercules's crazily muscled body, the graceful Hippolyte, Wonder Woman's mother and queen of the Amazons, easily kicks his butt in open combat (4A). She is able to do so specifically because of her femininity—a femininity that is figured as twoness and as love. Hippolyte gains her power from a magic girdle, a belt given to her by Aphrodite. Peter draws the gift giving as a moment of intimacy. Aphrodite bends down tenderly to place the belt around Hippolyte's waist—the goddess of love bowed by love before her servant (3A). As long as Hippolyte wears the girdle, Aphrodite's love and that moment of intimacy remain inscribed within her, a multiplicity that makes her and her sister Amazons invincible.

The girdle itself, strapped around the stomach, suggests a kind of bondage gear. And in later Marston/Peter comics, the Amazons bind Venus girdles around mostly female disobedient prisoners, magically teaching them the joys of girl-on-girl loving submission. Indeed (as discussed in chapter 1), if you open a random page of a Marston/Peter

FIGURE 16. *Wonder Woman #1* (1942)

comic, you are more likely to find a woman trussed up than not. The most spectacular instance of this is arguably in *Wonder Woman #3*, in which the Amazons engage in a ritual game in which some of them dress up as deer, while others hog-tie them, truss them up, and pretend to eat them (7A–10A; and see figure 23 in the next chapter).

A man showing women tied up suggests not masochism but something else. That was the opinion of one early Marston critic, Josette Frank of the Child Study Association of America. In a February 17, 1943, letter, Frank wrote to Marston's publisher, M. C. Gaines, objecting to Wonder Woman's "costume (or lack of it)" and to the "sadistic bits showing women chained, tortured, etc." (qtd. in Daniels 61).

It would be silly to argue that Marston and his readers did not enjoy the tying up as well as the being tied, the humiliating as well as the humiliation. However, the specifics of who is binding whom with what is perhaps less important than the multiplicity of possibilities and identifications. Silverman notes that masochistic fantasies are characterized both by a "propensity for impersonation" and by multiple forms of cross-gender identification (208, 204). Gaylyn Studlar concurs, arguing that "in the masochistic ideal, gender identity is transmutative and triumphantly bisexual" (32). And Linda Williams argues that a woman (or, presumably, a man) presented with a masochistic scenario may identify with the woman (or man) being beaten, with the man (or woman) beating, or with a male (or female) onlooker (215). The male masochistic fantasies discussed by Deleuze, and via Deleuze by Silverman, characteristically involve a submissive man and a dominant woman. The polyamorous Marston certainly enjoyed that pairing but felt no need to limit himself to it. Instead, his stories take a joy not just in multiple gender identifications but in the slippage between them. *Sensation Comics #2*, for example, has several male-male masochistic scenes, in which the nefarious Dr. Poison uses an intimidatingly large needle to menace a strapped-down Steve Trevor (4). At the story's end, the leering masked doctor has his green garments stripped away and is shown to be a shapely woman—retroactively making those torture scenes female-male instead of (or, rather, in addition to) male-male (43). The last page of the comic shows Wonder Woman's ally Etta Candy spanking the now-female Dr. Poison with a paddle (12–13). Marston's comics, then, are supposed to initiate their audience into masochism and submission. But part of that initiation is precisely that the gender of the audience is not specified and, indeed, can be considered malleable.

As Marston explained in a 1944 article in the *American Scholar*,

> It seemed to me, from a psychological angle, that the comics' worst offense was their blood-curdling masculinity. A male hero, at best, lacks the qualities of maternal love and tenderness which are as essential to a normal child as the breath of life. Suppose your child's ideal becomes a super*man* who uses his extraordinary powers to help the weak. The most important ingredient in the human happiness recipe still is missing—*love*. It's smart to be strong. It's big to be generous. But it's sissified, according to exclusively masculine rules, to be tender, loving, affectionate, and alluring. "Aw, that's girl stuff!" snorts our young comics reader. "Who wants to be a *girl?* And that's the point; not even girls want to be girls so long as our feminine archetype lacks force, strength, power. Not wanting to be girls they don't want to be tender, submissive, peaceloving, as good women are. Women's strong qualities have become despised because of their weak ones. The obvious remedy is to create a feminine character with all the strength of a Superman plus all the allure of a good and beautiful woman. This is what I recommended to the comics publisher. ("Why 100,000,000" 42–43)

So good women, for Marston, are tender, submissive, and peace loving. The problem with society is that *not even* women want to be good women, which suggests that *not only* women but also men should learn to be women—tender, submissive, and peace loving.

EMPOWERED SERVANTS

True superheroism for Marston, then, is not embodied in the Just Warrior. On the contrary, for him, the good and the powerful are definitively separate. From this perspective, the education mother, or love leader, can be seen less as a technology of control and more as a way to release control. Love leaders are teachers not because they are better than men at being tops but because they are better than men at being

FIGURE 17. *Sensation Comics #31* (1944)

bottoms. Thus, in *Sensation Comics #31*, Wonder Woman is presented as an ideal mother because she enters so readily into erotic bondage games with children—erotic bondage games in which the children are emphatically on top. A panel in which Wonder Woman kneels to be paddled by toddlers while an audience of diapered babies cheers has to be one of the most startling images in the series. "This is the way we brand you," one toddler declares. "The Red mark of displeasure will remain with you until the smart from this spanking wears off!" (9; see figure 17).

Thus, ideal mothers are the perfect commandresses because they are the perfect servants. Perfect education mothers are perfect because they submit (with the full erotic connotations of the word) even to their own children. As Ben Saunders explains, Marston believed "the world will become a better place when men learn to take pleasure in sexual submission, as most women have already learned to do; and the best teachers of men in this regard will be 'actively developed,' dominant-but-kind women who are willing to serve as their 'Love Leaders'" (51). For Marston, gender is absolute and essential, but it is not necessarily tied (as it were) to specific female and male bodies. Women must learn to be women, and men must learn to be women. If C. S. Lewis claims in *That Hideous Strength* that "what is above and beyond all things is so masculine that we are all feminine in relation to it" (391), Marston insists that Aphrodite above and beyond is so feminine that we are all, tragically, male in comparison. But with the proper discipline, we may at least learn from her to be, like women, more loving and more submissive. Thus, the submissiveness of women does not mean that women must submit. Rather, it means that men must learn from women how to submit lovingly. Women are, after all, better than men at both love and submission—and since love and submission are, for

Marston, goddess-like, that means that women are also stronger and wiser than men. We finally have a definitive answer, therefore, to the question first raised in chapter 1. The many, many, many, many images of Wonder Woman in bondage—tied with ropes, tied with chains, tied in her own magic lasso, trussed up with her eyes and mouth taped shut, in a gimp mask, in nets, in prison, in manacles, in phallic, pink, ectoplasmic tendrils—are not there (or are not there solely) so Marston's audience—whether men or women—can get off on women disempowered. Rather, they're there to teach men (and women too) the joys of restraint. Or as Marston wrote in a February 20, 1943, letter to his publisher, "The only hope for peace is to teach people who are full of pep and unbound force to *enjoy* being bound. . . . Women are exciting for this one reason—it is the secret of women's allure—women *enjoy* submission, being bound" (qtd. in Daniels 63).

Again, as we noted in chapter 1, the connection between Marston's bondage fetish and his feminism has understandably caused a certain amount of consternation among critics. But for Marston, there was no opposition between the two. Rather, Marston saw the masochistic dynamic as linked explicitly to the political, matriarchal triumph of women-as-a-class over men-as-a-class. We've already seen this in the story of Elva and Torgson, but it is repeated throughout Marston's work. For instance, in *Sensation Comics #11*, Wonder Woman travels to the planet Eros, where women rule and the greatest joy is going to prison. Disaster results, however, when one of the women is so taken with submission that she lets men take charge—and they immediately institute a cruel prison regime based on punishment rather than love (Wonder Woman soon sets things to rights, of course; 4–11). In *Wonder Woman #4*, from April–May 1942, Wonder Woman goes to a subterranean kingdom ruled by Mole Men, who treat women as their slaves. By the end, Wonder Woman and her friend Paula have opened the Mole Men's eyes to "the beauty of women." Thus awakened, the men beg the women to take control of the underground kingdom. As the new queen says gamely, "That's harder than being your slave, but I'll try!"(12B).

In all these stories, masochism is the erotic charge that powers visions of matriarchal ascendancy—the sexual frisson that gives men a stake in feminism, just as sadism gives men a stake in patriarchy. In this sense, masochism is, in fact, a challenge to patriarchy, as Deleuze and Silverman suggest it can be. But, as *Venus in Furs* shows, that challenge doesn't necessarily have to take on a political form. Instead, it can easily function as an individual rebuke to individual men who, like Amish Superman or Peter Parker or Severin, have failed in one way or another to live up to the manly ideal. There is, in masochism, "no necessary shift in power dynamics" (Modleski, *Feminism* 74). Such a shift only occurs, or is only imaginable, in Marston's writing because he has a deliberate, ideological commitment to feminism and female empowerment. Masochism is central to Marston's feminism, but his feminism cannot be reduced to his masochism. If it were, it would disappear.

At the same time, however, Marston's masochism cannot be reduced to his feminism—which means that his feminism can never be just about empowerment. In the Marston/Peter *Wonder Woman*, there is always at least some tension between the good and the powerful and some critique of the idea that the powerful is necessary for the good. It is true that Wonder Woman, and woman in general, must adopt the coercive role of love leader / education mother. But for Marston, women are fitted for that role specifically because they, unlike men, know how to submit. It is the experience of being disempowered that makes you a hero. Only those who eschew dominance are fit to control others.

The Mole Men story is a good illustration of Marston's thinking. In this tale, the rule of men is linked explicitly to violence and, for that matter, to wounds and illness. The Mole Men are tyrannical and want to sow war. It is up to Wonder Woman and Paula to show them the light—literally. Until Wonder Woman's scientist friend Paula cures them, the Mole Men are blind. In one panel, Peter gives us a close-up of the profile of a Mole Man, with sharp teeth, elongated nose, and orbless eyes, ranting on and on about how the scars of World War II will allow the Mole Men to take over the Earth. It's a creepy image but also a parodic one; war is the province not of masterful dominators but of pathetic rodents (8B). It's only when the Mole Men agree to let the women "rule the underworld in peace" that they are transformed. Following Paula's treatment, Peter draws the cured Mole Men not just as sighted but as handsome (albeit still with somewhat enlarged noses;

12B). Being ruled by women has made them men—because, for Marston, the best men are those who submit and love, like women. By being disempowered, they have become good and also, contradictorily, empowered.

The paradox of disempowerment as power, of submission as strength, is an important way in which Christian pacifists have tried to separate notions of power from notions of goodness. For instance, theologian Mark Moore specifically defines pacifism in terms of the rejection not only of violence but of control: "So what is pacifism? It is the uncompromising realization that we as humans are incapable of bringing about justice through violent retaliation. Hence, we relinquish all such acts to God in his sovereign and eschatological plan of judgment, justice, and mercy. Indeed, God have mercy on us." John Howard Yoder puts it even more explicitly in terms that superheroes can understand: "The triumph of the right, although it is assured, is sure because of the power of the resurrection and not because of any calculation of causes and effects, nor because of the inherently greater strength of the good guys" (232). Ben Saunders paraphrases this Christian philosophy this way: "It is better to give than to receive. . . . It is better to serve than to rule, better to surrender than to fight." He also notes that this vision is echoed in its "most difficult, most radical form" in many of Marston's comics (65). Saunders points specifically to the last line of the last script Marston published in *Wonder Woman* before he died of cancer, Hippolyte's devotional homily: "The only real happiness for anybody is to be found in the obedience to loving authority" (*Wonder Woman #28*, 12C; Saunders 65). I think Moore and Yoder, and Christian theologians in general, could recognize that as a kind of Christian witness.

Still, there are a number of differences between Marston and Christianity. Most notably, Marston's emphasis on submission and pacifism is insistently gendered. Submission, and therefore pacifism, is not Christ-like; it's Aphrodite-like. It's the particular, and particularly erotic, province of women. Saunders correctly points out that there are some major feminist difficulties with the idea of submission as a particularly female calling. As Moore and Yoder demonstrate, there has been an effort in contemporary Christian theology to accept and champion submission and to separate the powerful and the good.

However, Christian feminists have viewed this movement with understandable suspicion, since "patriarchal Christian males have often valorized doctrines of submission to reinforce oppression on the basis of gender" (Saunders 67). Saunders, in a lovely move, goes on to investigate these issues through a reading of the Christian feminist Sarah Coakley, whose book *Power and Submissions* is devoted to trying to reconcile the feminist ideals of equality and empowerment with the Christian injunction to "vulnerability" and "self-effacement" (5). For Coakley, the concept of *kenosis*—meaning, very loosely, Christ's embodiment and his subsequent subjection to human flesh and human frailty—is central to the Christian witness. "If I could not make spiritual and theological sense of this *special* form of power-in-vulnerability," she says, "I would see little point in continuing the tortured battle to bring feminism and Christianity together" (5).

Marston, too, is committed to making spiritual (if not Christian theological) sense of power-in-vulnerability and feminism. He wants to make women powerful, whether as Just Warriors or education mothers. But he also wants to universalize the morality of masochism—to teach the virtues of pacifism and submission. *Wonder Woman* is, then, in part an effort to reconcile powers and submissions or to separate the powerful and the good.

DIANA, DIANA

If Marston believes in separating the powerful and the good, it makes sense to look for goodness where there is not power. We've already seen that the wounded Steve Trevor is, for Marston, in many ways more radically just than he would be as an armed and battling warrior. Similarly, it is possible to see the real hero of *Wonder Woman* not as the titular star but as her nonsuper alter-ego, Diana Prince.

Diana is unusual in that she never gains superpowers. Superhero origin stories are in general about a transformative event that renders the transformed magically good *and* powerful.[17] Thus, a typical origin story might go like this: "Little Melvin Microbits is toddling along minding his microstuff when suddenly—transformative trauma! He is castrated by a radioactive giant tubular marine mammal! Quickly, miraculously, he grows a thing bigger than his dad ever had and decides to serve the Law as—Walrus-Man!" Batman is perhaps

FIGURE 18. *Sensation Comics #1* (1942)

the most paradigmatic example (small boy, dad shot, takes dad's place while still also remaining traumatized child). It works for Superman too, though (baby, father dies, takes dad's place while still also remaining puny child)—and (as we've already seen) for Spider-Man (young man, father-figure dies, takes dad's place while still also remaining traumatized child). There are some variations, such as Green Lantern (young man, father-figure dies, takes dad's place while still remaining asshole) or the Hulk (wimpy guy, traumatized, takes dad's place while still also remaining wimpy guy). But the general outlines always remain discernible. There is a somewhat good person whose goodness is either compromised or ineffectual or both. He (and it is usually he) then becomes powerful, and the goodness takes on meaningful shape—is effectively weaponized—by power.

But Wonder Woman's origin doesn't work like that. She's born (or magically fashioned, actually) with superpowers already in place. Her secret identity, Diana Prince, isn't the "real" trace of the traumatized child she was and remains. It's just an act. And moreover, it is a gendered act. Wonder Woman becomes Diana Prince specifically to pander to the needs of her man, as we see in *Sensation Comics #1*, page 8 (see figure 18).

This is a very odd sequence. Wonder Woman trades places with a nurse who looks exactly like her and has the *same name*. Moreover, the nurse has the same problem Wonder Woman does; both of them need to abandon their current identities in order to go to the men they love. The women switch places, but they're able to do so only because they were already in each other's places to begin with.

Female bonding, or sisterhood, is central to feminism. In fact, in much contemporary lesbian and feminist theory, female friendships and relationships are seen as centrally important to empowerment and to the opposition to patriarchy. According to Sharon Marcus in *Between Women*,

> Lesbian studies place women's friendships on a continuum with lesbian relationships and equate both with resistance to the family and marriage. As Adrienne Rich influentially argued, women's friendships and lesbian sexual bonds both defy "compulsory heterosexuality." The move to valorize women's friendships as a subset of lesbianism and a subversion of gender norms continues to be the dominant paradigm. (29)

During the Victorian era, in contrast, Marcus argues, female friendships were seen as an *aid* to heterosexual love—as reinforcing traditional femininity and relationships with men. Having close female friendships for the Victorians didn't make women homosexual or unmarriageable; on the contrary, it made them *more* successfully heterosexual. Marcus in particular points to Lucy Snowe in *Villete*, who resents and dislikes other women and who also (and not coincidentally) finds her own heterosexual romance plot continually and, indeed, ultimately thwarted. As Marcus says, "In Victorian fiction, it is only the woman with no bosom friend who risks becoming, like Lucy

Snowe, one whom no man will ever clasp to his heart in marriage, a friendless woman who remains perpetually outside the bosom of the family" (*Between Women* 108). It makes sense that Marston—who had a longstanding relationship with two polyamorous women—should believe that female friendships were conducive, and even vital, not just for women but for male heterosexual happiness. (For a further discussion, see chapter 3.) And perhaps that also explains why we need this bizarre scene of doubling before Wonder Woman can have her sort-of-tryst with Steve. Female-female relationships for Marston are vital for the creation of a stable, domesticated femininity. Wonder Woman needs Diana Prince to teach her how to be a woman. For male superheroes, then, the achievement of a double identity is usually an accession to power and, as Spider-Man shows, to a more fully realized masculinity. For Wonder Woman, though, doubling is the path to a more realized femininity—and to submission.

This is not an especially empowering vision. As I mentioned before, it is possible to read Wonder Woman's love of Steve as a love for the possibilities and powers of man's world. But it's also very legitimate, I think, to read it straight—as Wonder Woman giving up everything she has, even immortality, to be with the love of her life. Wonder Woman chucks her goddessness so she can go change her guy's bedpans. What kind of feminist message is that? Why on earth should women think that this is a good idea?

Theologian Chris Boesel has an interesting response to some parallel questions raised by Kierkegaard in regard to the incarnation of Christ:

> First the Why. Why does the god (the teacher) give herself (the eternal, the truth) to be known by the creature (the learner)? It must be for love—not by any necessity, but a free self-giving for the sake of the possibility of the relation itself. And love has a twofold dimension here. It is not only the *god's* love for the creature that the god . . . [gives herself]; it is also *for the sake of love*, so that *the creature* might love the god, that the god and the creature might be joined in a relation of "love's understanding." (315)

Boesel's use of the female pronoun here is serendipitous—but even without that, I think the analogy to Wonder Woman's situation is clear.

Like Christ, Wonder Woman, the goddess, gives herself to be known by Steve, and she does so specifically out of love. Moreover, she does so also, in Boesel's terms, "for the sake of love"—so that Steve, and man's world, may live in a world without war, guided by love.

Boesel goes on to explain why Christ (aka Wonder Woman) has to shuck off the godhead, that is, why he (and she) can't simply love man from on high. Again, Boesel is paraphrasing and sometimes quoting Kierkegaard here:

> Second, the How. How is the god to create the "equality," or "unity," necessary in order to "make himself understood" without "destroy[ing] that which is different," that is, the creature *as creature?* How does the god give herself to be known by the creature in and for love without obliterating the beloved?
>
> Climacus [that is Kierkegaard's pen name] rejects both the possibility of an "ascent," an exaltation of the beloved creature to the heights of heaven, . . . and of a divine "appearing" in overpowering, sacred "splendor," on the grounds that they would violate the integrity of the creature's existence, *as creature.*
>
> The "unity" of "love's understanding," then, must be "attempted by a descent." And a descent, by the god, to the level of "the lowliest" of all. . . . Therefore, "in love [the god] wants to be the equal of the most lowly of the lowly," and so comes to the creature "in the form of the servant." This "form," however, "is not something put on like the king's plebian cloak, which just by flapping open would betray the king . . . but is [the god's] true form." The god does not deceive, but in the "omnipotence of love," remains truly god while fully embodied as a particular human creature, just like any other human, even the lowliest of the low. (315–316)

The whole analysis by Boesel/Kierkegaard fits Wonder Woman almost perfectly. As a goddess, Wonder Woman can't appear to (be apprehended by?) Steve. For him to love her, and for her to love him, she has to descend and become not just human but a servant. She even takes over the form of a "real" human being—her double, both her and not her. The moment in the sixth panel of figure 18 is emblematic. Wonder Woman, newly transformed into Diana Prince, approaches

Steve's bed, and Steve delirious mutters, "An angel . . . a beautiful an-gel!" Steve both knows Diana (which is her real name and also her alias) and does not know her. The angel is thus loved not (only) as an angel but as a servant. From this perspective, you might argue that gender is irrelevant or secondary. Marston is not telling a story about what women should be or about how they need to be weak and servile to attract a man. Instead he's telling a story about the encounter with the divine and the paradoxical manner in which one, of whatever gen-der, can only love the transcendent through the particular.

The problem it that, as I've mentioned before, Marston is obsessed with gender and especially, one could argue, with the relationship between gender and Godhead. The particular divinity that Wonder Woman is, the transcendence she represents, is female. Femaleness is, in fact, intrinsic to the transcendence. Irigaray argues in her essay "Divine Women" that a female God is necessary if women are "either to communicate or commune with one another" (62). But Marston goes further, I think, suggesting that a female God is necessary if any-one, of any gender, is to experience communion. Moreover, when that transcendence is embodied in Diana Prince, it is also, even doubly, female. Obviously, Wonder Woman and Diana are both women. But the particular formal representation of that embodiment in the comic is also coded female.

I'm thinking specifically of that passage from Irigaray's essay "This Sex Which Is Not One," quoted earlier: "Woman 'touches herself' all the time, and moreover no one can forbid her to do so, for her genitals are formed of two lips in continuous contact. Thus, within herself, she is already two—but not divisible into one(s)—that caress each other" (24). Irigaray adds, "Whence the mystery that woman represents in a culture claiming to count everything, to number everything by units, to inventory everything as individualities. *She is neither one nor two.* Rigorously speaking, she cannot be identified either as one person or as two. She resists all adequate definition. Further, she has no 'proper' name" (26). Following Irigaray's formulation, when Wonder Woman moves from transcendence to immanence, she becomes two who remain one—neither one nor two. As Irigaray says, even her name is doubled and therefore inadequate. She is a Diana pretending to be Diana, so that her name is both hers and her sister's.[18]

The comic form itself embodies the indeterminacy. Comics are built around repetition of the same figure; on a given page, Peter will draw Wonder Woman over and over again. The panel borders separate these images; each is each, identity in its place. But when Wonder Woman needs to cast off her transcendence, the panel borders collapse, and suddenly two images of her occupy the same delimited space. We see Diana and Diana, together in the same box.

Once Diana and Diana are embodied together, they can touch. This self-caressing opens the way for love—and not only love of one another or of one as another. Marcus noted that affection between women was seen as aiding, not hindering, love between men and women; similarly, Irigaray sees women's duality as opening into multiplicity: "So woman does not have a sex organ? She has at least two of them, but they are not identifiable as ones. Indeed, she has many more. Her sexuality, always at least double, goes even further: it is *plural*. . . . *Woman has sex organs more or less everywhere*" ("This Sex" 28). The page on which Diana meets Diana tracks the movement from two to many. The duality of Diana and Diana is multiplied on one page as they talk from panel to panel, so that we see not just the one Diana that is two but doubled Diana's multiplying profligately. And then, inevitably, in the sixth panel, the one Diana replaces the other Diana, while the other Diana is replaced in the frame by Steve.

A female self-caressing, self-opening to love for another—that's a metaphor for motherhood. And indeed, Diana, incarnated as a nurse, treats Steve with matriarchal affection, telling him, "Be a good boy now and keep quiet" (*Sensation Comics #1* 8). Diana's love of Steve isn't (just) romantic love and isn't (just) divine love—it's (also) the love of a mother for a child. If Wonder Woman is a Christ figure—and I think she is—then she remains a female Christ figure. "Being and remaining two is necessary for keeping love," Irigaray says in her discussion of religion and incarnation in her *Key Writings*. "Woman has to be attentive to that and help man to be capable of such a kind of behavior which is more difficult for him" (246). Women, for Irigaray, are better at being two in one and two at once in no small part because of the feminine potential of parturition. Incarnation for Irigaray, and for Marston, becomes, then, first a metaphor for pregnancy and then a model for the simultaneous balance of individuality and union, of submission and strength, that is necessary for love.

What's perhaps most interesting about that formulation is how easily it fits into Boesel/Kierkegaard's. Wonder Woman does not try to overawe Steve with her transcendent power. Instead, she lowers herself to him, showing her transcendent power through the servitude of love. The transcendent matriarch becomes human precisely to change bedpans. That's what divine love is. That's the point. The good is not the powerful. It's giving up power. Or as Marston says, in one of his most lyrical passages from *Emotions of Normal People*,

> Love is a giving, and not a taking; a feeding, and not an eating; an altruistic alliance with the loved one, and not a selfish conflict with a "sex object." *Whatever the organism has acquired during the expression of its appetitive emotion must be given away again in the expression of love, and "everything" includes the organism itself.* "Giving away" however, does not mean destruction or depreciation of the giver. It means only a submission of everything that the giver possesses, including his own body, to the service and needs of the loved one. (382, italics in original)

This passage I think explains why the first Wonder Woman story opens with an unconscious Steve Trevor. The initial hero in *Wonder Woman* is not a Just Warrior or even an education mother. He's a convalescent. To find his way to the island of the Amazons, to return to the matriarchal womb of wisdom and love, Steve must first set aside the manly prerogative of agency and violence. If masculinity is war, then to escape from war, Steve also has to escape from masculinity. For Marston, then, Steve's injuries are a kind of gift. They mark him as blessed, for only the wounded, the abject, and the castrated can know peace and enter Paradise.

CHAPTER THREE

CANDY YOU CAN EAT

Wonder Woman has often been seen as a queer or lesbian figure. This chapter begins by questioning Marston's involvement in, and knowledge of, this queerness and discusses how questions of knowledge are tied to the closet. I then look at Marston's psychological and fiction writing to argue that he was very conversant with, and approving of, lesbian relationships. This has implications for the reading of Marston's own polyamorous relationship and for the comics, which can be seen as deliberately and consciously advocating lesbianism.

The chapter moves on to discuss the contested relationship between men and lesbianism, looking at the figure of Pussy Galore. The exploitive nature of male representations of lesbianism is juxtaposed with Janice Raymond's prejudiced attacks on transsexuals, which are also attacks on lesbophiliac men.

Finally, Marston's investment in lesbianism is linked to both his interest in drag and his essentialist vision of femininity. Essentialism is usually seen (via Judith Butler) as opposed to queerness, but Marston's work suggests other possibilities. In particular, I talk about the work of trans theorist Julia Serano to try to show ways in which Marston's lesbophilia, and identification with women, is consistent with his feminism.

WHAT DOES EATING MEAN?

"When you've got a man, there's nothing you can do with him—but candy you can eat!" Etta Candy declares in *Wonder Woman #1* as she delicately holds a little nub of something that just so happens to be lined up with Diana Prince's crotch (3D; see figure 19). Etta's hand looks enormous—bigger than Diana's head, thanks to Peter's wavering perspective. Still, despite the thick masculine digits, her thumb and forefinger hold the candy with a large, swaggering delicacy. You can't see it very clearly in this panel, but her outfit is also insouciantly, even flamboyantly butch: a green suit with a white cravat at the throat, topped off with an orange cowboy hat. In comparison, the uniformed Diana, with her tie and her hair tucked under her hat, seems almost femme; at least she's wearing a dress. Meanwhile, off to the side, a clearly superfluous man obligingly blends into

FIGURE 19. *Wonder Woman #1* (1942)

his seat. You can't do anything with him—and Etta certainly doesn't need this barely there nonman to provide her with either masculinity or desire.

In a discussion of this panel, Lillian Robinson notes, with some humor, that Etta's words are "seemingly free of double entendre" (41). That is an interesting formulation, not least because of the clumsy nimbleness (not unlike Etta's) with which it raises questions in order to simultaneously sidestep them. There's only one reason to disavow a double entendre, after all, and that is to underline it. And if this image is "seemingly" chaste, then "seemingly" to whom? To Etta? Diana? Marston? The effaced man? Lillian Robinson herself? To me? To you? There are various ways to resolve such questions of knowledge, identity, and desire. Here are some (by no means exclusive) examples.

1. Marston and Peter Do Not Know, but Their Audience Does
This seems to be what Robinson herself is pointing to. Thus, when Robinson says that the panel is "seemingly free of double entendre," she is not saying that there is no sexy lesbian content. Rather, she is saying that the sexy lesbian content is visible to the reader (that is, to

Robinson and, presumably, to you) but not to Etta or to Marston. The fact that you, the reader, understand the joke but Etta does not is more than simply incidental—it is intrinsic to the humor itself. The delight in this panel, the sweet, guilty pleasure, is not just in the sex but in the knowing. Indeed, it is in the sex as knowing and the knowing as sex: the two are intertwined and inseparable. If Etta was in on the joke, it would not be a joke, or at least not the same joke.

You can see many similar examples of this type of humor in the aptly named Internet page "Unintentionally Sexual Comic Book Covers." Curated by "Maddox," the site includes one cover featuring an astronaut in an intimate clasp with a monkey, another showing a young boy hitting an older man with a strategically positioned salami, and so forth. These images are amusing not just because they are sexual but (as it says in the title) because we presume that the sexual content is something we see and that the creators did not. When the cover of a Dell comic called *The Rifleman* shows a boy holding a log just at the level of a cowboy's crotch, the significant look between man and boy and the placement of the log at log level are assumed to be serendipitous rather than deliberate. They amuse precisely because they are not meant to amuse—or not in that way, anyhow.

"That way," is, of course, not merely sexual but homosexual. Three of Maddox's five unintentionally sexual comic-book covers are predicated on the "discovery" of homosexual content; the other two show unintentional bestiality. None depict heterosexual relationships. Nor should this be especially surprising. Heterosexual content is overt and acceptable. Everybody knows that if you put a man and a woman together, you need to watch your implications. Other sexualities, though, are less open, less obvious, more closeted—so closeted, in fact, that in these instances the person in the closet is not even aware of his or her own secret. You know the truth about Etta and Diana (and perhaps Marston?). In fact, you know what they want and who they are better than they know themselves. The reader who sees Etta and Diana, then, can be seen as that half-erased, barely there man off to the side in the panel—a phantom presence, unobserved, whose lack of legibility is both power and knowledge. He sees but is not seen, while Etta is painfully, garishly readable to everyone—except herself.[1]

2. Marston and Peter Know, but Their Audience Does Not
This was the position taken by Frederic Wertham in *Seduction of the Innocent*. Published in 1954, Wertham's bestseller contributed to a moral panic that many fans charge with permanently crippling the comics industry. In his book, Wertham accused comics of fostering every sort of immorality, including homosexuality:[2]

> The homosexual connotation of the Wonder Woman type of story is psychologically unmistakeable. The *Psychiatric Quarterly* deplored in an editorial the "appearance of an eminent child therapist as the implied endorser of a series . . . which portrays extremely sadistic hatred of all males in a framework which is plainly Lesbian."
>
> For boys, Wonder Woman is a frightening image. For girls she is a morbid ideal. Where Batman is anti-feminine, the attractive Wonder Woman and her counterparts are definitely anti-masculine. Wonder Woman has her own female following. They are all continuously being threatened, captured, almost put to death. There is a great deal of mutual rescuing. . . . Her followers are the "Holliday girls," i.e. the holiday girls, the gay party girls, the gay girls. Wonder Woman refers to them as "my girls." (192–193)

For Wertham, Wonder Woman is a kind of code. The Holliday girls are "gay" girls, and one assumes he would see Etta's desire to eat "candy" as a direct and deliberate allusion to lesbian oral sex. The closet here, the coded gay subtext, is intended to pull the reader into she knows not what. Whereas Maddox's readings place power and knowledge with the audience outside the closet, Wertham's places them with the creators inside. The man fading into the seat, then, is not the powerful holder of the sadistic gaze but rather a sadistically alienated and effaced victim, the healthy male and his heterosexual potential sidelined by aberrant perversion. Etta knows just what she is offering to Diana when she waves that hand, and Diana's naivete is also her seducibility. If someone like Wertham does not tell her what she does not see, she will fall into the closet as into a *vagina dentata*, to be a gay girl forevermore.

3. *Marston and Peter May Know or May Not Know;*
There Is No Way for the Audience to Tell

This approach is exemplified by Trina Robbins in her essay "Wonder Woman: Lesbian or Dyke?" Robbins points out many instances in the Marston/Peter *Wonder Woman* in which there are intimations of female-female attraction. Robbins especially singles out *Wonder Woman #19*, in which Wonder Woman is aided by an eight-foot-tall Mexican mountain woman named Marya.[3] Marya clearly has a crush on the Amazon. In one panel, Marston writes of Marya, "Driven desperate by her great love for Wonder Woman," the giant breaks out of a cement casing, shouting, "My Preencess—I come!" (Wonder Woman praises her by declaring, "Great work, girl friend!") So Marya loves Wonder Woman, and Wonder Woman calls her "girlfriend." That seems fairly explicit. And yet, Robbins argues, there is no way to determine whether such hints were meant to be taken as indicative of same-sex attraction or whether they were simply an innocent byproduct of Marston's commitment to providing girls with models of same-sex friendships. As Robbins says, "Whether Wonder Woman's creator really intended any hidden lesbian agenda in his comics, or whether suspicions of Sapphism were simply products of Wertham's McCarthyist mentality, William Moulton Marston provided a safe place for girls in the pages of his comics, away from Man's World" ("Wonder Woman"). For Robbins, then, the point is not with what appetite Etta and Diana discuss candy but rather the fact that that man off to the side is so elaborately not the focus. Etta's disavowal of romantic interest in males is important. Her avowed interest in "eating," on the other hand, can bear no theoretical weight. The closet is closed, and what we don't know is, for practical purposes, illegible.

THE KANGAROO IN THE CLOSET

So again, in reading the interchange between Etta and Diana, we have three options. They are (1) Marston did not know the interaction could be seen as gay; (2) Marston did know the interaction could be seen as gay; (3) there is no way to tell how gay Marston intended the interaction to be. I don't wish to suggest that these options are all equally reasonable or equally correct. On the contrary, as I'll discuss later in this chapter, I think at least two of them are fundamentally misguided.

However, for now, what I want to focus on is the way that all these readings leverage, and are leveraged by, a particular relationship with knowledge and ignorance, speech and silence. They are all powered by their relationship to the closet—a phenomenon that gives any speech act in its vicinity "the exaggerated propulsiveness of wearing flippers in a swimming pool," as Eve Sedgwick puts it (*Epistemology* 3). Maddox positions himself as the knower and so can mock the unknowing for their ridiculous gayness. Wertham positions Marston as the knower and so can demonize him for his dangerous gayness. Robbins insists there is no knower and so can erase gayness altogether, at least as an object of theoretical inquiry. And Maddox, Wertham, Robbins, and certainly I as well are all implicated in the "structure of contagion" whereby, as Sedgwick says, "*It takes one to know one*" (*Epistemology* 156, italics in the original). How can Wertham read that code? Why doesn't Robbins want to? Why is the man in that train looking, or why *isn't* he looking? "Silence," Sedgwick writes, "is rendered as pointed and performative as speech, in relations around the closet, . . . [and] ignorance is as potent and as multiple a thing there as is knowledge" (*Epistemology* 4).

You don't have to believe Eve Sedgwick, though. If you want an illustration of the multiple powers and potencies of the closet, all you have to do is read *Wonder Woman*. Superhero comics, with their secret identities, have always flirted, and more than flirted, with the closet. But *Wonder Woman* does a lot more than flirt. In one scene, from *Wonder Woman #18*, for example, the evil Dr. Psycho suddenly and ectoplasmically transforms himself into, as he declares, "Tyrone Gayblade, the great lover" (6C).

There isn't really any good way to follow that, but another example that is nearly as flamboyant can be found in *Wonder Woman #2*. In a two-page sequence (7C–8C), an "oriental dancer" named Naha captures Wonder Woman with our heroine's own magic lasso. Naha then dresses Wonder Woman in a hat and trench coat and (still herself dressed in a diaphanous, skin-baring dancer's outfit) takes Wonder Woman across town to a yacht club, where the two lounge on deck chairs. Finally, Naha brings Wonder Woman to a private cabin, where she removes the Amazon's coat, gloves, and hat, ties her legs together, and tapes her eyes and mouth shut (see figure 20). "Why make me do

all this?" Wonder Woman asks, and, indeed, there is no real diegetic reason for Naha to create such an elaborate pantomime. The dancer's casual response ("To fool the police if they follow us") seems more excuse than explanation. Certainly, even if she is worried about the police, Naha's actions seem excessive. For instance, rather than just

FIGURE 20.
Wonder
Woman #2
(1942)

compelling Wonder Woman to follow her orders, Naha binds the Amazon's arms to her sides and then fits her trench coat with "false hands." When the two arrive at the club, Marston lovingly explains that "Wonder Woman's hand seems to present a membership card," while Peter draws the card gripped between the yellow thumb and forefinger—a gesture reminiscent of the way in which Etta held her candy in issue 1.

The false hands demand that the reader look beneath the presented surface. We see Wonder Woman standing outside the taxicab, one arm held by Naha—but we know that under the coat her arms are tied to her side. We see Wonder Woman reclining on a deck chair with her arms crossed on her lap and one red boot resting casually on the other. But we know that her *real* arms are tight to her body, making her position uncomfortably awkward—and her crossed legs even more cheekily and incongruously languid. Thus, two women, both in costume, share a secret knowledge about one woman's hands. And that secret floods each panel with excessive, exciting meaning and tension, turning the sequence into a kind of flirtatious parody of *Benito Cereno*.

As these examples indicate, *Wonder Woman* is deliriously, obsessively, almost incredibly camp. Philip Core's discussion of camp seems especially a propos: "There are only two things essential to camp: a secret within the personality which one ironically wishes to conceal and exploit, and a peculiar way of seeing things, affected by spiritual isolation, but strong enough to impose itself on others through acts of creation" (9). I'll talk about Marston's peculiar way of seeing things shortly, but I want to focus on the first part of Core's definition—the idea that camp involves a secret that one wishes both to conceal and to exploit. This seems like an excellent description of how *Wonder Woman* functions and of why it is so idiosyncratic. Again, in the Naha sequence, Naha herself has a secret (her control of Wonder Woman) that she both hides and utilizes. At the same time, Naha's secret-within-a-secret is, or can be, that she is not Wonder Woman's antagonist but her lover—that the fictional captive narrative presented in-story as real is, in fact, fictional. The artificial surface, the pantomime, is the highly visible secret—and that secret is exploited (like the Orientalist fetishization of Naha herself) to add exotic whimsy, or whimsical exotica, to the "straight" adventure narrative. The fact that the bondage fantasy is *so* obvious that it virtually flips from subtext to text isn't a contradiction but an elaboration, so that the "straight" adventure narrative, too, becomes the visible hidden truth. Truth and justice, sex and control, switch in and out of the closet, so that knowledge and naivete are always both condescending to and surprising each other.

Eve Sedgwick has argued that this kind of manipulation of knowledge is not merely one effect of texts but is the actual organizing principle of narrative itself. Novels, Sedgwick says, create an "inexplicit compact by which novel-readers plunge into worlds that strip them, however temporarily, of the painfully acquired cognitive maps of their ordinary lives," in return for "an invisibility that promises cognitive exemption and eventual privilege" (*Epistemology* 97). At the beginning of a novel, Sedgwick says, the disoriented reader is presented with a total ignorance that appears as total knowledge. Thus, for example, when Jane Austen introduces us to a social milieu that is utterly unknown, she can for that very reason assume, and/or compel, universal acknowledgment of its truths.

Sedgwick does not use Austen as an example, but she wouldn't see it as a coincidence that the truths initially discussed in *Pride and Prejudice* involve the unpredictable matrimonial habits of single men.[4] On the contrary, Sedgwick suggests that knowledge in novels is essentially constructed like, and through, the closet. Between narrator and reader, she says, there are established "relations of flattery, threat, and complicity" (*Epistemology* 97). Narrative, for her, is a complicated form of epistemological coercion. The author flatters the reader by telling her that she is worldly and wise—that she, for example, understands the motivations of single men, as others do not. And in exchange, the reader acknowledges the narrator's even greater knowledge. The novel, then, becomes a secret to peruse together. To open a book is to open a closet.

Sedgwick's linkage of narrative and the closet is built specifically on late nineteenth-century high-art realist narratives (*The Bostonians*, *Billy Budd*) and on the specific relations of knowledge and ignorance around homosexual men. Still, her discussion fits *Wonder Woman* surprisingly well. For instance, the title page of *Sensation Comics #31* from July 1944 emphatically links narrative disorientation to narrative complicity. As you can see in figure 21, the cover image is both bizarre and confusing. Peter's perspective is always unusual at the best of times, but here he seems to be deliberately dispensing with it entirely, so that the action all appears to occur on a single surface. In addition, a good third of the panel is taken up with a giant explanatory text scroll by Marston, which both seems to be imposed on the image and to be a kind of beribboned fabric hanging from the curtains that frame the panel on one side. Next to that curtain, on a raised dais, sits a toddler with Wonder Woman over her knee. The toddler in comparison to the adult Wonder Woman looks enormous, even grotesque—her eyes are so wide open, and so weirdly expressionless, that she looks more like a doll than like a real child. The toddler is paddling Wonder Woman vigorously with a hairbrush (the motion lines seem to disappear behind her chair, which is emblazoned with a kind of coat of arms showing a lollipop and a bottle). Crowded into the front and right side of the panel are infants who applaud the paddling vigorously from amid their toys. These toys include a stuffed raccoon that appears to be floating in thin air and a wooden doll that hangs morbidly from a ribbon—its head limp and its eyes and mouth gaping open.

But is our heroine disturbed at being assaulted by a nightmare monster-child in a surrealist flatland? Not at all! Butt and boots in the air, Wonder Woman cheerfully turns to the reader and closes one eye in a conspiratorial wink. To paraphrase Sedgwick, this *Wonder Woman* comic robs you of your cognitive map and in return lets you know that you are observing from a position of safety and worldly wisdom. You are assured that you know what is happening behind that curtain or inside that closet.

Although Sedgwick and Wonder Woman both present narrative-as-closet, though, what is inside the closet, and the reader's perspective on it, is somewhat different. In the realist novels that Sedgwick discusses, the content of the closet is, broadly, mimetic. Single men with large fortunes have the same closets in the novel as they do outside it. Wonder Woman's wink, on the other hand, means something rather different. She is not telling the reader that this is *really* happening but that it is *not* really happening; she is beckoning the reader to partake in a fantasy. The complicity is in the reality of an illusion, rather than in an illusion of reality. Whereas Sedgwick's novelists and readers enter into an agreement to pretend that the contents of their closets are true, Wonder Woman and her winking collaborators enter into an agreement to pretend that they aren't.

This compact allows Marston and Peter to create a narrative in *Sensation Comics #31* that would make Fellini blush and Dalí do a spit take. Things start off coherently enough, as Wonder Woman rescues a

FIGURE 21. *Sensation Comics* #31 (1944)

couple of children from alligators and then reprimands their negligent mother. On page 5, though, the children are afflicted with some kind of sleeping sickness, and to rescue them Wonder Woman joins them in the dreamworld of "Grown Down Land." She is quickly imprisoned by toddlers, chained, and then tied with her own lasso by the girl she came to rescue. Kneeling before her new child mistress, Wonder Woman is commanded to go kidnap the child's negligent mother and father. She does so, and they all (blindfolded and kneeling) are forced to consume grown-down medicine, which turns them into children (though the father as a six-year-old still rather hideously retains his pattern baldness, mustache, and hairy legs). Steve and Etta then show up to lead Wonder Woman back home, and they all eventually wind up safe—with the formerly negligent mother and father now loving and affectionate since they've been reconnected to their inner children. In the last panel of the story, Etta teases Wonder Woman about how dumb she was when she was grown down into a kid. Steve, ever gallant, demurs, insisting, "At least you were affectionate! You gave me a nice kiss!" "Which proves Etta is right," Wonder Woman volleys back. "I *was* a silly little girl!" (13) The teasing disavowal of childhood kisses is absolutely central to the narrative, which revels in fantasies of eroticized childhood by pushing them into a supposed dreamworld.

Yet the orally obsessed Etta's presence in the panel, and in the story, is a marker of how porously Marston and Peter actually treat the line between adult and child. Peter, by this point, was drawing Etta to look like she was a pudgy eight- to ten-year-old. Usually, no one comments on her strange infantilization—it is visible to us but does not seem to be seeable, or readable, by Etta's friends. But in this story, suddenly we learn that everybody knows—and was, supposedly, just keeping quiet out of politeness (11).

In any case, Etta's queer appearance is, in this context, a decided boon. When Steve enters Grown Down Land, he is instantly captured. But all the kids assume that Etta is a child, allowing her to plot to free her allies. Thus, rather than a closet constructed around heterosexual/homosexual identity, in this narrative, the binary is adult/child, with Etta as an adult passing for a prepubescent, and Wonder Woman (who "never grew all the way up"; 5) as a playful child masquerading as an adult. And just as the closet highlights and segregates homosexual desire, so does the binary here both facilitate and banish the sexualization of parent-child relationships. "Dear old Stevie!" child Wonder Woman says as she jumps up to give Steve a kiss. "I'm so glad you came too—wanta play ball or cops 'n robbers?" (11). In Grown Down Land, anything you imagine is real—but what exactly are we imagining here? And is it more or less real if we don't want to know?

In *Epistemology of the Closet*, Eve Sedgwick argues that "the typifying gesture of camp is really something amazingly simple: the moment at which a consumer of culture makes the wild surmise, 'What if whoever made this was gay too?' . . . What if the right audience for this were exactly *me*?" (156, italics in original). In the Grown Down Land story—and in Marston/Peter in general—the consumer of culture is encouraged to make the wild surmise "What if whoever made this was gay too?" in exact parallel with the wild surmise "What if whoever made this was a child too?" Wonder Woman's wink is both an openly secret acknowledgment of sexual knowledge *and* an openly secret acknowledgment of childhood play. From the perspective of Marston and Peter, then, all of children's literature—from Narnia's secret world-in-a-wardrobe to Calvin's secret friend to those blundering mirror images Thomson and Thompson—can be seen from the vantage of the closet. The point here is not that Thomson and Thompson or Calvin or Harry Potter are *really* gay. Rather, the point is that the binaries of knowledge and innocence that Sedgwick identifies as typical of the closet are also typical of children's literature—and that Marston and Peter insistently conflate the two. What else to make of that transparent secret, the invisible plane? Or of the marvelous panel in *Wonder Woman #5* shown in figure 22 (second part, 11).[5]

Jacques Lacan argues in his famous essay on the mirror stage that an infant sees itself in the mirror and joyously recognizes itself as an "I." Here, though,

FIGURE 22. *Wonder Woman #5* (1943)

Wonder Woman's enthusiastic finger "SNAP!" sound effect seems redolent of the joy that the infant feels when it looks in the mirror and recognizes itself as a kangaroo. In Marston and Peter, there's a secret through every porthole, a shadow at every step—and that shadow is not (like Wonder Woman's in this panel) shapeless and black and ominous but is instead curious (queer?) and helpful. A closet with a kangaroo in it is a closet everybody would want to open. For Sedgwick, the closet tends to create narrative effects of paranoia, threat, and condescension—of Billy Budd hung from the yardarm. For Marston, it produces a cheerier vision, not least because he believes so definitively that gay literature is for kids and that kids' literature is for gays. The closet is not a nexus of murderous fear but a playful site of pretend, the door that always, surprisingly, opens onto love, in all its manifestations.

These divergent discussions of the closet are, surely, tied into divergent experiences of the closet. Sedgwick was a heterosexual woman who identified strongly with gay men during the height of the AIDS epidemic.[6] The closet, in her experience, killed. Marston's commitments were quite different.

THE MOST PERFECT LOVE

As I've (more than) hinted, I don't believe that there is much doubt about the deliberateness of the lesbian subtext in *Wonder Woman*. Indeed, I basically agree with the pseudonymous writer Jones, One of the Jones Boys, when he says that said subtext is "more than subtext; hell, it's more than text-text." Probably the most dispositive evidence within the *Wonder Woman* comics themselves is in the fairly spectacular *Wonder Woman #3*. In this story, Wonder Woman and Etta travel to Paradise Island to take part in a celebration of an Amazon holiday called Diana's Day. During the festivities, some Amazons dress up as deer while other Amazons try to hunt and catch them. The captured deer are then trussed up and placed on a table for "eating" (see figure 23).

Peter depicts the results on page 10A in one of the most startling sequences in the history of comics. In the first panel, a row of six "does" are shown hanging by their wrists from a wooden beam. Their faces are obscured by their arms, rendering them anonymous—they are literally presented as curvy, mouth-watering slabs of meat. Their

FIGURE 23. *Wonder Woman #3* (1943)

tails stick up perkily erect behind them, a row of adorably parodic womanly penises. In front of them, an Amazon inspects the wares. She is dressed in a cook's hat and a white dress and apron—the supposedly utilitarian work outfit only emphasizing her naked shoulders and casually limned cleavage. In her right hand, the cook holds a long, slender, slightly curved sword, which of course is positioned so that it extends out from her crotch. She shakes her left finger in the face of an Amazon who has been "skinned"—her doe hide apparently sliced off with the sword and rolled down to her ankles as she hangs suspended. "Aha, my fine doe, you'll soon be ready for cooking!" the cook declares, to which the skinned Amazon replies, "Oh what a relief to get rid of that hot, stuffy doe skin!" Meanwhile, to the right of the skinned doe's head, Peter has drawn what appears to be a floating, scribbly pink mass, with smaller scribbles dancing about beneath it. Presumably it's supposed to be some kind of Amazonian topiary, but in this context, it comes across as a joyfully displaced yonic eruption, as if the very hills are celebrating the does and their soft, yummy, soon-to-be-exposed interiors.[7]

You wouldn't think you could top that image, but the next panel is if anything even more brazen. "You'll make a lovely chicken, darling! Wait until I give you a crisp skin!" exclaims an eager Amazon chef, brandishing two big, pointy knives. The Amazon dinner smiles cheerfully, flat on her back on a platter, her bound legs tucked up, knees together, and pointed toward her ravisher. "You make my mouth water," she enthuses. "How about feeding me to myself?" In the background stand several other Amazons in those stiff Peter poses, staring with oddly blank expressions, frozen in place by an excess of flirtatious banter. In a third panel, nine Amazons are shown with their arms tied behind their backs kneeling on a circular pie crust—displayed for the enjoyment and delectation of their peers.

These kinds of female-female erotic games occur throughout Marston's comics. They are clearly inspired by his academic work on sorority initiation rituals.[8] At Tufts University, Marston observed sorority "Baby Parties," in which freshmen were made to dress up as, and act like, infants. If they rebelled, upperclassmen captured and chastised them. According to Marston's observations, as well as interviews with the participants, both the girls who did the punishing and those who were punished found the experience stimulating—especially the parts involving capturing and being captured. On the basis of this research, Marston concluded that female erotic responses are "*not limited to inter-sex relationships*" (*Emotions* 301, italics in original). There is little doubt, then, that if you asked Marston if the Amazons experienced erotic pleasure during their games, he would reply (possibly in italics), "*Of course! And good for them!*"

To reiterate: Marston spent substantial time and energy observing sorority bondage and domination rituals that he identified explicitly and enthusiastically as based on homoeroticism. He then included similar rituals in his comics, deliberately and extravagantly playing up the homo-eroticism. I do not see how it is possible, given this evidence, to see the erotic female-female play in *Wonder Woman* as anything but intentional.

However, as Eve Sedgwick has pointed out, even in the face of substantial evidence, many readers are eager to minimize gay content. This is in part the nature of the closet, which encourages us to respond to questions about sexuality with the brief answer, "Don't ask. Or, less laconically: You shouldn't know" (*Epistemology* 52). Sedgwick goes on to list a number of typical ways in which evidence of same-sex attraction has been dismissed. I won't reproduce all of them, but here are three that seem likely to be relevant for our discussion:

> Passionate language of same-sex attraction was extremely common during whatever period is under discussion—and therefore must have been completely meaningless. . . .
>
> Attitudes about homosexuality were intolerant back then, unlike now—so people probably didn't do anything. . . .
>
> There is no actual proof of homosexuality, such as sperm taken from the body of another man or a nude photograph with another woman—so the author may be assumed to have been ardently and exclusively heterosexual. (52–53)

Sedgwick's examples do not fit Wonder Woman precisely since she is talking about the gayness of authors rather than of characters. Still, I think her insights are useful—not least because the sexuality of Marston, and of those he slept with, is more fraught than it at first appears. At the very least, Sedgwick highlights some of the ways in which, and some of the reasons why, the lesbian content of *Wonder Woman* might be minimized. For instance, if you were skeptical of Amazonian lesbianism, the mere existence of same-sex eroticism might not be enough to convince you. You might argue that in the Diana's Day games, Marston was merely advocating and approving of Platonic, albeit erotically charged, female friendships. Yes, Marston was all for girls tying each other up and pretending to eat each other. But lesbianism was much less discussed in his time than in ours. Who is to say that he linked these kinky games to genital activity? Who's to say he even knew how lesbian sex worked?

As I said, you might argue along those lines—until you found this passage from Marston's psychological treatise *Emotions of Normal People*:

> Furthermore, though the fact seems little known, the clitoris of one woman may be stimulated nearly as effectively by the vulva of another woman, as can the penis of a male with the vagina of the female. The female emotion resulting from stimulation of the clitoris by another woman (as apparent in the behaviour of women prisoners) seems fully as extensive as the male emotion resulting from stimulation of the penis. In this type of physical relationship, both women most frequently experience simultaneous stimulation of the clitoris with appropriate emotional states following. Neither woman, of course, receives stimulation of the mouth of the vagina. (318)

As you can see, that is Marston explaining clitoris-to-clitoris sex, or tribadism—a practice that he says appears to be "little known." Queer theorist Judith Halberstam agrees with Marston on that; according to her, tribadism has been little discussed or visualized in modern times, even by lesbians themselves. This has been especially true since the time of Sigmund Freud, who, Halberstam says, never mentioned the practice (65). Thus, there is reason to believe that when it came to the mechanics of lesbian sex, Marston was not only knowledgeable but was among the *most* knowledgeable American males of his day. And in case you're worried that Marston was familiar *only* with tribadism, in another passage, he helpfully mentions that one woman can bring another to orgasm through the use of "tongue or hand" (*Emotions* 327).

But perhaps Marston knew about the mechanics of lesbian sex but disapproved of it. Maybe he thought female-female erotic ties should be expressed only through chaste romance and not through clitoral rubbing. Well:

> Girls of five or six years, or older, are quite likely to experience passive love for other girls of similar age, with or without mutual stimulation of the genital organs, as the case may be. . . . At least two completed love affairs of this type between girls five to seven years old have been brought to my attention. In both cases the

children were wholly normal so far as could be determined by medical and psychological examination. (*Emotions* 303)

So there is Marston publicly arguing that it's perfectly normal and healthy for five- and six-year-old girls to fall in love and have sex with each other.

Nor did Marston's approval of female-female intercourse cease at pubescence. On the contrary, he devotes a whole subheading of *Emotions of Normal People*, titled "Women's Passion," to expounding on the commonness, normality, and general pleasantness of lesbian relationships. He starts by asserting that "nearly half of the female love relationships concerning which significant data could be obtained, were accompanied by bodily love stimulation" (*Emotions* 338). While it's difficult to parse this statement precisely (is he actually saying that half of all female friendships involve lesbian sex?), it's clear that female-female attraction is not, for him, a minority identity but is instead a potential available to, and enjoyed by, a very large number of women.

Marston backs up this claim by citing his observations of women dancers, among whom, he says, "physical love relationships with other women seem to be the rule rather than the exception." He adds that for one married couple of his acquaintance, "physical love contacts . . . were more enjoyable" for the man after "passion responses had been evoked from [the wife] by another girl" (*Emotions* 338). In another instance, he says, a "male psychologist" of his acquaintance watched as "two girl lovers, who had been separated from one another for some weeks by the college authorities, . . . performed the love act unhesitatingly in his presence" (338). The "male psychologist" in question was quite possibly Marston himself—perhaps taking notes for his description of tribadism.[9] In any case, Marston concludes by suggesting that stigmatizing female-female intercourse is pointless, since as long as women are biologically capable of being stimulated by both men and women, they will "continue to enjoy both types of love relationships whenever possible," regardless of "social prohibition" (339). After detailing this stimulating but strictly anecdotal evidence, Marston moves to a more (putatively) scientific mode. He says, "I have been unable to verify a male medical opinion given me at the beginning of my investigation, that such love affairs between girls were always injurious to their physical health" (339). The one caveat that Marston offers is in regard to lesbian relationships among prison inmates. Research among these populations suggests that in a small number of cases (he cites two out of ninety-seven) lesbianism may cause some "physical deterioration." He speculates that this is because the women were not able to "counterbalance" their lesbian affairs with heterosexual ones. But for the most part, and in all cases outside institutional settings, he says that he detected "no emotional or physical results of a deleterious nature" (339).

For Marston, then, lesbian relationships are normal—even inevitable—for many (half of all?) women and are also virtually always utterly harmless. Indeed, at several points, he suggests not just that lesbianism is harmless but that it is actively good for women themselves and for society as a whole. Again, in one anecdote, Marston says that a woman who sleeps with another woman will be a better lover for her husband. No doubt many feminists, lesbian and otherwise, would find the male-centered rationale here offensive. But perhaps they would be mollified (or at least surprised) by Marston's suggestion in the same paragraph that lesbian sex makes women more affectionate mothers. And certainly there is nothing especially patriarchal about Marston's claim that men rarely manage to give women clitoral orgasms through heterosexual intercourse—while other women are able to do so as a matter of course (*Emotions* 327–328).

Marston's most enthusiastic endorsement of lesbianism, however, is not in his academic work but in his (circa 1932) pseudohistorical pulp soft-core novel *Venus with Us: A Tale of the Caesar* (also known as *The Private Life of Julius Caesar*). The work is effectively *Wonder Woman*'s older, more explicit sister. In it, Marston imagines a sensual Orientalist Roman past filled with eroticized slavery and same-sex love. It includes one notable scene in which Caesar watches as "Lesbian dancing girls abandon themselves in an orgy of rhythmic ecstasy" (213). In an even more definitive, if not more explicit, speech, Cleopatra expounds on the virtues of lesbianism:

"Ah!" Caesar commented thoughtfully. "You and Berenice—"

"We loved each other—oh! *terribly*. I worshiped her; she was my Isis. Our love was the most sacred thing that I have ever had in my life." Cleopatra's voice became soft as velvet and indescribably sweet. "You know, Gaius, they teach a great truth in our school: 'Woman is made for love. She knows how to love, and how to be loved. Consequently, if a loving couple is composed of two women, it is perfect.'" (217)

Marston, then, included lesbianism in both his academic work and in his fiction. He saw lesbianism as normal, healthy, and even ideal. But even that probably understates the extent of his commitment to lesbophilia.

As I have mentioned several times in this book, Marston's living arrangements were unusual. He was initially married to Elizabeth Holloway. While teaching at Tufts University, he met a graduate student named Olive Byrne—she was in fact his assistant in his sorority "Baby Party" experiments (*Emotions* 299). Olive moved in with the Marstons in the late 1920s, and the three of them established a polyamorous relationship. Olive and Elizabeth each had two children by Marston. After Marston's death in 1947, the two women lived together until Olive's death in the late 1980s.

The Marston household seems to have been at least fairly open about their arrangement, according to Les Daniels, who offers the most complete discussion of their relationship. Still, that doesn't mean that they broadcasted it. According to Daniels, Sheldon Mayer, Marston's editor, was "nonplussed" as he "became aware of the situation" but was "ultimately won over." Mayer goes on to say that Marston "had a family relationship with a lot of women, yet it was male-dominated" (31). It is hard to know what to make of such fragments—how did Mayer "become aware" of the Marstons' situation, exactly? What does he mean by "a lot" of women? Is he talking about Marjorie Wilkes Huntley, a longtime friend of the family who came in and out of the house both before and after Marston's death. Or were there even others? And what does Mayer mean by "male-dominated"?

All these questions pale beside the biggest issue, though. Daniels notes that Olive and Elizabeth "were friendly enough to name their kids after each other" (31). They were also, as I've mentioned, friendly enough to live with each other for four decades after Marston died. That is really exceedingly, unusually friendly—queerly friendly, one might even say. Yet Daniels never so much as mentions the logical ensuing possibility.

Daniels's circumspection has been shared by most other writers on the topic. In an essay on queer themes in Marston's work, Trina Robbins doesn't even mention Marston's polyamory, much less the relationship between Elizabeth and Olive ("Wonder Woman"). A 2001 online biography of Elizabeth Marston by Marguerite Lamb suggestively refers to the polyamorous relationship as a "ménage à trois," but the rest of the article (including quotes from family members) presents the Olive-Elizabeth relationship as strictly pragmatic and functional.[10] Ken Alder calls the arrangement a "ménage à trois" (185), and Ben Saunders notes that "the bonds of affection between all three partners were strong" (42), but neither elaborates beyond that. Lewis Call mentions the fact that Olive Byrne's bracelets inspired Wonder Woman's and speculates that this could indicate that the Marstons' polyamorous relationship "may have had room for female submission as well as female dominance" (32). But the possibility of female-female erotics, much less female-female BDSM, is not raised. The one exception here is Tim Hanley, who forthrightly acknowledges that "Marston may have lived in the middle of a female love relationship, and this could have influenced his work" (135).

Perhaps the most telling instance of the general, odd silence is an otherwise excellent article about Marston's life and work by Geoffrey C. Bunn. In his analysis of Marston, Bunn notes that the man was "well acquainted with deception and masquerade"—which was no doubt true. To prove his case, Bunn cites as evidence the fact that Marston used a pseudonym when he wrote *Wonder Woman* (94). Surely if you want to prove that Marston knew about masquerade, the evidence to cite is not the pen name. The evidence to cite is the life with its sexual secrets and secrets within secrets, many of which scholars are still reluctant to whisper about more than sixty-five years after the man's death.

Even Jill Lepore's *The Secret History of Wonder Woman*, released while this book was in proofs, is reticent. Lepore had unprecedented access to the Marston papers. She found that Marston, Elizabeth, Byrne, and Huntley all participated in nude New Age sex meetings. She discovered that Elizabeth was a devotee of Sappho and died with a volume of the poet's work by her beside. She found that Olive, the niece of Margaret Sanger, was familiar with and unjudgemental about homosexuality. But Lepore never comes out and speaks directly to the obvious questions. Of course, to some degree those questions are unanswerable.[11] But we can perhaps use an analogy. If Marston had written academic treatises in which he declared sex between men to be normal, if he had written a novel in which he declared sex between men to be ideal, and if he had then spent his life living with a man, what would you conclude? Marston made his sexual preferences abundantly clear in his public work and writing—work and writing that both Olive and Elizabeth helped him with. He was a lesbophiliac who lived with two women who were willing to flout the sexual conventions of their time and, for that matter, of ours. I suppose it's possible that at some point we will find evidence that Elizabeth and Olive were not lovers. But on the basis of what we know, I think the assumption has to be that they were.

To summarize, then: Marston was aware—even, one could say, hyperaware—of the existence of same-sex love between women. He knew, and referred explicitly to, various kinds of lesbian sex, including tribadism, oral sex, and mutual masturbation. He believed that these practices, and female-female love in general, were normal, natural, healthy for women themselves, healthy for society, and ideologically and spiritually "perfect." Moreover, in his comics, much of the same-sex play was clearly inspired by sorority rituals, which in his academic work he specifically identified as sites of same-sex eroticism. Finally, he lived in a socially stigmatized polyamorous relationship with two very probably bisexual women. As a result, he likely had firsthand experience with lesbian relationships and undoubtedly had firsthand experience of the closet, with its multiple secrets, silences, and codes.

Given all this, I do not see how it is possible to see the lesbian romance and lesbian play in *Wonder Woman* as anything but intentional. Moreover, I think there is good reason to believe that Marston wanted his child readers to find the material erotically stimulating and hoped that it would encourage both boys and girls to be more open to the idea of lesbian sex. Remember, Marston believed it was "normal" for five- and six-year-old girls to engage in lesbian genital play. Cleopatra's "perfect" lesbian love affair is supposed to have occurred when she was somewhere between eleven and thirteen years old. Marston thought that lesbianism made women better lovers and mothers—a fact with broad political implications since Marston believed (as discussed in chapter 2) that matriarchal feminine love would save the world. Thus, Marston had numerous reasons to promote lesbianism, even discounting the fact that he very probably had a personal stake in the social acceptance of lesbian relationships.

In that scene on the train with which I began this chapter, then, I think it is safe to say that Etta and Diana are flirting—and that Marston would enthusiastically embrace and endorse any plausible, or even implausible, double entendre. The sexual content is not unintentional, as Lillian Robinson intimates. Nor is it undeterminable, as Trina Robbins says—we know much, much more about Marston's attitude toward lesbianism than she suggests. Surprisingly, it is Fredric Wertham whose reading seems most accurate.[12] Marston may not have meant "Holliday" to be a pun on "gay," but he certainly fully intended the Holliday girls to participate in and model erotic same-sex play. Wertham saw that as sinister, and Marston adamantly did not. They disagreed about lesbianism. But I think they would have agreed that lesbianism was what they were disagreeing about.

WONDER PUSSY, WOMAN GALORE

Settling Marston's attitude toward lesbianism, though, doesn't end the discussion. Far from it. We know that in *Wonder Woman #1*, Etta and Diana are, in fact, talking about what Etta and Diana are talking about. But that still leaves us with the question, what is that half-effaced man doing there off to the side? What does he see when he sees two women flirting—or two women living in his home, as the case may be—and what's in it for him? Or, to put it another way, now that we know Marston's intentions, what, exactly, are his intentions?

Male erotic fantasies about lesbians are ubiquitous, notorious, and, as Elisabeth Ladenson has written, "somewhat underexamined" ("Special Issue" 372). For many people, Ladenson says, the topic of men and lesbianism seems "at once obvious and improbable, even unworthy of interest" (373). When she organized a special issue of *GLQ* on the topic, "Men and Lesbianism," Ladenson was surprised to discover that she couldn't convince any men to contribute. Many of those she approached claimed they had nothing to say on the topic. This is, as Ladenson pointed out, a most unusual state of affairs for academics or, indeed (as Ladenson was too polite to say), for men in general (374).

Ladenson's observations were made a decade ago, but they still mostly hold true. As Sharon Marcus told me by email, men's interest in lesbians, and especially lesbian porn, is still brought up "as a passing observation, that is taken as too self-evident to require analysis."[13] More extensive discussions tend to vary between animosity and wariness. The specter of Howard Stern (who Ladenson mentions at the end of her introduction), or of someone like him, is never far away. Nor would I say that this wariness is exactly misplaced. After all, perhaps the most iconic narrative of men and lesbians from the past half century is the book and, especially, film *Goldfinger*, starring James Bond and the single-entendre wonder that is Pussy Galore.

In the 1964 movie, Galore (Honor Blackman) is the leader of a team of lesbian pilots. She works for the criminal mastermind Goldfinger out of purely mercenary motives. Galore is independent and tough—perhaps, like the boy named Sue, because she has to fight every time she introduces herself.[14] In any case, however she acquired them, her fighting skills are inevitably no match for those of superspy Bond (Sean Connery), who drags her into the hay (literally) and rapes her. This is a transformative experience. Immediately thereafter, Galore eschews lesbianism to become Bond's girl, joining him in the fight against evil. (Her team of Sapphic pilots changes allegiance along with her, though how she convinces them, and what they think of her motivations, is never articulated.)

What's most indicative, and not incidentally most offensive, about the Bond-Galore love affair is the extent to which Miss Galore is so completely beside the point. The rape and transformation is never about her. In fact, we don't ever get a sense of her as a character except that she's inaccessible—and then, suddenly, not so much. She falls for Bond because he's just so darn overwhelmingly attractive, and she abandons her lesbianism as if she were doffing a hat. There's no actual psychological progression attempted; it's just insert phallus, hello enlightenment. The whole point of the encounter is, in fact, to annihilate her as a character—which is why her wit evaporates with her lesbianism. After she's been heterosexualized, she never quips again.[15]

The thrill of erasure is also why Galore has to be a lesbian to begin with. As Ladenson argues (in reference to the novel, but it works for the film as well), "it is [Galore's] sexual indifference that has attracted Bond in the first place" ("Lovely" 422). Galore is defined by her impenetrability specifically so she can be penetrated. Her will is inviolable, both in the sense that she doesn't want to be violated and in the sense that not being violated is all there is to her will. When Bond rapes her, then, he enters not just her body but her mind, replacing her desires with his own so that she becomes simply his cat's-paw. Male power fantasies don't come much cruder. What Bond gets from his investment in lesbians is a maximized return on his own power. The excessive difference ("Pussy Galore") is exciting precisely because it can be eradicated—the lesbian is thrilling not in her lesbianism but in the way in which even her aggressive lack can be insouciantly filled. As Ladenson says in *Proust's Lesbianism*, "The name Pussy Galore is successively understood as an interdiction, a challenge, and a gift withheld and then ultimately delivered. The lure of James Bond as a character is that he represents the impossibly phallic man who can win the impossible prize represented by Pussy Galore" (9).

In Bond's swaggering conflation of mind control and rape, Ian Fleming's suave, handsome hero seems to have a lot in common with one of Marston and Peter's ugliest villains, Dr. Psycho. The dwarfish, misshapen, but brilliant scientist Psycho is introduced in *Wonder Woman* #5. There we learn that he was jilted and framed for the theft of radium by his fiancée, Marva. In revenge, Psycho captures Marva and hypnotizes her, in a panel that quivers with violence. Against an ominous, shadowy background, Marva is tied with her arms over her head while Dr. Psycho stands in front of her, his enormous head as large as her whole upper torso. His demonstrative eyebrows flex mightily as lines of inky black smudges shoot from his distended eye sockets into her half-lowered lids. Peter fills the area around Psycho with scribbly, horizontal lines, so the doctor's whole body seems to tremble and thrust forward, while Marva gapes in anticipation, mouth receptively open (4A; see figure 24). The scene is obviously a rape, and as in *Goldfinger*, violation leads quickly to transformation and control. In the next panel, we see Psycho and Marva before a judge, as the caption explains, "Under Psycho's hypnotic control Marva is forced to marry him."

FIGURE 24. *Wonder Woman #5* (1943)

For Bond, gaining control of Pussy Galore is the key to victory; when she switches allegiance, she ensures Goldfinger's defeat. Thus, Bond's phallic victory over Pussy is the victory of Pussy obtained as phallus; she's simultaneously the fruit and the rod of his mastery. In a similar manner, Psycho's control of Marva literally empowers him. By using Marva as a medium, Psycho is able to summon ectoplasm from the spirit world, which he can use to transform his own appearance or to create various kinds of deadly blobby traps and weapons. Whereas the dynamics of *Goldfinger* are just obvious enough to be tedious, though, Psycho's mastery of feminine ectoplasm is flamboyantly self-parodic. The first thing he does with his newfound abilities is to build "muscles like Hercules on his own spindling arms," after which he transforms himself first into Mussolini and then into John L. Sullivan. "I'm the champ's ghost!" he chortles, striking a pose as red ectoplasmic light flows toward him from the seated Marva. The panel is a perfect negative image of the hypnotism/rape scene on the previous page. There, Psycho's eyes gaped wide as power flowed from him toward her; here, Marva is blindfolded as power flows from her toward him. Having built his manliness on rape, he is contradictorily at his victim's mercy, poised to disincorporate as soon as she walks out—or, the blindfold suggests, as soon as she looks at him. Psycho, then, is Marston's critique of stunted, ludicrous evil sociopaths like Bond who think that rape makes them men (4A–5A).

But while Psycho is meant to be the bad guy, there is also a sense in which his actions are paradoxically more justifiable, or at least more understandable, than Bond's. Pussy Galore is just a phallus and so could presumably be replaced by another handy phallus, be it gun, car, or martini. But that ectoplasm that turns Psycho into Sullivan, that's a magical pink you can't get just anywhere. Indeed, in the first panel showing Psycho drawing forth the ectoplasm, the disconnected blobs look like scribbly, ghostly fetuses, as if the evil hypnotist is leaching out specifically maternal power. Psycho goes to other women for his ectoplasm when Marva is not available—but it has to be to other women. Nothing else will do. For Bond with Pussy Galore, the point is to *dominate* her; for Psycho with Marva, it's to dominate *her*—not to obliterate her but to gain what she has.

In *Proust's Lesbianism*, Ladenson argues that Proust's world is one in which there is a "sexual economy that is not based on a phallic standard" (134). That is certainly the case for *Wonder Woman* as well. Marston's women don't want the penis; rather, his men want the absence of a penis—a unique female power. Psycho is wrong to try to get that power by force. But by Marston's lights, he's certainly *not* wrong to find it appealing.

Psycho's desire for, and provisional acquisition of, female power is why he's such a dangerous villain—and also such an enjoyable one. Particularly in his return engagement in *Wonder Woman #18*, Marston, Peter, and co-writer Joye Murchison seem to find him a blast to write, as he races from panel to panel, changing from Steve to General Darnell to that notorious lover Tyrone Gayblade, animating ectoplasmic dinosaurs one instant and proposing marriage to Etta the next. Psycho even gets to be our Amazon heroine for a page or two, allowing Harry Peter to draw a flat-out evil Wonder Woman, complete with heart-stoppingly devilish eyebrows (3A). At least for a little bit, then, Psycho gets to use women's power to be the paragon of womanhood, and one of the comic's most dastardly villains manages, for a moment, to fulfill what had to be one of its creators' fondest dreams. Marston certainly finds Psycho despicable, but he also finds him exciting.

You can see this, I think, in the bottom left panel of page 11A of *Wonder Woman #5* (see figure 25). Steve is half sitting, half reclining in a wooden chair, his legs straight out in front of him, right arm hanging

FIGURE 25.
Wonder Woman
#5 (1943)

down so his knuckles touch the floor. Off to the side stands Dr. Psycho, enormous head thrust forward, eyebrows eyebrowing, outsized hands extended and flexing, diminutive legs receding under him, as if determined to tip him over onto his titanic chin. The two are drawn with such different proportions that they seem like they could be different species.

And yet despite (because of?) the oddity of the juxtaposition, the scene has an undercurrent of odd, expressionist eroticism. Steve's face is screwed up in a tight expression that could be pain or ecstasy, his body limply stiff, legs spread, while Psycho—the rapist—leans forward, his nose and chin pointed eagerly between Steve's legs. Steve's foot almost brushes Psycho's knee, but there is no contact. The only touch is the white mass on Steve's chest, which seems visually divorced from everything around it. You could almost think it was a scribble defacing the panel rather than part of the scene.

But it's not a scribble pulsing and quivering there in Peter's lovely lines. It's ectoplasm—which, as we know, is pulled out of women. If this is a sexualized encounter, any intimacy between the two men is routed not through a woman (à la James Bond and Goldfinger's struggle for the loyalty of Pussy Galore)[16] but rather through femininity. Male lust is transformed into female sensuality as that scribble rubs over and against itself, and the result is an uncanny vision of men having lesbian sex. They don't do it very gracefully, perhaps, but who would have thought that they could manage it at all?

THE VENUS PENIS

In *Goldfinger*, the point of lesbophilia is to watch as "the very phallic Pussy succumbs to the even more phallic James Bond"—to celebrate as the hero expands into another and so becomes even more like himself (Ladenson, "Lovely" 422). Marston and Peter, on the other hand, don't want to erase gender distinctions. On the contrary, as that giddily heterogeneous fantasia of doll man, big-head guy, and scribbly blob shows, they are fascinated and thrilled by difference. The result is a kind of male lesbianism analogous to that which Naomi Schor attributes to Barthes. Here there is "the abolition of male penetration, with its valorization of depth, in favor of an *adhesive* mode of sexual relations, where the transvested male becomes . . . a textile membrane stretched over the female body: male lesbianism as a second skin" (392). Thus Dr. Psycho's ectoplasmic effusions. On the one hand, they flow over him like a second skin, turning him into Wonder Woman. On the other hand, they materialize and glom onto Steve in an "*adhesive* mode of sexual relations"—lesbianism as a slippery gluten.

This description is reminiscent of Susie Bright's notably (and unusually) tolerant explanation of male fascination with lesbianism:

> Most men who like this kind of [lesbian] erotica don't want to *save* the lesbians, they want to *be* the lesbians. Lesbian lovemaking is soft and slippery and it never, ever ends. There's no hard-on to worry about, and one orgasm leads to the next, sometimes fast and furious, sometimes gentle as a breath. It combines feminine intimacy with multiple climaxes, and in those notorious group sex scenes, there are more nice pairs of tits than you can count. Who doesn't want to be a lesbian if that's what you get to do all day? (98, italics in the original)

Lesbophilia in Bright's view is a soft and slippery feminine dream. Its delirious pleasure comes not from finding a new, impenetrable place to stick the phallus but rather from the way in which the phallus is whisked away as gently as a breath, never to bother anyone again. It's a polymorphous prelapsarian vision, in which everyone and everything is the mother and her plentiful bosom, pleasurably sucking and loving through all eternity.

For both Bright and Schor, male investment in lesbianism is also, or can also be, an investment in transvestism—in appearing as, or taking on the identity of, a woman. Schor, reading Gustave Flaubert, argues that the author "projects himself as a woman in order to make love to himself as a woman," so that his lesbophilia is ultimately "not so much narcissistic as it is masturbatory" (397). Similarly, Bright says that as a lesbian sex-advice columnist, she's received "many letters about lesbian sex from men, and photographs" (97). Many of those photographs, she says, are of the men themselves, dressed in women's clothes.

If Marston were alive today, there is little doubt in my mind that he would love Susie Bright and all she stands for.[17] I suspect he might even send her pictures of himself in drag. And I'd be willing to bet money that he'd send her an autographed copy of his novel *Venus with Us*, which would amount to pretty much the same thing. As I mentioned before, *Venus with Us*, Marston's soft-core "historical" Roman novel, is filled to its slippery surface with lesbian eroticism.[18] It's also (and not coincidentally) a sustained exploration of Marston's longing to be a girl—or, at least, girly. The novel's main character, Julius Caesar, is as big a Mary Sue as I think I've ever encountered in literature.[19] He is a miraculously skilled fighter, able to slaughter as many swordsman as Marston can fit in the prose on a single page. He is shockingly handsome and sleeps with women of every race, creed, color, and nation—quite often two at a time, naturally. He's cultured, refined, and worldly wise but always fighting for right. Indeed, he might as well be James Bond—if James Bond were undisputed emperor of the entire civilized world.

Another major difference between James Bond and Marston's Caesar is that Caesar wears makeup. The first time we see him, he is hidden in one of his mistresses' apartments, his "slender white fingers . . . engaged in spreading rouge delicately over one cheek" (7). Marston goes on to inform us that Caesar's "voice was high, almost like a girl's." Caesar uses this voice to tell his mistress's slave girl that he can't find the right color: "Your mistress is a blonde—at least she has been lately—and she has nothing but this damnable orange rouge stick. Now you are a brunette, and can sympathize with my troubles. How am I ever going to get the right coloring here in the highlight, just over my cheekbone?" (7). The campiness is irresistible—and, indeed, the slave girl, Alda, falls in love with him directly, pausing only to show him how to fix his blush.

Caesar's effeminacy is not an incidental accouterment; it's central to his character and, for Marston, central to his greatness. Marston's Caesar (or Gaius, as his lovers call him) has dedicated his life to the goddess Venus—which for Marston means that he has dedicated his life to love and women. The plot of the novel (such as it is) is mostly concerned with demonstrating that every one of Caesar's successes and triumphs was motivated by the women in his life. He destroys the pirate fleets besetting Rome not in order to help his nation but in order to free Alda, captured by the pirates. He makes Octavius rather than Brutus his heir, at the suggestion of his political adviser and lover, the magnificent British barbarian princess Ursula. Gaius's death results when he presents himself at the Roman Senate against Ursula's express advice.

Gaius, then, is the Overman as chivalric transvestite. This formulation is not quite the feminist battle cry that Marston seems to think it is. The trope of women-propping-up-the-great-men is of long patriarchal pedigree, both in fiction and in life. In a study of Sappho's legacy, for example, Joan DeJean writes that many male writers would use a "fiction of the female as an initiatory coming-of-age rite" and "transvest themselves in order to use the appeal of female stereotypes for self-promotion" (47). Along the same lines, Naomi Schor notes that many French male authors in the nineteenth century identified with lesbians as a way of proving their antibourgeois bona fides (393). And as Susie Bright wryly says, "Most men are disgusted with other men. . . . Every time I get a letter from a man who lauds lesbian superiority, I can guess how competitive he is with his fellow men" (98). Identifying with women doesn't have to be about women per se; it can just be another move in the same patriarchal power play.

Thus, while Marston may *say* that Caesar doesn't really care about power, he is nonetheless the person who gets to exercise it, while the women mostly roll around together and/or help him with his makeup. Occasionally, Ursula or Cleopatra will go off to rule this or that bit of the domain, but irresistible Gaius always retains their ultimate loyalty, so that their glory only makes his more splendid. Women are the source and sign of power rather than autonomous individuals able to wield power themselves—all of which sounds depressingly familiar. For Marston in the novel, femininity itself seems to function as the phallus—Venus as the penis. Again, Dr. Psycho is the exemplar; in *Wonder Woman #5*, he uses the feminine power of ectoplasm to turn himself into the founding father George Washington. Psycho-as-Washington then dedicates himself to calumniating women war workers and the female sex in general (6A–7A). Psycho expropriates women's essence on behalf of patriarchy.

We have, then, gone in a circle. On the one hand, men erase women in order to aggrandize and reify male identity. And, on the other hand, men identify with women . . . in order to aggrandize and reify male identity. Male androcentrism and male gynocentrism seem to end in the same place. Whether it's Bond filling Pussy with the phallus or Caesar wielding Venus like a penis, it's still Dr. Psycho using women for his own ends. Male lesbophilia always seems to end in rape.

WHO'S IN WHOM?

Marston, of course, did not believe that lesbophilia must end in rape. On the contrary, as we've seen, he appeared to believe that lesbian sexuality benefited all people—adults, children, mothers, fathers, women, men, and everyone else. Perhaps he was mistaken. But before we dismiss him, I'd like to take a look at one of the worst, most morally reprehensible arguments ever made against male lesbophilia: Janice Raymond's "Sappho by Surgery," a chapter of her influential 1979 book *The Transsexual Empire.*

Raymond's monograph is a viciously prejudiced attack on transsexual women. Trans activists and researchers Susan Stryker and Stephen Whittle have compared it to the *Protocols of the Elders of Zion*, which seems like an accurate assessment (131). The book, and particularly the chapter in question, is a hate-filled, ignorant atrocity—which is precisely why it is worth looking at its antipathy to lesbophilia closely. If Raymond is against lesbophilia, it can't be all bad.

The chapter "Sappho by Surgery" focuses on what Raymond awkwardly and insultingly refers to as "the transsexually constructed lesbian feminist." By this she means transsexual women who are both lesbians and feminists. However, for Raymond, these women are not women but men masquerading as lesbians. Thus, the chapter is essentially presented as an attack on male lesbophilia—which is why it concludes by arguing that lesbian feminist trans women are "in the same tradition as the man-made, made-up 'lesbians' of the *Playboy* centerfolds" (118). Raymond's argument is that lesbian transsexual women are all treacherous deceivers who take on the female form in order to infiltrate, desecrate, and appropriate female spaces and female bodies. "All transsexuals rape women's bodies by reducing the real female form to an artifact, appropriating this body for themselves," Raymond insists (104). She adds, "The transsexually constructed lesbian-feminist feeds off woman's true energy source, i.e., her woman-identified self" (108). She goes on to suggest that transsexual women are drawn to lesbianism because they know that that is "where strong female energy exists" (110). Thus, lesbophiliac men (of which lesbian transsexual women are for Raymond a subset) are twisted masculine vampire rapists, hungry to feed on gynoenergy. Shades of Dr. Psycho.

Given all this talk about female energy, and given the revulsion Raymond expresses toward people she calls "men," you would think that she would extol the virtues of femininity. In fact, though, the opposite is the case. In much of her book, Raymond rails against transsexual women for *promoting* femininity. Transsexual women, she insists, "conform more to the feminine role than even the most feminine of natural-born women" (79). In fact, she argues that femininity is a male invention and that women who conform to femininity are "in this sense . . . transsexuals, fashioned according to man's image" (106). To be feminine is for Raymond to be a Stepford Wife: manmade, artificial, and enslaved.

The association of transsexual women with femininity is not unique to Raymond. Julia Serano argues that it is endemic. Serano is herself a trans woman, and she says that most of the prejudice she encounters as a lesbian woman and as a trans woman is not transphobia or homophobia so much as it is misogyny:

When a trans person is ridiculed or dismissed not merely for failing to live up to gender norms, but for their expressions of femaleness or femininity, they become the victims of a specific form of discrimination: *trans-misogyny*. When the majority of jokes made at the expense of trans people center on "men wearing dresses" or "men who want their penises cut off," that is not transphobia—it is trans-misogyny. (*Whipping* 14–15)

Thus, for Serano, Raymond's animosity toward trans women is *not* based on a hatred of men, however much she claims that men are the enemy. Instead, Serano says, Raymond's transphobia is at bottom misogyny—a hatred and mistrust of femininity. This is why, Serano says, Raymond barely mentions transsexual men (Serano 48–49). Seeking to be masculine is understandable and unremarkable. But Serano argues, "in a male-centered gender hierarchy, where it is assumed that men are better than woman and that masculinity is superior to femininity, there is no greater perceived threat than the existence of trans women, who despite being born male and inheriting male privilege 'choose' to be female instead" (15).

Obviously, transgender bisexual women such as Serano face much more discrimination than do cisgender straight men such as Marston. And yet I think that the points Serano makes here in refuting Raymond's attack on trans women also function to partially refute Raymond's simultaneous attack on lesbophiliac men. Lesbophiliac men do not choose to be women, but some of them at least choose to identify with women. Is that identification entirely deceptive—is it just a means to steal female energy? Or is valuing femininity, perhaps even to steal it, a challenge to a society "where it is assumed," as Serano says, "that men are better than woman and that masculinity is superior to femininity"?

Another way to phrase this question, perhaps, is "what happens when penises go into lesbian spaces?" Raymond's answer to this is simple: when a penis (or even someone who used to have a penis) goes into a lesbian space, the result is rape. "One of the definitions of *male*," she says, "as related in Webster's, is 'designed for fitting into a corresponding hollow part.'" This, of course, means heterosexual sex, but for Raymond, it also means "that men have been very adept at penetrating all of women's 'hollow' spaces, at filling up the gaps, and of sliding into the interstices" (103). She adds that women moving away from patriarchy have many such gaps and that transsexual women will fill them all up if they are allowed. As an example of this sort of sneaky penetration, Raymond singles out Sandy Stone, a trans woman who worked as a recording engineer at Olivia Records, an all-women recording studio (101–102). Raymond's attack on Stone was a forerunner of womyn-born-womyn policies at places such as the Michigan Womyn's Music Festival, which still excludes trans women from its grounds (Serano 233–234).

Raymond sees herself as defending women from patriarchal penises. But in doing so, she falls back helplessly on the hoariest stereotypes. Men for Raymond are the thrusting aggressors, women are the hollow spaces; men are the penetrators, women are the gaps. This is the same rhetoric by which, as Serano argues, patriarchal culture equates femininity with "helplessness, fragility, and passivity" (328). Raymond might as well be writing a pulp novel—her virginal damsels are always in distress.

Serano argues, in contrast, that femininity does not necessarily have to be weak, that passive femininity is constructed, not natural. To see the constructed nature of feminine weakness, she suggests to her readers,

> Imagine what would happen if instead of centering our beliefs about heterosexual sex around the idea that the man "penetrates" the woman, we were to say that the woman's vagina "consumes" the man's penis. This would create a very different set of connotations, as the woman would become the active initiator and the man would be the passive and receptive party. One can easily see how this could lead to men and masculinity being seen as dependent on, and existing for the benefit of, femaleness and femininity. (329)

As it happens, there is a sexologist who saw intercourse in just this way. His name was William Marston:

> The [woman's] captivation stimulus actually evokes changes in the male's body designed to enable the woman's body to capture it physically. . . . [During sex] the woman's body by means

of appropriate movements and vaginal contractions, continues to captivate the male body, which has altered its form precisely for that purpose. (*Emotions* 333)

For Marston, it is not the man who penetrates the woman but the woman who captures the man. And as Serano suggests, this reversal makes the woman the "active initiator" and the man the "receptive party"—so much so that the erection is seen as an adjunct of *female* sexuality (*Emotions* 332–333). Penises don't defile Marston's vaginas; on the contrary, Marston's vaginas swallow up penises.

This is the case in the *Wonder Woman* comics as well. Wonder Woman's magic lasso is the most obvious example. By means of captivation stimulus, it immobilizes and compels responses from male bodies—and not incidentally from female ones as well. It is a vagina as surely as James Bond's gun is a penis. Nor is the lasso the only instance in Marston of the captivating, capturing vagina as metaphor. For instance, take the scene in figure 26. In this image from *Wonder Woman #5*, Psycho is placed dead center in the middle of a wide panel, his giant face with its caricatured features almost seeming to leap out of the page—indeed, his foot actually crosses over the panel border (16A). From the reader's perspective, Psycho's giant head is growing even larger—and that perspectival head growth is being induced by a phalanx of encircling women. Spread out in the background, Etta and three other Holliday girls rush to the attack. "Paddles up, sisters, give him the works!" one of the girls shouts. Another pursuer, her legs pressed tight together, has her arm bent so that the paddle rubs her billowing skirt—surely in this case a clitoral symbol rather than a phallic one. All four of the girls' mouths are open; Etta's lips, in particular, gape threateningly as she encourages the pursuit. "Watch him kids—give him the Lamda Beta treatment!" Thus, the ritual of Sapphic domination opens to consume the male, with lubrication supplied by the globules of ectoplasm drifting nearby. Little wonder that in the next panel Psycho pulls his pistol or that it is instantly shot from his hands. Diegetically, it's Steve who renders Psycho harmless and Steve who saves the day, but visually, it's Etta who stands in the center of the panel, hands on her hips, legs spread defiantly, her crotch just about level with Psycho's bulging eye, as he looks in horror at his useless gun tilting flaccidly down.

FIGURE 26. *Wonder Woman #5* (1943)

Gloria Steinem, in her introduction to the 1972 *Ms.* collection of *Wonder Woman* strips, expresses concern that in touting female superiority, Marston is simply encouraging women to switch with men in the hierarchy, rather than eliminating hierarchy altogether. It's undoubtedly true that Marston sees women as superior. But as the tension between visually marginal, narratively central Steve and narratively marginal, visually central Etta demonstrates, women-on-top is not, and cannot be, simply a mirror image of men-on-top. Men in *Wonder Woman* are never as disempowered and objectified as women in James Bond or gangsta rap or Gauguin—a couple thousand years of tropes don't just vanish because you have a vision of active vaginas. Thus, when Marston flips the binary from masculine/feminine to feminine/masculine, the result is not simply hierarchy inverted. Rather, it's heterosexuality inverted—which is another way of saying it's queer.

You can see this even more clearly in instances when Marston and Peter work directly with longstanding heterosexual images and narrative conventions. For example, *Sensation Comics #41* includes a sequence that strongly evokes the plot and illustration tradition of Sleeping Beauty. Look, for example, at Peter's drawing of the unconscious "princess" Lyra in figure 27 (9). If you compare this to traditional drawings of the legend, such as the 1906 illustration of the Sleeping Beauty tale by Herbert Cole, you can see definitive differences. In both illustrations, the beauty lies twined in vines, with sensual drapery (whether clothes or covers) emphasizing her languid lack of resistance. In Cole's image, however, the image of the bound and waiting woman is overtopped by the active man—arm thrust forward, crotch cocked—who will unwrap her and take her away from all this. Marston and Peter's narrative functions rather differently. For them, it is not a man but the vines themselves that wake the sleeper. She is then dragged out of the room, and Peter shows her wrapped tightly by the curving tendrils, her eyes wide in horror as she is lowered into the giant, purple-mottled flower/vulva/mouth of the octopus plant. In the next panel, we see a cutaway to show her inside the plant, curlicues of white gas drifting around her like flowers, her blond hair streaming down to the side. The blue background makes it look like she is floating in the air or in the water, while the vines around the edges of the image suggest the stylized, overripe floral borders of Beardsley. Instead of Sleeping Beauty and her bower as embodied heterosexual hymen to be penetrated, Marston and Peter have given us Sleeping Beauty as yonic lesbian fever dream. The princess's sexual awakening involves not marriage but a return to the hungrily yearning maternal womb.

However, the original Sleeping Beauty story, with its penetrated-and-saved damsel in distress, isn't entirely overwritten. In the Marston/Peter narrative, the octopus plants are (barely) controlled by a standard male mad-scientist type—the aptly named "Creeper" Johnson. On the previous page, we actually see Johnson placing the plant below Lyra's window (8). We then watch the invasion of the bedroom as the vines creep upward into her room. The consequent violation

FIGURE 27. *Sensation Comics* #41 (1945)

could definitely be seen, therefore, as a male penetration and rape—if the means of accomplishing it weren't so decidedly feminine. Similarly, you might see the octopus plants as a horror-film *vagina dentata*, an expression of the uncontrollable evil of femininity—except that the plants are actually controlled by a male villain. To further complicate matters, Creeper initially wanted to capture not Lyra but her father in his giant octopus lips. And then at the comic's conclusion, Wonder Woman wraps both Creeper and Lyra's father in her magic lasso and commands them to patch up their relationship. It's a sort of fairy-tale ending with two grooms and a compelling vagina as officiant (13). When Marston and Peter run Sleeping Beauty through a vision of consuming femininity, the end product is not a disempowered prince waiting for his princess to suck him bodily from his bower but a flamboyantly gendered mess.

AMAZON WOMYN'S SPACES

Just as Marston's take on Sleeping Beauty is not a simple reversal of the myth, so his take on female spaces does not simply replace the idea of an impermeable female community with the idea of an impermeable male one. Rather, Marston shares with Janice Raymond a fascination with pure, impenetrable female communities. The Amazon's Paradise Island—where no man may set foot—is as militantly man-free as the Michigan Womyn's Festival. This enforced purity prompted Charles Reece to compare the ideology of *Wonder Woman* to fascism. Reece argues that the Amazons express a Nazi-like "fear of contamination" couched in terms of "ideological purity and nationalism." In this, Reece echoes critics of Raymond who, as I mentioned earlier, have on occasion compared her work to virulent anti-Semitic propaganda.

What Reece misses, I think, is the extent to which Marston's rhetoric of purity (which is consonant with Raymond's) is complicated by his vision of an active, powerful, and not at all vulnerable femininity. Thus, in *All-Star Comics #8*, the first Wonder Woman comic, Steve Trevor crash lands on Paradise Island, violating the taboo against men. So do the Amazons toss him in the gas chamber? Of course not! They rush him to the hospital and then send Wonder Woman off with him to aid in the fight against the Nazis. That hardly seems like ideological purity. And while there is a nationalism expressed there, it's not a specifically *Amazonian* nationalism but just good, old-fashioned, very-male-tolerant U.S. patriotism. For Marston, the Amazons aren't, like Raymond's women, in constant danger of being violated, which means that they can make reasonable exceptions to their rules if they need to. Indeed, the very first thing we see them doing is making an exception to their rule—almost as if the rule is there just to be done away with.

An even more suggestive test of the Amazon's no-men-allowed rule occurs in *Wonder Woman* #23. In the third story in the comic (set during Wonder Woman's childhood), evil space aliens wearing cat masks and flaming cloaks invade Paradise Island while riding giant kangaroos.[20] Hippolyte is, as you'd imagine, startled and concerned by this turn of events—though not quite for the reasons you'd think. The flaming cloaks and the giant kangaroos don't bother her, but, "How terrible," she thinks: "*Men* on Paradise Island! This breaks Aphrodite's law!" (4C). Things go from bad to worse as the invaders fire blue rays that wrap up and weaken all the Amazons, and soon Paradise Island is filled full to the brim with beautiful women wrapped head to toe in bondage. Business as usual, in other words.

That business as usual is, it turns out, even more usual than it looks at first. After the expected round of everybody being tied up and everybody breaking free, child Wonder Woman pulls the cat mask off an alien and discovers that "he" is a she (12C). As Diana declares, "Great Minerva—these sky riders are masked women! Aphrodite's law hasn't been broken—we can beat them!" Immediately thereafter, the Amazons realize that it's the invaders' clothes and cloaks that give them power, and so they strip all the invading women to their underwear. Defeated, the aliens ask to become Amazons, and Hippolyte agrees— after a suitable period of imprisonment and retraining, of course.

We are supposed to believe that the alien invaders were *always* women, from the moment they first appeared. But we're talking here about illustrations; a drawing may have the appearance of a gender, but it isn't actually gendered—whatever an "actual gender" might mean. To the extent that the alien invaders had a sex when they came riding in on their kangaroos, that sex was male. If you look back at the aliens in the beginning of the comic, they look like men, without breasts and with facial hair (cat whiskers). Certainly, they look nothing

FIGURE 28. *Wonder Woman #11* (1944)

like the shapely, seminaked, amply bosomed women into whom they are supposed to have transformed in the final panels (see figure 28). Indeed, the only way we know that these female images are identical with the earlier male images is that Marston and Peter tell us so. The narrative says that the women were always men, but functionally the comic simply asserts that those men and these women are the same. As so often with camp—and, indeed, with the closet—the secret is not what's under the mask but the mask itself. Men or women, they are what you see, and what you see is queer.

Marston's vision of active female sexuality has, then, important implications for his vision of lesbian sexuality. As we've seen, Marston rejects the Bond–Pussy Galore model of relations between men and lesbians, in which the first must penetrate and convert the second. But Marston also rejects what Ladenson sees as a Proustian model, in which a self-sufficient lesbianism is viewed as transcendentally seamless and "impenetrable" (*Proust's Lesbianism* 134). The heterosexual Fleming sees lesbianism as an exclusionary resistance to be overcome. The homosexual Proust sees lesbianism as an exclusionary impassable barrier. The polyamorous Marston, however, does not see female-female relationships as exclusionary at all. Rather, for Marston, lesbianism and female communities can take men in without violation or contradiction, because when it comes to sexuality, it is women who are determinative, not men. In this sense, Amazon society in *Wonder Woman #23* was not kept pure and did not need to be kept pure. The Amazons simply took men in and by so doing made them women. In Raymond's view, a man who penetrates a woman's space conquers it— he makes it male. But for Marston, a woman's space that holds a man conquers him and turns him female. Paradise Island thus has more than enough space for trans women. And it certainly has space too, if anyone doubted it, for lesbophiliac men. Who is Wonder Woman, after all, if not Marston in disguise?

WOMAN VERSUS NOTHING

For Marston, essentialism and queerness are not in conflict. Instead, queerness is anchored in, and made possible by, an essentialist vision of femininity. Femininity for Marston doesn't just appear to be strong and loving; it is strong and loving. Women for him capture men not just as a metaphor but as a scientific fact. And it is from those beliefs that you get Sleeping Beauty rescued/captured by a semisentient vagina, or men turning into women on Paradise Island. Femininity makes the world safe for polyamory. You can't have the second without the first.

Perhaps it goes without saying, but this is not necessarily the standard view within either feminism or queer studies, where sex of all sorts is now acceptable, but "gender essentialism" is often considered a dirty word. As I mentioned earlier, Gloria Steinem in her intro to the *Ms.* collection was uncomfortable with Marston's views on female superiority, arguing that, though no tests could tell for sure, the "consensus seems to be that society, not biology, assigns some human traits to males and others to females." She added that once society had ceased to assign these traits, everyone would be able "to develop the free range of human qualities." Marston's view of women as superior, she said, leaves us with "yet another social order based on birth."

Steinem's critique of Marston anticipates in very broad outline Judith Butler's extremely influential arguments in 1990's *Gender Trouble.* Butler's thesis has been popularly summarized as "gender is performance." The phrase does not actually appear in her book but works as a decent thumbnail description of her view. Like Steinem, Butler argues that gender is not biological or original; it is culturally and socially learned. As a result, all gender is false—a performance. For Butler, then, the truest, most liberating genders are those genders that are most self-consciously performative. She singles out particularly drag, which she says plays up the dissonance between gendered performance and anatomy. Such parodies do not mock an original, Butler argues; rather, they mock the notion *that there can be* an original. "The original identity after which gender fashions itself is an imitation without an origin," she argues. Instead of seeing gender as a cause of gendered actions and desires, she says that drag shows gender as a "personal/cultural history of received meanings," which are interpreted through imitative performances. And those imitative performances are not based on an original but are themselves based in turn on other imitative performances. There is then a "parodic proliferation"—an endless stream of copies and copies of copies infinitely regressing. There is no true gender to imitate, and so everyone is free to imitate whatever they wish—to build their own fake gender from the parts that suit them, rather than being forced to conform to someone else's drag (188).

From Butler's perspective, then, drag should undermine gender essentialism, not be its handmaiden. And yet, as we've already seen, Marston, a gender essentialist if ever there was one, seems to love drag with all his campy heart. We already mentioned the cross-dressing cat-headed aliens in *Wonder Woman #23* and Dr. Psycho masquerading as Wonder Woman in *Wonder Woman #5*. But those drag kings and queens are hardly alone. Indeed, cross-dressing is a staple throughout Marston's tenure, from *Sensation Comics #2* in 1942, one of Marston's first issues, to *Wonder Woman #28* in 1948, probably his last.[21]

Almost all these transvestites are antagonists, though; Marston rarely has Wonder Woman or Steve or even Etta masquerade as the opposite gender. This, then, might be a way to reconcile the essentialism with the drag. Maybe, after all, the deviance is part and parcel of the villainy, and Marston's cross-dressing baddies are the distant forebears of such imagined transvestite monsters as Norman Bates from *Psycho* and Buffalo Bill from *Silence of the Lambs*.

There are some grounds for this comparison in Marston's attitude toward gay men in *Emotions of Normal People*—an attitude grounded precisely in his gender essentialism. Marston believes women are more loving and more giving than men are; he therefore believes, as I've mentioned, that love between two women is perfect. The natural corollary would be that love between two men would be uniquely *imperfect*, and that does appear to be Marston's view of the matter. Though he says he has only observed "one or two" such relationships among boys in school, he draws fairly sweeping conclusions. Boys, he argues, are physiologically unable to induce love responses in each other. Therefore, male homosexual relationships are based on satisfying "appetitive" desires, rather than on love, and are essentially egotistical and, between older and younger boys, exploitive (252–253). Thus, the all-male (though not explicitly homosexual) world of Neptune in *Wonder Woman #15* is described as entirely built on power and dominance. As the Neptunian leader declares, "We live in a state of armed truce—the strongest masters rule the weaker ones and take their possessions. A *very* strong master may capture others and make them into mechanos" (2B). Mechanos are, as the name suggests, human drones created by chemical processes.

Marston's gender essentialism and misandry, then, result in his endorsement of some unpleasant and familiar stereotypes of gay men, who, in his view, are either promiscuous, opportunistic exploiters or weak, victimized exploited. If Marston's gender essentialism and misandry could lead him to vilify gay men, it seems as if it could also lead him to see female cross-dressers as inherently villainous in their embrace of masculinity.

Despite Marston's stated dislike of male homosexuality, there is not much in the way of homophobia directed against gay men in the comics. The Neptunians might perhaps be seen as an exception, though even here, Marston's attitude doesn't seem especially condemnatory. When we first meet the slave-mechanos, for instance, they are dressed in loin cloths, slave bracelets, and little else. One quickly leans down so that his master can step on his neck. We are certainly supposed to see the unloving submission here as problematic, but it's problematic because of the lack of love, not because of the submission or the eroticism. On the contrary, and as in Marston's female-female dominance games, the ritual here seems as if it's supposed to be titillating. Beefcake, like cheesecake, is presented for the enjoyment of children of all genders—and so, inevitably, Wonder Woman gets to step on the slave's neck as well ("I don't want to seem unfriendly," she muses; 3B).

Similarly, while it would make logical sense for Marston to dislike drag kings, there's little textual evidence to suggest that he does. In films such as *Psycho* and *Silence of the Lambs*, the narrative takes some pains to link the perversion with the crime. Norman Bates has mommy issues, so dresses up as mommy. Buffalo Bill wants to transform himself, so butchers women and takes their skin. Marston never makes any such connection. Dr. Poison and the Blue Snowman (to name two cross-dressers) wear male clothes and are villains, but the villainy is never explained in terms of the cross-dressing.[22] Indeed, there is never any narrative explanation given for the cross-dressing at all. It's just something, apparently, that Dr. Poison, the Blue Snowman, and cat-headed aliens enjoy doing. Additionally, there is at least one occasion when the good guys cross-dress. This, again, occurs in *Wonder Woman* #15. To infiltrate the men-only planet of Neptune, Wonder

Woman and the Holiday girls dress up as Tigeapes (part tiger, part ape, naturally; 5C). It's not clear whether the Tigeapes are supposed to be male or female, but in any case, the women are concealing their femininity. In addition, the Tigeape costumes are originally used as part of a sorority ritual, which means for Marston that they are eroticized (4C). Thus, in this sequence, drag kings for Marston are not evil or wrong. They're sexy.

So what exactly is Marston's view of drag, and how is it inflected by, or reconciled with, his gender essentialism? If femininity and masculinity are real, and masculinity is worse, why is it apparently so enjoyable to show women expressing masculinity? To answer that question, we'll look at *Wonder Woman #11* from winter 1944, the story with the most complicated and most thematically central use of drag.

The villain in *Wonder Woman #11* is Hypnota, a stage magician with a turban, a diabolical accent, and even more diabolical facial hair. Hypnota controls others with blue rays of dominance that shoot from his eyes. Early in the story, Marston and Peter show the reader Hypnota's stage act. This involves him tying up his assistant, the aptly named Serva, and placing her in a cabinet. He then hypnotizes the audience, and they see him transform into Serva. He assures them that Serva is still inside the cabinet. He then transforms back into himself and opens the box to reveal Serva still inside. The show is less a magic show than a drag performance, in which the audience sees a man turn into a woman and then back into a man.

Peter's drawings of the magic/drag show seem, at least on the surface, to buttress Butler's assertions about drag and artificiality. Granted, Peter's illustrations always look stiffly fake, but when he draws a stage, it further emphasizes the degree to which reading his comics is like traveling through a pasteboard world. The first panel of the sequence, showing Serva announcing the act (4A; see figure 29), is an agglomeration of stage-magician clichés arranged almost at random. Off to the right side, a bunny (real? wax?) stands with ears and tail erect at the foot of a table with a blue, glowing crystal ball. The cabinet, with rose designs that Peter draws exactly the way he draws real roses, stands in the center, flanked by what looks like two veiled manikins—Peter colors them gray, like statues, though later we learn that they are in fact flesh-and-blood women. On the left, we see two

FIGURE 29. *Wonder
Woman #23* (1947)

birds flying—it's impossible to determine whether they're supposed to
be real or merely a design on the wall. Out front stands Serva, her red
skirt frilling out over legs that seem too big for her body, her right arm
gesturing back at a weird angle, her head too small, looking for all the
world like a mismatched doll.

The artificiality extends to the pacing of the sequence, which is as
awkward and jumbled as that initial panel. The perspective moves in
and out of the scene with stochastic irregularity while Peter throws
in liberal puffs of smoke here and there, either for the sake of excitement or simply so he doesn't have to draw backgrounds. The cabinet
in which Serva is locked is shown from different angles and with sufficiently wavery draftsmanship that it's not instantly clear that it's the
same cabinet from panel to panel or whether in any given panel it is
supposed to be opened or closed. The result is meant to be mysterious
and awe inspiring (Diana in the audience declares at the end that Hypnota is "the most dangerous man alive!"; 6A). But it ends up just being
confusing. Wait, did he show us the girl in the cabinet? She's still in the
cabinet though. But she wasn't before? Um . . . I guess I'm impressed?

I doubt the clumsiness is exactly intentional, but it does work thematically. The magic show, with a man maybe obscurely changing into
a woman and then maybe confusingly back into a man, functions as the

stumbling gender-swapping blueprint for the entire comic. Not only is Hypnota actually a woman, but he (which is apparently his preferred pronoun) and Serva are twins. Hypnota hypnotizes Serva to help him in his evil plots and, at times, to take his place in them. The two trade identities back and forth so frequently that even on a second or third reading it is not always clear who is who. For instance, the opening scene of the comic shows a woman in a pink dress and a green cloak backing out of Steve's office as he declares, "I have obeyed!" Wonder Woman, incensed to hear that Steve is obeying anyone but her, pursues "that hussy!" but the girl manages to escape (1A). So is that girl Serva, or is it Hypnota? Even on rereading, there's no way to know.

Similarly, the magic act that doesn't make sense on the first time through is supposed to be clearer once you know that Hypnota is a woman. But is it? Are we supposed to think he didn't *really* hypnotize anyone and just changed clothes? But he can actually hypnotize people, so why would he need to pretend? Or again, in one scene in which Hypnota is captured, it turns out that it's not Hypnota at all but Serva hypnotized to pretend to be Hypnota (11A). So in retrospect, are we supposed to believe that it was really Hypnota pretending to be Serva pretending to be Hypnota? Or was it just Serva pretending to be Hypnota? Or what?

For Butler, the uncertainty here would have to be a feature rather than a bug. Drag in this comic is, in line with Butler, an imitation without an origin. We know that someone is in a costume, but what's under the costume is just another costume or more often a question mark. The comics form itself seems especially well suited to make this point, since each "character" is made up of a sequence of repeated images, copies referring to a nonexistent prototype. Thus, in the magic show, we see Hypnota in one panel in a puff of smoke, then Serva in the next panel in a puff of smoke. Their identity, or for that matter their lack of identity, is conventional and narrative—their gender is simply a surface inscription. There is no real authentic "there" there, not even in the cabinet or closet, which may appear to be closed or open but which is in fact simply a surface, containing no truth or even any falsehood. In Butler's view, drag is a giddy revelation of emptiness, a nihilistic triumphalism. The point of the magic show is not so much the transformation from man to woman to man as the erasure of man and woman in the movement from panel to panel. The pictures of drag are only there to define the ecstatic blank white of the gutters between the panels.

Marston undoubtedly thought the drag was fun too—but not, I think, because of the deconstructive joys of limning an absence. Rather, for Marston, secret identities, masquerade, and endless gendered reversals are all exciting not because they open on absence but rather because they open on femininity. Surely Marston, who more than half wanted to be Wonder Woman himself, wrote so many cross-dressing villains because he loved those panels in which a guy pulled aside his mask and showed that under all that dreary masculinity there was a woman just waiting to come out. For Marston (and for the reader on a second time through), the joy of the drag is that there is a woman changing into a woman changing into a woman. There is a woman in every puff of smoke, a woman in every cabinet, a woman in every woman, and a woman in every man. Even after the magic show is completed, the magic goes on—the very next page shows us Wonder Woman behind the curtains changing into her costume, yet another transformation the meaning of which is "woman!" (7A). Marston is like a child playing a game of peek-a-boo. Uncover the eyes—and there's mommy! Uncover the eyes—and there's mommy! Uncover the eyes—and there's mommy! Repeating the trick doesn't deconstruct or invalidate the trick, any more than loving your child three days in a row makes that love less real.

For Butler, this is the wrong way about. Gender (and presumably love) are not truths that are repeated; rather, the repetitions that form them create an ungrounded "truth." Or, as Butler says, "signification *is not a founding act, but rather a regulated process of repetition*" (198, italics in original). For Butler, the erasure of the origin should allow for a disintegration, or at least a problematization, of binaries such as natural/unnatural, homo/hetero, and man/woman, with their inevitable attendant exclusions and restrictions. Dissolve gender, and a woman can conquer man's world, while men will be welcome on Paradise Island.

Of course, for Marston, a woman does conquer man's world, and men are welcome on Paradise Island with some frequency. But putting that aside for the moment, the problem with Butler's formulation is that she doesn't so much erase binaries as replace them with a binary of her own. That binary is *foundation/repetition*, which is simply a new name for the very old binary *presence/absence*. In Butler's formulation, repetition becomes reality; foundation, or presence, becomes illusory and dangerous. Origin is erased—but only to return as origin as nothing. To secure freedom, diversity, and autonomy, presence itself is excluded, which inevitably results in the surreptitious saturation of everything and everyone with the presence of nonpresence. Nonidentity, instituted through an insistently nonpresent repetition of surfaces, becomes the inescapable, emptily mechanical identity of everyone, while the Cartesian "I think therefore I am" is replaced with the supposedly liberating but actually indistinguishable insistence that "I think therefore I am not." In order to avoid the imperialism of presence, Butler institutes an imperialism of nonpresence, in which women are free to be and do anything except identify as women, and selves are free to be and do anything as long as everything they are and do is nothing.

This is not to belittle the joys of nonpresence or the rush of nongender. Slipping free of categories and letting yourself slide along the endlessly replicating chain of identity and desire can be immensely satisfying. As Hypnota-dressed-as-Serva chuckles at the conclusion of *Wonder Woman #11*, "Ha! Ha! It was amusing to pose as Serva, hypnotize people and then escape by blaming it on myself!" (16C).

Hypnota's ironically self-conscious embrace of nonidentity is not, however, a particular boon for the marginalized. Hypnota's fluidity doesn't undermine oppressive power but simply allows it to bypass normal channels and circulate more freely. As the plot twists and turns and dives into plot holes here to emerge from plot holes there, Hypnota/Serva and his/her blue hypnotic ray of power seems to be both everywhere and nowhere. Gangsters attack the Saturnian ambassador and don't remember why they did so; hunky male human slaves shipped to Saturn in swimsuits refuse to be freed; and in one particularly preposterous panel, "a queer thing happens," as Etta Candy, dominated by Serva and her seductive blue ray, suddenly and startlingly forgets how to play ice hockey (8B). From geopolitics to domestic labor to leisure-time activities, every aspect of life is controlled not by a centralized hierarchy but by an ineffable technology of dominance and desire. An invisible hand, if you will.

Obviously, transvestites have not enslaved us all, much as Marston might like them to. If taking off Judith Butler's turban reveals Adam Smith, it's not because queer people have conquered but because non-presence is the ideology of our time. In postmodernity, everybody's closet is empty. That's certainly a relief, and even a salvation, to some people, gay and otherwise. For others, though, being nothing can feel less like freedom and more like death. As Julia Serano says in her essay "Performance Piece,"

> Instead of trying to fictionalize gender, let's talk about all of the moments in life when gender feels all too real. Because gender doesn't feel like drag when you're a young trans child begging your parents not to cut your hair or not to force you to wear that dress. And gender doesn't feel like a performance when, for the first time in your life, you finally feel safe and empowered enough to express yourself in ways that resonate with you, rather than remaining closeted for the benefit of others. And gender doesn't feel like a construct when you finally find that special person whose body, personality, identity and energy feels like a perfect fit with yours. Let's stop trying to deconstruct gender into non-existence and instead start celebrating it as inexplicable, varied, profound and intricate.
>
> So don't dare dismiss my gender as a construct, drag or a performance, because my gender is a work of non-fiction.

MY FAIR MIRROR

Andrei Tarkovsky's 1972 film *Solaris* is set on a space station orbiting the titular planet, where people's thoughts become real.[23] In the early scenes of the film, we see our hero, Kris Kelvin (Donatas Banionis), wandering around his father's house on Earth. In the final scenes, we again see him at his father's, though things are somewhat odd. The water in the pond does not move, and when he looks through the window, he sees his father drenched by an indoor deluge. Still, he embraces his father's knees, and the camera pulls back, back, back, revealing that he is not at home but on an island on Solaris. It's all just a set—a staged fantasy of contact and catharsis. The film is, in other words, a film, imagined by a brain that, if you squint at it right, seems to look something like Tarkovsky's and something like God's.

Artificiality in *Solaris* is not an imitation of an imitation that shows there is no original. Rather, it is an imitation of an imitation that shows the original is far realer than anything we've ever seen. In a similar way, the artificiality in Marston and Peter can be seen not as an ode to the artificiality of gender but rather as a demonstration of the artificiality of everything *but* gender. *Wonder Woman* is a mask, and underneath that mask is the real, which is femininity. The artifice of the art is a truth not because nothing is behind it but because something is. For Tarkovsky, that something is God. For Marston, on the other hand, that something is the feminine—which means the world (even female bodies) is the drag Aphrodite puts on.

So if there is a true essence of femininity, what is it? Although there is no single answer, one popular contender is childbirth. For example, Shulamith Firestone, a thoroughly dour materialist, argues that the mechanics of human reproduction and childrearing—the dangers of labor, breast-feeding, extended infancy—are at the root of all human culture. Thus, in her view, "The natural reproductive difference between the sexes" is responsible not only for sexism but for all economic exploitation and prejudice (8–9). In contrast, Julia Kristeva, a mercurial visionary, ties the desire for motherhood to a "nonsymbolic, nonpaternal causality," comparable to "Heraclitus' flux, Epicurus' atoms, the whirling dust of cabalic, Arab, and Indian mystics, and the tippled drawings of psychedelics" (238–239). For Firestone, having children is a lead chain; for Kristeva, it is an Orientalist ecstasy.[24] In both cases, though, pregnancy defines what it means to be a woman.

As far as I've been able to find, Marston and Peter include only one scene of childbirth in their run on *Wonder Woman*. It is in *Wonder Woman #1*, and it is certainly one of the most unusual takes on parturition in superhero comics, if not in pulp fiction more generally (5B).

I find the three panels in figure 30 heartbreaking, though the narrative is so compressed that you can miss the emotion if you are not paying attention.[25] This sequence occurs in the narrative after the Amazons, who have suffered much hardship, are finally led by Aphrodite to Paradise Island. There Athena teaches Hippolyte how to sculpt—and what Hippolyte chooses to create is the image of a little girl. She wants

FIGURE 30. *Wonder Woman #1* (1942)

a child, in other words, but she can't have one. And so she becomes obsessed with the image she has created. She prays to Aphrodite, and a miracle occurs; the baby comes to life. Peter draws the scene so that the moment that Diana is "born" seems almost ritualized: the mother and daughter both stiff, shown in the instant before they touch in a frozen tableau, rather than in the moment when they embrace.

The sequence reminds me a little bit of the end of Grant Morrison's *Animal Man*, where the hero's family is magically resurrected by Morrison himself, acting as deus ex machina. It also (and perhaps deliberately) evokes Shakespeare's *Winter's Tale*, in which the statue of Hermione inexplicably returns to life. The power in all three moments is in having the heart's desire granted and in the recognition that the heart's desire just doesn't actually get granted in this way. Love demands miracles, and a creator granting a miracle to a creation is sometimes an act of love. That's certainly part of what the Christian faith is about (a connection both Morrison and Shakespeare make). Marston's vision is more pagan and, not coincidentally, more female. In Morrison and Shakespeare, men pray for the resurrection of their wives/lovers, and their wish is granted. Here, though, a woman prays to have a child. And the granting of the wish emphasizes the miraculous nature both of this particular birth and of all births.

In *The Dialectic of Sex*, Shulamith Firestone demands *"the freeing of women from the tyranny of their reproductive biology by every means available,"* up to and including "artificial reproduction," to liberate them from the tyranny of childbirth (206, italics in original). Kristeva, in a directly opposed and yet oddly similar vein, lyrically celebrates pregnancy as inspiration: "The language of art, too, follows ... the other aspect of material jouissance. . . . At the intersection of sign and rhythm, of representation and light, of the symbolic and the semiotic, the artist speaks from a place where she is not, where she knows not. He delineates what, in her, is a body rejoicing" (242). Firestone rejects utterly the idea of pregnancy as creative or even marginally worthwhile; Kristeva imagines pregnancy as the semimystical origin of creativity itself. Marston and Peter deliver a fantasy that answers and expands on both. Hippolyte is not bound by the biology, or the history, of pregnancy, and yet (or as a result?) she is able to turn a lump of clay into "a body rejoicing." To satisfy Firestone, artifice is pregnancy; to satisfy Kristeva, pregnancy is artifice. And as a result of those syllogisms, creation ends up as feminine—which is to say, inspired by women, performed by women, and always, in its essence, metaphorically female. "Passion for a woman is the *sine qua non* of artistic creation," Marston writes in *Emotions of Normal People*, and he goes on to insist that, although more men than women have been artists historically, "the female passion response, when, and if devoted to artistic creation might be expected to prove itself unusually potent, and delicate in its form of expression" (355–357).

The connection between childbirth and art is longstanding: Marston himself in the sequence shown in figure 30 mentions Pygmalion. Often, such comparisons are designed to redound to the benefit of the artist, to cast a borrowed glamour on his (and it is usually his) work. As one example, consider Michael Fried's remarkable reading of Courbet's *Grain Sifters*:[26]

In the *Grain Sifters* ... the fall of sifted wheat onto the canvas ground cloth immediately in front of the kneeling sifter ... [can be] compared to a rain of pigment and hence to the actual making of the painting. Now I want to suggest that the fall of grain and pigment—pigment representing grain representing pigment—can also be seen as a downpour of menstrual blood—not red but warm-hued and sticky-seeming, flooding outward from the sifter's thighs—and thus as expressing an even more extreme fantasy of "feminine" painterly productivity (this despite the fact that menstruation is an equivocal sign of *biological* productivity). We might gloss that fantasy by saying that it imagines painting to be a wholly natural activity—to be unmediated by anything beyond the (female) body itself. (46–47)

In Fried's view, Courbet links painting with menstruation in order to make art into nature. Fried says that this comparison is made "despite the fact" that menstruation is biological. But surely the force of the comparison is precisely *because* it is biological and earthily unmediated.

Fried's reading is ingenious. But it fails, I think, to entirely take account of its own ingeniousness. After all, if Courbet wished to link art and female biology, why not paint a pregnant woman?[27] Or, for that matter, why not paint a pregnant woman painting? Instead, the connection of art to birth is made elliptically, routed through a vision of unconscious female agrarian toil. The cleverness of that deferral—the virtuosity with which the painting slips down the chain of signifiers—suggests a conception of painting not as biological effusion but as masterful artifice. Painting-as-nature and painting-as-artifice are not in conflict, however. Rather, they depend on each other. Courbet's naturalness testifies to his mastery, and the mastery in turn secures for him the naturalness. By taking the feminine as his own, the artist becomes a perfected hermaphrodite, the superbly naive craftsman. And all that has to happen for this apotheosis to occur is for the woman herself to become a (literally, in this painting) faceless cipher. She is a biological placeholder and a winking reference.

Courbet leverages the image of women for his own greater glory. The sequence from *Wonder Woman #1* works differently. Hippolyte is not just *like* an artist; she *is* an artist. If Marston's conscious creation is natural because it is comparable to a pregnancy, then so is Hippolyte's. And if Marston's conscious virtuosity allows him to lay claim to biology, then so too does Hippolyte's. Hippolyte is both artist and mother; the two roles aren't separable. The love of artist for made thing, of mother for child, and of goddess for creation are commensurate rather than opposed. Aphrodite is mistress of them all.

Courbet fantasizes that painting is female; Marston fantasizes that he himself, in the act of creation, is female. Indeed, the fantasy is I think specifically that the quintessentially female act of creation, the breath of Aphrodite, will make him a woman. Thus, he is—and how could he not be?—both creator and created, both Hippolyte and her daughter. What he has made from his love is himself, her wonder girl.

A FUTURE WITHOUT WONDER WOMAN

In the introduction, I argued that *Wonder Woman*, the original comic, was much more interesting, beautiful, and worthwhile than Wonder Woman the popular icon. I have tried in the bulk of the book to show why I value Marston/Peter so much. In this conclusion, I want to briefly explain why I feel that most other versions of the character are—let's be kind and say "superfluous."

The three chapters of this book focus on three of Marston/Peter's major concerns: feminism (or bondage), pacifism (or violence), and gayness (or heterosexuality). For this conclusion, I have selected for discussion one iteration of Wonder Woman that addresses each of these themes. In doing so, I have tried to choose work that is at least marginally competent. There are many, many Wonder Woman stories through the years that are thoroughly worthless in almost every respect. But it seemed unsporting to single out, for example, Samuel Delany's dreadful 1970s stories from *Wonder Woman #202–203* (the undoubted nadir of his illustrious career) or Christopher Moeller's blindingly bad 2002 *JLA: A League of One* (in which Wonder Woman dies beautifully and is kissed back to life by Superman) or, for that matter, the terminally dull Lynda Carter television series. Or anything by Robert Kanigher. Or . . . well, you get the idea.[1]

Instead, I've focused on work that has received at least some level of critical acclaim and that is, in my own estimation, not completely aesthetically and intellectually worthless. I have tried, in short, to pick some of the more interesting and inventive responses to Marston and Peter's character—for better or worse.

FEMINISM: THE TRUTH WILL MAKE YOU CONVENTIONAL

The team on *Wonder Woman* from 2011–2014 was is writer Brian Azzarello and artist Cliff Chiang with occasional fill-ins by artist Tony Akins. Their run has been controversial, for reasons that should become clear. Nonetheless, it has received a good bit of praise for both its storyline and its art.[2] Azzarello and Chiang are among the most respected currently working superhero writers and artists, respectively, and the series is entirely professional, which is something that cannot be said of much of DC's output. I will be discussing issues 1–7 of the series, which include the first collected trade plus one additional issue. The comics do not have page numbers, so I will simply reference individual issues.

Azzarello and Chiang began *Wonder Woman* with a new issue 1 in 2012. This was part of DC Comics' massive "New 52" marketing initiative. In line with the reboot, their story line deliberately undoes or reworks much of the Wonder Woman mythos and backstory in favor of an exploration of what might be termed the gritty underbelly of Greek mythology. Like Marston, they explore themes of feminism, bondage, and (inevitably when focusing on Greek myths) sexual violence. Their perspective is deliberately and diametrically opposed to that of *Wonder Woman*'s creators. Though this is intended to be shocking, the result is much more conventional in just about every way than the original *Wonder Woman* series.[3]

The opening sequence of the first issue of *Wonder Woman* #1 sets the tone for much of what is to follow. In the first panel, we're treated to the soaring skyscrapers of a cityscape; we then zoom in to see three women looking down over the balcony of a penthouse suite. One of the women leans far forward; her rear end is dead center in the frame. Off to the side, in extreme foreground, we see the host's torso. The top of a wine bottle is also visible, its opening casually pointed toward the aforementioned ass.

The host is, as we quickly learn, the Greek god Apollo, and by page 2, he's moved up behind the three women, who all say "Ahhhhh" in unison, as if his magic power is simultaneous triple rear penetration. A few pages later, we learn that that *is*, effectively, his power—the three women float in the air, eyes white, mouths gaping, as they spew forth oracular pronouncements for the enlightenment of their host/rapist/

controller. Their speech is his speech, their minds are his minds, and when their work is done, they float off the balcony and are incinerated. The last we see of them is some charred bones and a skull floating earthward.

Azzarello and Chiang, then, open with a display of sexualized male violence. In Marston/Peter, a man such as Dr. Psycho pulled power out of women, but that power filled him, rather than the other way around. Here, the women are not so much the source of power as they are tools. They are vessels that Apollo fills, things to be exploited and then destroyed. Again, Marston and Peter often used themes of sexualized male dominance and control—especially in the stories focusing on Pluto and Dr. Psycho. What is different here, I'd argue, is the extent to which the book's narrative aligns itself with the rapist. The creative team uses the women as objects just as much as Apollo does. Thus, Azzarello and Chiang do not tell us the women's names, nor do they tell us anything about them. We know only that they've come up on the roof to have a good time and that they will be punished for that indiscretion. They exist narratively only to titillate, first with sex and then with violence. The fact that there are three of them turns them into a deindividualized collective. This is especially the case since Chiang gives them all the same basic look connoting sexual attractiveness/availability: slim bodies; tight dresses; long, lustrous hair. The creative team doesn't even bother to build suspense or to make us feel their terror; we do not masochistically identify with them as we might with a victim in a slasher film. We merely watch their annihilation—an annihilation that is their whole purpose. Just as Pussy Galore is inviolable so that James Bond may violate her, these nameless women exist solely to demonstrate that their destroyer (diegetically the god; extranarratively Azzarello/Chiang) is a potent, cold-hearted bastard. Azzarello/Chiang open their series by aggressively letting us know that they do not care about women and that they do care about power. Moreover, whereas Marston and Peter consistently saw female sisterhood and female beauty as a potential source of strength, Azzarello and Chiang see it as vulnerability. Women in this world do not have power.

Or, rather, women can have power—but only male power, because that is the only kind of power there is. In issue 7, Wonder Woman ties the god Hephaestus in her magic lasso, declaring that it enforces truth.

"And that—the Truth—is my weapon."[4] Chiang draws a close-up of Hephaestus's ugly, red-eyed, toothy visage as the ensnared monster declares, "No . . . your weapon is intimidation. You blame the rope. That's the truth." The only power is violence; the only truths are ugly. Wonder Woman is a brute because there are only brutes, which means that only brutes speak the truth.

Wonder Woman deceives herself by believing that there is a power other than force—or other than the phallus. The series is devoted to demonstrating to her the enormity of this error. The major reworking of the mythos, revealed in *Wonder Woman #3*, is that the Amazon princess was not created out of clay by Hippolyta.[5] Instead, she is the daughter of Zeus. As Hippolyta says, "Diana, before there was you, there was a man." The caption is placed next to an image of Zeus, naked except for a cloak, his eyes glowing, his penis tactfully tucked behind Hippolyta's honking big sword. Their courtship is then presented as a swordfight / wrestling match, which is glorious because of its violence. "Strength supporting strength . . . sinews entwined . . . Absolute control . . . given up," Hippolyta says, as we see in silhouette her astride the king of the gods, his head thrown back in the throes of orgasm.

In some sense, this appears to be in line with Marston's belief in loving submission, since Zeus is on the bottom giving up control. But it's difficult to see his potency as reduced in the moment when he's conceiving the hero of the book. Hippolyta's dominance doesn't make Zeus less phallic, just like Zeus's dominance doesn't make Hippolyta less phallic. On the contrary, their love affair, with swords standing in for penises and "strength supporting strength," is expressed as an apotheosis of leap-frogging penises. Zeus cedes control to the phallus that is Hippolyta and therefore has his phallus and his control validated, just as Hippolyta cedes control to Zeus and has her phallus and her control validated. They put aside their bits and grab the other's bits, and everybody is more father-ruler than they were before.[6]

This is certainly more egalitarian than James Bond entering Pussy Galore or than Apollo murdering those three women at the beginning of the book. The relationship between Hippolyta and Zeus is not unequal, except in the sense that the equality is defined in terms of patriarchal bits. This is emphasized by the change in Wonder Woman's origin. As I discussed at length in chapter 3, Wonder Woman was, in Marston/Peter's telling, created without male intercession. She was made out of clay by her mother and brought to life by Aphrodite's breath. While tales of men creating life without women are staples of our culture—from *Pygmalion* to *Frankenstein* to the 1985 humor/sci-fi film *Weird Science*—tales of women creating life without men are extremely rare. Besides Marston/Peter, in fact, I can't think of another example of female parthenogenesis in either high or low culture.

Rather than building on perhaps the most original origin in super-hero comics, Azzarello simply dumps it. In his telling, the clay-come-to-life narrative was only a story made up by Hippolyta to fool Zeus's wife, Hera, and prevent her from killing baby Diana in a jealous rage. Thus, Wonder Woman no longer is born from the female intersection of Hippolyta's craft and Aphrodite's love. Instead, her powers are because she is Zeus's daughter; they're a patriarchal blood right. "I'm a lie. You're a fool. And you made one out of me," Wonder Woman tells her mother as she stomps off, holding herself oddly and unpleasantly rigid, her arms flexed and off to the side, like her body is accommodating itself to its new phallic reality.

Hippolyta's lie was that there could be a female community and a female magic that is not inhabited by, and powered by, men. Wonder Woman's foolishness was in believing her. The stupidity, therefore, is specifically in accepting and believing in Marston's work and in his ideology. The Wonder Woman origin was for children. Now that the comics audience is older, we can all laugh—or at least smirk—at those dumb kids back then who didn't know about the birds and the bees and their penises. If, as I said in chapter 3, Marston and Peter gleefully open the closet to discover woman and then open the closet to discover woman and then open the closet to discover woman, Azzarello and Chiang just as assiduously open the closet to discover the penis. In issue 3 of their run, we learn that the truth of Wonder Woman is manness; in issue 7, we learn that this is the truth of the other Amazons as well.

In a three-page sequence, Hephaestus explains that the Amazons do not become pregnant by divine will, as Wonder Woman thought. Instead, three times a century, they go out on the ocean, board vessels, and sleep with the men. When they are done, they toss the men overboard. The girl children of the resulting pregnancies are kept;

the boys are traded to Hephaestus for weapons. When the boys grow up, they work in his forge. As Azzarello and Chiang tell this story, it's about, or related to, sexual gendered violence. Hephaestus compares the Amazons to pirates, and the specter of rape is quite clear. This narrative could, then, be a way of putting women in the position of rapists and aggressors. As we've seen, this is something that Marston/Peter occasionally did, as in the image of Clea and Giganta threatening a stripped-down Steve (see figure 7). Similarly, as discussed, Susan Brownmiller's enthusiastic endorsement of kicking male rapists in the balls gets a good deal of its force from the not-very-buried reversal of roles—the idea that rapists themselves can be sexually assaulted.

Imagining female rapists can be, and sometimes is, used as a way to avoid or undo or complicate phallocentrism. If Azzarello and Chiang had shown men being raped en masse, it would, at the least, have provided some imagery that would have been quite unusual for superhero comics—or, indeed, for pop culture in general. On another tack, Azzarello and Chiang could have made some effort to reference the history of women's oppression as a motivation for the Amazons' actions. In that case, the narrative would have moved toward rape-revenge—an exploitive genre but not necessarily an unfeminist one.[7] This is not the path Azzarello and Chiang take, however. Instead, they seem determined to put the Amazons in the position of rapists in a way that does not upset, or even tinker with, patriarchal gender norms. Thus, the men on the ship are not actually raped, because, presumably, Azzarello and Chiang can't figure out, or are uninterested in figuring out, a way to violate men the way that men have historically and in great numbers violated women. Instead, the creators just assume that all the men in question would be happy to screw random women at the drop of an anchor. As Kelly Thompson notes in her March 26, 2012, review, this neatly erases gay men ("She Has No Head!"). It also, as Thompson says, assumes that every man everywhere will have sex with any woman who just shows up. It positions all men, in other words, as patriarchal drones, ruled by the phallus—or at least by their own phalluses.

Women, too, are relegated to stereotypical gender roles. In the sequence in which the Amazons appear on shipboard, the reader is positioned with the sailors, staring at an Amazon who is posed in the familiar come-hither posture. (We are, presumably, supposed to infer that the Amazons subscribe to *Maxim*.) Thus, the women, even as they take the iconically and statistically male position of rapist, are still objects of a male narrative and, indeed, of a male gaze. This female warrior society depends for its continuance not just on men but on conforming to the most banal male erotic stereotypes. The Amazons cannot simply take the phallus but must conform themselves to it, so that the only possible female society is one defined by male wet dreams.

Again, in issue 1, sexualized violence is treated as validating, exciting, and cool; killing women makes Apollo (and by extension his creators) tough and interesting—it is a way to build him up. Something rather different happens with the Amazons. When the *Maxim*-posing Amazon appears, Chiang draws a sailor in the foreground turning to look, with three white motion lines connoting surprise/excitement surrounding his head. The cartoony touch fits jarringly with Chiang's mostly naturalistic style—and with the narrative itself, which is after all about sexualized violence and murder. Azzarello, too, adopts an "ironic" tone; in the panel after the Amazons appear on ship, he has some random divine guy make jokes about "booty" and "seminal mortal vessels."

Along similar lines, when Apollo kills, the violence is emphasized and the sex downplayed; in fact, the sex (three women at the penthouse partying) is diverted into violence, which is the payoff. With the Amazons, the focus is reversed. Azzarello and Chiang are happy to show us women astride rutting sailors, but the murder is only suggested by some blades and then by bodies falling into the water at a distance. When a man is the assailant, the reader does not see the sex but participates vicariously in the violence. When women are the assailants, the reader participates vicariously in the screwing but gets to back off for the consequences. Thus, Azzarello/Chiang do not use a rape-revenge structure, or the flipping of gendered violence, to make men participate viscerally or emotionally in the experience of oppression. On the contrary, for them, gendered violence is carefully organized and conceptualized through traditional phallic roles and moralities. Rape is cool. Castration, on the other hand, is sometimes funny (because anyone who is not a man is funny) and sometimes a kind of thing we don't really want to look at too closely (because men are okay with seeing the burned bodies of women, but chopped-off penises, not so much). Either way, it is male experience and male interests that matter. The one time we really get a sense of a woman's interiority in either sequence is in a single panel in which one of the Amazons is shown reaching out to try to prevent her male child from being taken away from her. It's a thoughtful moment in a comic not replete with them, but it is hard to miss the fact that we get to sympathize with the Amazon only when she is mourning her male offspring.

In chapter 2, I discussed the way in which Sigmund Freud took the typically female experience of father-rape and substituted for it the typically male experience of the Oedipal complex, thereby transmuting female trauma into male angst. Azzarello/Chiang perform a similar patriarchal alchemy. In the real world, of course, when there has been a gender bias in infanticide, as in China, the victims have been disproportionately girls, not boys (Mungello 1–8). Moreover, infanticide is linked not to the empowerment of women but to their "economic and social vulnerability," according to Lionel Rose (15). When women kill their infants, it has historically been because they do not have the resources to raise them or because they live in a society where out-of-wedlock pregnancy is severely punished. Infant death is, in the real world, disproportionately the result of women's *weakness*, not of women's Amazonian self-sufficiency. Nonetheless, Azzarello and Chiang present infanticide as a practice performed by strong women against male children—or as a practice that would be committed against male children if it were not for the intervention of the kind patriarch, Hephaestus.

The male Amazon babies grow up to work in Hephaestus's forge. Wonder Woman in issue 7, mistaking Hephaestus for an exploiter, ties him up and tries to free her "brothers." They, however, do not want to be freed and ask her to release the "Master." Again, Wonder Woman is shown as being a fool, not just for believing in the virtues of an all-female society but for doubting the virtues of an all-male one. Men, for Azzarello and Chiang, do not need to be protected from patriarchy or class exploitation. Rather, they need to be saved from their mothers, from their sisters, and from strong women generally—from feminism, in other words.

As with the other reversals in the series, the iniquity of the Amazons is presented as the truth behind the myth or at least as a truth closer to the actual mythological heart of the Greek tradition. Hephaestus scoffs at Wonder Woman's suggestion that the Amazon babies were provided by the will of the gods. "As a God, I will tell you that [Gods] don't care about anyone but themselves," he insists. The power of these revelations is seductive; hidden knowledge, or closeted knowledge, always has, as Eve Sedgwick says, a powerful propulsion (*Epistemology* 3; see chapter 3 for a more complete discussion). In this case, the unveiling of the new truth is used to hide the fact that that new truth is every bit as ridiculous as the old one. A child made from clay is no less plausible than a child conceived by a god. A nonexploitive all-male society is not more likely than a nonexploitive all-female one. And in the real world, feminism is not the greatest threat children face. On the contrary, Linda Gordon argues, on the basis of her historical survey of child abuse in the nineteenth- and twentieth-century United States, that "the presence or absence of a strong feminist movement makes the difference between better and worse solutions to the social problem of child sexual abuse" (61). She adds, echoing the findings of Judith Herman and Lisa Hirschman that we looked at in chapter 1, that "probably the most important single contribution to the presentation of incest would be the strengthening of mothers" (62). Women's empowerment as a protector of children is the reality; the supposedly more realistic Amazon fever dream of castration and violence is the fantasy.[8]

Even with regard to the Greek myths themselves, Azzarello/Chiang are not necessarily more accurate than Marston/Peter. There are, for example, no Greek myths in which Apollo has a penthouse. More consequentially, perhaps, Hephaestus as moral protector of the weak contradicts or obscures the legends in which he attempts to rape Athena.[9] Marston/Peter, for their part (as we've seen), did not gloss over the sexual violence in Greek myths. It's just that Marston/Peter used that sexual violence as a way to negotiate issues of sexual violence, while Azzarello and Chiang use it mostly to present themselves as edgy.

What's at stake, therefore, is not truth but ideology. The Amazon legends were originally ambiguous, presenting strong woman who were both worthy opponents and inevitably defeated, who were feminine but engaged in the quintessentially masculine pursuit of war, who both perpetrated gendered violence and were the victims of gendered violence in turn.[10] From these ambivalent patriarchal myths, Marston and Peter created an explicitly matriarchal vision—one that managed to retain the stories' richness while rejecting their misogyny. Azzarello and Chiang then took Marston and Peter and replaced the peace-loving Amazons not with the Greeks' admirable, war-loving Amazons but rather with a society built on falsehoods. The most salient fact about Azzarello/Chiang's Amazons is that they are liars. Thus, whereas Marston and Peter are much less antiwoman than the Greeks were, Azzarello/Chiang are arguably more so. If Marston/Peter's revision of the Amazons was determinedly feminist, Azzarello/Chiang's is . . . what? explicitly antifeminist? determinedly misogynist?

I think Azzarello/Chiang's *Wonder Woman* does have a lot of misogyny in it—and that misogyny is probably in part deliberate. Jamaal Thomas suggests that Azzarello wants to "tweak the collective noses of those who (rightfully) view Wonder Woman and the Amazons as feminist icons," and that assessment sounds right to me. But just because the misogyny is in service of tweaking doesn't make it less misogynist. The negative portrayals of women in Azzarello/Chiang are powered by a left-wing desire to desecrate women in the process of desecrating the status quo, rather than by the right-wing desire to denigrate women in order to preserve the status quo. Either way, the results are much the same as far as the women in question are concerned.[11]

In part, then, Azzarello is misogynist because Wonder Woman is a feminist icon, and he likes to spit on icons. But the series's ideological antifeminism is also probably a function of genre. Azzarello is best known for his noirish series *100 Bullets*, and a lot of that sensibility has transferred over to *Wonder Woman*. Azzarello's is a dark and gritty Wonder Woman, living in a world where every man (or god) is out for himself and every woman is either a dupe (like Wonder Woman), a trophy (like Zola, the woman whose main function in the story is to give Wonder Woman someone to protect), a dame you can't trust (like the bitchy, vengeful Hera), or all three at once. To win in noir, you have to be hard—and "hard" here definitely includes screwing over the women. Wonder Woman's least hapless moment in the first part of the series occurs in issue 6, when she orchestrates a plot against Hera. This plot involves pimping the queen of the gods out to her two brothers-in-law. It's true that this is just a feint, and Hera is never actually raped. But the fact that Wonder Woman is strongest when she aligns herself with patriarchal exploitation is, I think, indicative.

Azzarello/Chiang's *Wonder Woman*, in its conflation of easy nihilism with insight, functions as standard, amoral, "controversial," male genre pulp—better than Ian Fleming, worse than Raymond Chandler, okay if you like that sort of thing and to be avoided if you don't. It is also, however, at least to some degree, a critique of the original Marston/Peter series. As Ben Saunders has noted, contemporary female superheroes tend to be "moody, haunted, erratic and untrustworthy" (156). Saunders adds that in contrast, Wonder Woman remains "noble [and] optimistic" (157)—which is why Azzarello and Chiang treat her like a fool ignorant of the most basic facts about her origin, her family, her weapon, and everything else. She's out of place in man's world—which means that either man's world is wrong or she is. Marston and Peter insist on the first interpretation; Azzarello and Chiang, much more conventionally, opt for the second.

In making this choice, Azzarello and Chiang inadvertently reveal how carefully those original comics were constructed. Azzarello/Chiang dumped Marston/Peter's feminism—but as a result (or, if you wish, as a prelude), they have to dump everything else as well. Without the commitment to understanding female experiences of oppression, there is no ground on which to build a female community different from a male community and thus no alternative to violence and force. Similarly, the focus on patriarchy makes it impossible for Azzarello and Chiang to imagine anything but heterosexuality. Even though their Amazon community is supposedly more adult and more realistic, there is no hint in the first seven issues of lesbian possibilities or potentials. At least as far as we're shown, this is a female community whose sexual focus is exclusively on men. Marston and Peter were radical because they were feminist, pacifist, and queer—not as separate goals but as a single, indivisible vision. Azzarello and Chiang, in rejecting that vision, end up as antifeminist, violent, and patriarchal. And while that's supposed to be daring, the truth is that in comparison to the original, it feels more like a predictable cultural genre default.

PACIFISM: WONDER WOMAN ASKS YOU
TO PLEASE STOP FIGHTING

Azzarello and Chiang are ideologically determined to reject Marston/ Peter's Wonder Woman. Gail Simone, working with Terry Dodson and Bernard Chang, was much more enthusiastic about the character's legacy. Whereas Azzarello's Wonder Woman is in many respects a fool, Simone's is wise, strong, and generous. She is also quite witty—Simone has a quick ear for dialogue and a fine sense of comic-book goofiness. Thus, in the 2008 collection *The Circle*, we get superintelligent gorillas battling Nazis on Paradise Island. Even better is Diana Prince musing on the contradictions of man's world at a surprise birthday party: "It is a strange culture that outlaws the hug. On the other hand, there is cake. And that excuses much" (23). Simone's light touch, deft characterizations, and respect for Wonder Woman's mythos has won her work on the title a good deal of praise. Trina Robbins in an essay on the *Hooded Utilitarian* calls Simone "one of the two best Wonder Woman writers" other than Marston because of her sense of fun ("Reinventing"), while Saunders praises Simone for "restor[ing] some of Diana's lost prestige" after a series of disastrous reboots (163–164).

As is probably apparent already, I much prefer Simone's impish but reverent *Wonder Woman* run to Azzarello/Chiang's earnestly ironic desecration. "Better than Azzarello/Chiang" is, though, a fairly low bar, and Simone's *Wonder Woman* still has serious problems. These are best encapsulated in *Wonder Woman #18* and *#19*, with art by Bernard Chang, in which Simone directly engages with Marston/Peter's themes of war and pacifism.[12] The two-part story, "Expatriate," focuses on the Khund Empire. The Khund are a race of extremely vicious, unrelenting warriors—Wonder Woman describes them as "perhaps the most brutal alien race ever to land on this world or any other" (114). Wonder Woman had defeated the Khund in the past, and so they respect and even revere her. They come to Earth to ask her aid—their people are being systematically wiped out by an ultrapowerful alien ichor. (Like I said, Simone embraces the comic-book goofiness.) Wonder Woman is faced with a moral dilemma. Should she prevent the destruction of the Khund, knowing that they will continue on their genocidal rampage across the stars? Or should she acquiesce in the genocide of the Khund themselves? Which genocide to choose?

Wonder Woman doesn't hesitate; she instantly decides to protect the Khund. Her sidekick, Etta Candy (in this version a tough, competent military lieutenant colonel), also and just as instantaneously agrees with her. And not only do Wonder Woman and Etta come to the same conclusion, but they manage to convince everyone else of the rightness of their position. There's an alien Green Lantern named Procanon Kaa,[13] whose daughter was killed by the Khund. But Wonder Woman beats him in battle and then talks to him for a few minutes, and soon he's racing off to protect all Khund everywhere. Even more miraculously, Etta talks for literally three small panels, and—ta da!— the godlike ichor experiences a transformational change of heart (or whatever the ichor equivalent of that organ is), forswears its genocidal ways, and heads on home. It's like some sort of bizarre anticlimactic deus ex machina in reverse.

The problem here isn't exactly the improbability. After all, if you're willing to accept a godlike ichor, why not a godlike ichor that lacks the courage of its own convictions? For that matter, Marston/Peter plots were not distinguished by their adherence to the rules of logic. If Marston had been writing Simone's story line, he probably would have resolved the whole thing by having Wonder Woman slap Venus girdles on the evil male Khund rulers and the godlike ichor both. Then he would have put a queen on the Khund throne and let male Khund and ichor spend the rest of their existence in happy, peaceful, erotic servitude.

But while Marston's utopian pacifism was not realistically plotted in any sense of the word, it did have an internal coherence. Pacifism for Marston was, as we've seen, tied to gender, to a belief in the power of eroticized reeducation, and ultimately to a vision of loving submission as the spiritual relinquishing of power and force. As discussed in chapter 2, when Paula gives the Mole Men back their sight in Marston/Peter's *Wonder Woman #4*, we know what it is they see—the beauty of women, of love, and of submission, all of which lead to peace. But what exactly does the godlike ichor see when it has its mind (or whatever) changed by Etta? Here's what Etta tells it:

Look, I'm not saying I understand all this. But I do believe you're trying to do something good. To prevent the Khund from destroying other civilizations in the future, right?

But . . . won't this just continue the cycle of revenge and kill-ing? You can't destroy a planet in the name of compassion. I know I'm just a lieutenant colonel from a small planet a long ways away, but even I know that.

How can you be so powerful, so great, and not know that? I know we can't stop you—but haven't you shed enough blood here? (147)

This monologue occurs in a kind of sidebar running down the page. Artists Bernard Chang and Jon Holdridge barely illustrate it. First we see a close-up of Etta's face; then we see her moving around a ship sketched from a distance. There's no real sense of space, much less of place—supposedly we're meant to be impressed with Etta's smallness in comparison to the ship, but the panels themselves are too tiny, and the view too distant, for the scale to have much impact. Etta's words are the turning point of the plot; they are intended to be so powerful that they move even a superpowered colloid. Visually, thought, they're a giant dud, pushed off to the margins and rendered in such a way that you can barely figure out what she's doing or where she is. The godlike ichor may have been impressed, but Chang and Holdridge just shrug and urge you to turn the page.

I think they have the right idea; Etta's speech can't bear the weight that's put on it. Certainly, Etta echoes many pacifist thinkers in point-ing out the futility of revenge and killing. But it's an echo that thuds back and forth in a vacuum. How does pacifism exist in Etta's life? What do her words mean to her, and what are they supposed to mean to us, much less to the godlike ichor? This question isn't just rhetori-cal. From the perspective of most pacifist writing, the position taken by Wonder Woman and Etta simply doesn't make sense. There are, of course, pacifists whose dedication to absolute nonviolence is such that they would not agree to the destruction of the Khund. But as Thomas Merton suggests, this kind of unequivocal pacifism is usually predicat-ed on religious beliefs (or, as he puts it, "the fully consistent practice of nonviolence demands a solid metaphysical and religious basis both in being and in God"; 209). Simone gives no indication that either Etta or Wonder Woman is motivated by such blanket spiritual condemnation of violence. On the contrary, Wonder Woman fights all the time and often thinks about how much she enjoys battle ("a woman's amuse-ments are sometimes inexplicable," she quips; 115). Etta, for her part, is a military woman who carries a gun as a matter of course. Both Won-der Woman and Etta would, then, presumably be philosophically okay with fighting World War II—as were many practical pacifists such as Bertrand Russell.[14] But if you're willing to battle and kill Nazis, why wouldn't you be willing to acquiesce in the destruction of the Khund? It's true that the ichor is perpetrating not just war but genocide—but, then, the Khund are thousands of times worse than the Nazis. Not only have they enslaved and then utterly wiped out the populations of countless planets, but their culture is utterly devoted to genocidal warfare. Simone doesn't make it clear whether there are any Khund at all who forswear war. She suggests, indeed, that their culture does not even understand the meaning of peace, all of which implies that in a real sense there are no Khund civilians. And to top it off, the Khund are utterly unrepentant. They ask for Wonder Woman's help, but it's clear that if they're saved, they'll simply go back to killing as they did before.

Given all that, Etta's insistence that "you can't destroy a planet in the name of compassion" seems nonsensical. People kill in the name of compassion all the time. Virtually all violent U.S. interventions in our day are sold to the public in the name of humanitarianism. If Etta thinks that this sort of thing is unjustified, what is she doing in the military? And if on the other hand she believes that killing in the name of compassion is sometimes justified (as Etta must since she is in fact willing to kill), then on what possible grounds can you argue that it is not justified in the case of the Khund? Etta's argument wouldn't sway a high school debate team, much less a neoconservative—and much, much less than that an uberpowerful godlike ichor.

Simone's moral world, then, doesn't make sense: it's not ratio-nal. Still, to give her the benefit of the doubt, there are some moral approaches that don't rely heavily on rationality. It is logically incon-sistent to carry a gun and to save the Khund, but perhaps there is an emotional framework where those actions could be reconciled. One thinker who might possibly provide a context for Simone's moral uni-verse here is Nel Noddings, who argues that rules-based moral think-ing is inadequate and suggests instead using what she refers to as an "ethic of care." Rather than relying on abstract concepts such as justice, Noddings looks to the maternal bond of caring for the child as a way to understand ethical relations and the ethical self. For example, she discusses the case of Simon Wiesenthal, a Holocaust survivor who was asked for forgiveness by a blind and dying Nazi, named Karl. Under orders, Karl had murdered many Jews.[15] Noddings says that care ethics would not necessarily prescribe forgiveness or a single ethical response in such a situation. However,

> called upon to care, we would respond with some form of sympathy and comfort to Karl. Perhaps we would simply hold his hand. Perhaps we would cry with him—shedding tears he could not see. Perhaps we would talk about the horrors of corrupt education and obedience to authority. Perhaps we would share tales of happier times. Perhaps we would say nothing but, through touch, provide a bit of comfort. We would not ignore the face-to-face expression of need. (146)

The determination not to turn away from a personal "expression of need" echoes Wonder Woman's explanation of her decision to help the Khund: "It is almost impossible for an Amazon to resist a cry for aid" (Simone et al. 119). Along the same lines, in *Wonder Woman #15* by Simone and artists Terry and Rachel Dodson (also included in *The Circle*), Wonder Woman shows concern and understanding for a captured Nazi foe. "Even for him I follow the Amazon code when facing a vanquished foe," she says, "punishment for the adult, empathy for the child" (46). The Dodsons don't do a lot visually with the maternal implications—Wonder Woman's hand on the evil super-Nazi's shoulder seems more comradely than mothering. Still, the link between empathy, mothering, and reeducation as the Nazi confesses his sins under the power of Wonder Woman's rope seems clear enough. Wonder Woman for Simone is not a love leader using her feminine sexuality for purposes of reeducation. But she is perhaps a caring leader, responding to human need with sympathy and strength.

Noddings's formulation of morality as a caring relationship, then, seems to fit Simone's *Wonder Woman* much better than any kind of spiritual or pragmatic pacifism. Still, it doesn't fit all *that* well. Though

Wonder Woman's morality does seem to flow from, or take shape within, the assumption of an ethic of caring, that ethic is constantly itself defined by what amounts to an abstract rule. Wonder Woman empathizes with the Nazi captive not out of an experience or valuing of caring per se but because the Amazon code tells her to value caring. She chooses "diplomacy over bloodshed," as she says, "to the very last" not through a vision of caregiving or of a maternal ethic but because such is the "Amazon code" (117). And this is the case throughout Simone's writing—Wonder Woman is always referring her moral choices to what is presented as an Amazon warrior code. For Wonder Woman, the internal experience of morality seems to be not the emotional relation of face-to-face caring but rather adherence to a complicated system of rules that mimic the emotional relation of face-to-face caring.

If the outcome is the same, the distinction may seem unimportant. However, inevitably, the outcome is *not* the same, and at crucial moments, the tension between love by rule and rules of love leaves Simone's ethics not just intellectually incoherent but emotionally incoherent as well. This is perhaps most evident in the sequence during which Wonder Woman defeats and then converts the bereaved Green Lantern, Procanon Kaa. She accomplishes the defeat in part by using empathy; she notices that he flinches every time she says the word "Khund." Exploiting his weakness, Wonder Woman defeats him, and then, in a lovely turn of phrase, tells him, "Take my hand, Lantern. It is open. Will you fill it with your own?" (140). Instead, in one of the most dramatic sequences in the book, he beats her bloody while Wonder Woman just stands there and takes it. Chang and Holdridge avoid most of the violence, focusing on Kaa's raging face rather than on Wonder Woman's battered one. Still, when they show Wonder Woman's black eye, split lip, and slashed cheek at the end, it's a shock—especially in contrast to her magazine-cover flawlessness just a page back. Her damaged face is a mark not just of her courage but of her humanity, and as such, it leads Kaa to see her as a person rather than as an enemy. Empathy leads to nonviolence, and out of nonviolence comes empathy; love and peace are a whole.

But no sooner is this insight embraced than it's abandoned. Kaa explains that the Khund destroyed not only his home world and his daughter but also many other worlds in his space sector, under his protection. He is on the side of the godlike ichor precisely because of compassion and empathy. In this context, Noddings points out that an ethic of care is not an absolute ethic of pacifism: "Females know that they will fight for the lives of their children and that—with great sorrow—they will side with their own in times of conflict, even when their own are demonstrably wrong" (32).[16] In this case, Kaa's side is not demonstrably wrong; in working for the eradication of the Khund, he is inspired not merely by anger over his dead child but by fear of what further depredations the Khund will wreak on those under his protection.

If we are working from an ethic of care, in other words, Kaa's testimony—his description of where his own caring has led him—should have a great deal of weight. But when he says that his experiences as the survivor of what is essentially an uber-mega-Holocaust have left him questioning universal justice, Wonder Woman responds not with empathy but with a cold-hearted reaffirmation of the rules: "I'm sorry for your loss, my friend. But if loss makes you doubt your belief in justice . . . then you never truly believed in justice at all" (143). Condescendingly telling a Holocaust survivor that he is only despairing because his faith isn't strong enough strikes me as a callousness bordering on actual evil. Surely, the formulation should be inverted. If the murder of millions (or, in this case, billions) of people doesn't shake your sense of justice, it seems unlikely that you actually care about people at all. Her pro forma "I'm sorry for your loss" notwithstanding, Wonder Woman here does not come across as caring. On the contrary, she appears monstrously insensitive, waving away the destruction of innumerable planets while self-righteously condescending to a man who has suffered enough that his ability to even marginally function has to be considered a miracle of courage.

I don't actually believe that Wonder Woman (or, by implication, Gail Simone) is an unfeeling monster. Rather, the point is that the moral world here isn't anchored ideologically, structurally, or emotionally. Wonder Woman doesn't treat Procanon Kaa as if he's a Holocaust survivor because he isn't a Holocaust survivor. He's a stock DC alien superhero, whose function is to battle Wonder Woman and then be redeemed by her. Pacifism, empathy, genocide—they're tropes. They're not what the story is about.

So what is the story about? That seems obvious enough: it's about the heroine. Simone's writing doesn't suggest an ethic of caring so much as an ethic of caring about Wonder Woman. Indeed, that caring about Wonder Woman is self-reflective; the idolization of Wonder Woman becomes thematized and even literalized. In *Wonder Woman #14*, Wonder Woman defeats a group of intelligent apes and converts them not to the worship of women or the service of Aphrodite, as Marston might have had it, but to personal fealty to Wonder Woman herself.[17] In *Wonder Woman #17*, we learn that Diana's miraculous birth didn't just answer Hippolyta's prayers but saved all the barren Amazons from despair. In the Khund story line, there is one redeemable Khund: Kho. Kho is a self-declared Wonder Woman "fan," who has followed Wonder Woman's broadcast adventures from afar (Simone et al. 119). Whereas Marston celebrates the transformative power of erotic bonds, Kho is redeemed when her celebrity worship impels her to race to Wonder Woman's aid despite the wishes of her father. The comic becomes an advertisement for its own fandom. Worship Wonder Woman and all will be well—which is why Wonder Woman's black eye has more emotional weight than any number of anonymous burned-out planets.

It is not surprising, then, that when the godlike ichor flies, flies away, it says it is leaving on the condition that Wonder Woman stands personally responsible for any further depredations by the Khund. Peace is ensured not by the overthrow of patriarchal power in the name of love but through Wonder Woman's personal guarantee. She's not just a paragon; she's a totem.

And how does Wonder Woman ensure that the Khund will not kill again? By convincing the bereaved Procanon Kaa to take on Kho as a daughter and apprentice. In part, this seems like an effort to form a bond of family, to create a healing kinship between enemies. But the last panels of the story focus not on a reconciliation between victim and victimizer but on Kho's comically garbled efforts to recite the Green Lantern oath, long familiar to readers of DC comics. The answer to genocide is not so much forgiveness and a "complexity of the heart" (Simone et al. 149) as it is winking nerd knowledge and the introduction of a new female superhero.

In superhero comics, superheroes are always the solution—that's how the genre works. And yet Simone's run highlights the extent to which Marston and Peter were an exception to that rule. Marston's Wonder Woman was always the victorious savior—but that's because she embodied the ideals he cherished. For Simone, on the other hand, it often feels like peace and love are important because they are attributes of Wonder Woman, rather than because they have some value in themselves. Simone's Wonder Woman still looks like Marston's— she's compassionate, she's loving, she's strong, she wears a swimsuit. But the logic that gave those qualities meaning has largely evaporated, so that, for example, the peace that was reeducation and submission and love and castration now means little more than "Wonder Woman would like you to stop fighting." The result is a bit like the giant statues the Khund build to honor Wonder Woman, all of which depict her as a hideous troll-like warrior. The devotion is sincere, the execution is amusing, but still it's hard to escape the feeling that somehow, somewhere, something has gotten lost in the translation.

GAYNESS: NO PHALLUS AS BIG AS ALICE

Perhaps my favorite post-Marston/Peter version of Wonder Woman isn't a comic. It's a marvelously funny 1996 ink drawing by Nicole Eisenman titled *Wonder Woman*, in which Alice from *Alice in Wonderland* is shown with her head stuffed up into, and obscured by, an ecstatic Wonder Woman's crotch (see figure 31).[18]

One of the things I like most about this illustration is the way it delights in and elaborates on the queer themes and obsessions of Marston/Peter's run. Marston was (as discussed in chapter 3) fascinated not just by lesbianism but by incest. For him, mother's love was innately erotic; the persuasive force of Wonder Woman's lasso was explicitly maternal and sexual—and sexual because it was maternal. For Marston, then, Eisenman's intimations of birth, the fact that Alice could be seen as going up into, or pushing herself out of, Wonder Woman, would definitely be part of the lascivious charge. I think he'd also like Wonder Woman's effusive, unabashed joy, expressed as orgasmic athleticism.

Other aspects of the drawing can be seen not so much as an extension of Marston/Peter as a clever critique. Wonder Woman's legs, stuffed meatily into her flexing boots, give the character a muscular solidity she never had in Peter's elegantly slender drawings. During Marston's run, Lillian Robinson points out,

FIGURE 31. Nicole Eisenman, "Alice in Wonderland," 1996, ink on paper, 30 × 22.5 inches. Used with permission.

we know Wonder Woman has [muscles] because we see her using them. Ours is a narrative as opposed to a visual knowledge, however. . . . Throughout the [Marston] period . . . she accomplished her remarkable feats without any apparent definition in her biceps or thighs. Her calf muscles, highlighted by the red boots, are developed only to—but not beyond—the point required for "nice legs" in the pinup sense. (62)

Robinson concludes that "at no time did muscularity overshadow or even threaten the conventional notion of beauty" (63). Marston let his women be strong, but he was ambivalent about letting their bodies show that strength. Etta (whom Robinson does not mention in this context) was stout and strong and often even sexual in her butchness, but she was also there to be laughed at. Eisenman, on the other hand, gives us a Wonder Woman who looks like she's borrowed Etta's legs. Butchness is not only an option; it's an ideal.

Or at least that's one interpretation. However, fusing Wonder Woman and Etta cuts both ways. On the one hand, it can be seen as naturalizing a wider range of body types—as doing what Robinson asks and showing us a strong woman who looks the way a truly physically strong woman would actually look. On the other hand, though, it can be seen as making Wonder Woman a figure of fun, in the same way that Etta is a figure of fun. There's no doubt, after all, that this image is a joke—and that joke, in substantial part, is on Wonder Woman herself. From this perspective, Eisenman isn't responding to the explicit queerness in Marston/Peter by making it more explicit. Rather, she's treating Wonder Woman in the same way that Maddox treated those unintentionally sexual comic-book covers mentioned in chapter 2. As in the 1993 drawing *Betty Gets It*, in which Eisenman showed the Flintstones' Wilma taking Betty from behind, the humor and the shock here are in the sexualization of pop-culture detritus that was not originally, or not intentionally, sexual. Wonder Woman and Alice were in the closet, and we are opening the door to find out what they are doing in there. The laugh is in seeing, and knowing, something that the character, or the creators of the character or the audience of the character, do not see and know. Queering the character is a thumb in the eye to convention.

Again, this interpretation leads to the conclusion that Eisenman is not intentionally referencing Marston/Peter. Rather, the touchstone for her realistic, tactile portrayal seems to be, first of all, the television Wonder Woman, Lynda Carter. Other inspirations are the conventional innocent representations of Alice—and perhaps, with the juxtaposition of the flag costume and Americana realism, Norman Rockwell. Eisenman defaces these markers of straightness and innocence with queerness. The queerness includes not just the explicit lesbian oral sex but also those thick, butch legs (perhaps, Terese Ortega suggests, referencing R. Crumb) and the twisted grotesque German-expressionist features, one eye weirdly smaller than the other, the nose squished and piggish, and the mouth open to show all its gaping teeth.

For Marston/Peter, Wonder Woman's queerness was fundamentally normal; in their comics, homoerotic sorority games, or female-female dominance and submission, are presented as entirely healthy and even idealized fun for all typical girls and women everywhere. Wonder Woman's queerness—including mother-daughter eroticism—is never in conflict with her iconic perfection. It is part of that perfection. For Eisenman, though, queerness is used deliberately to challenge that perfection—and that perfection is, therefore, I think, perceived as straight. Eisenman is the snotty punk-rock kid using queerness to kill your idols, which for those who know Marston/Peter is a little disconcerting, since that idol was already quite, quite queer to begin with. For Marston, his BDSM polyamory, which theoretically (and probably actually) included lesbianism, was a universal utopia, which could and should incorporate everyone. Eisenman's lesbianism works more as a counterculture assertion—a way to define herself against mainstream characters and icons.

Using queerness as a way to demonstrate or solidify counterculture aesthetic edginess is a long-standing practice of the avant-garde. Indeed, Christopher Reed argues in his *Art and Homosexuality* that the identities of "avant-garde artist" and "homosexual" took shape together over the eighteenth and nineteenth centuries, reinforcing and inflecting each other (76). For example, Andrew Elfenbein describes the linking of the avant-garde and homosexuality in eighteenth-century British literary production:

Men and women who wanted a literary career but who lacked a university education, London connections, or inherited wealth seized the role of untutored genius to justify their entitlement to authorship. In striving to present their works as the works of geniuses, they needed to find ways to demonstrate the daring and wildness that, according to eighteenth-century treatises, geniuses supposedly possessed. Eighteenth-century treatises often associated this daring and wildness with androgyny and with unsuitability for traditional domestic arrangements. Although they stopped short of connecting androgyny with homosexuality, men and women aspiring to the role of genius did not. I argue that a frequent strategy for such authors was to challenge contemporary codes of sexual propriety in their works, and in some cases, in their lives. They used transgressive sexual representations, especially those of same-sex eroticism, to mark their perceived superiority to authors who merely reproduced codes of sexual propriety. (13–14)

Thus, Eisenman's use of queerness and her transgressive representations are deliberately deployed as daring markers of the avant-garde, separating her from pulp sources and their conventional consumers. In contrast, the plentiful queer themes in Marston/Peter's work were not self-consciously marked as daring or avant-garde—and, in large part as a result, they have not been recognized as queer. This erasure, in which the avant-garde uses queerness and queerness then becomes unrecognizable outside the avant-garde, adds a further irony to Christopher Reed's observation that "groundbreaking visualizations of the physical and emotional bonds between people of the same sex . . . often originated outside the avant-garde in realms of popular culture before being appropriated as avant-garde spectacle" (9). Reed argues that the avant-garde's disavowed-but-essential conservatism is closely tied to its eschewal of political engagement. The avant-garde, Reed says, is grounded "in ideals of self-expression" and individualism (204). He concludes that "though in theory individualism is given free rein in the avant-garde, in practice it is defined by rejecting association with subordinate groups (thus artists can express their Americanness and still be individuals, but to identify as a feminist or a homosexual is assessed as a limitation)" (204). Homosexuality as a group political identity in the 1970s and 1980s, according to Reed, "became a potent threat to avant-garde individuality" and provoked considerable backlash against artists who asserted that their homosexual identity was central to their art (204).

Obviously, it's difficult to look at Eisenman's *Wonder Woman* without thinking about lesbianism. Yet Eisenman's relationship to lesbianism as a collective political identity is ambivalent. Terese Ortega, in a thoughtful blog post on the drawing, suggests that "as a lesbian," the artist presumably identifies both with Wonder Woman and with Alice, both with "the big, triumphant Amazon woman and [with] the one who seeks knowledge by way of a woman's body." I don't disagree with that. But at the same time, it seems worth noting that it is difficult to identify with someone who has no head. In Marston/Peter's narratives, lesbian erotic dominance and submission occurs within hierarchical but sisterly communities. Eisenman, in contrast, imagines a lesbianism in which one partner is decapitated. Wonder Woman's triumph is one that cannot be mutually expressed; instead, it is built on Alice's transformation into a body, a tool—a phallus. Lesbianism becomes here not an alternative to masculine power but a way to trump it. No matter how big your penis may be, fellas, it won't be as big as Alice.

As Reed points out, many queer feminist artists in the 1990s, such as Del LaGrace Volcano and Catherine Opie, were attracted to, and utilized, representations of masculine power in their art. The results could be exciting and liberating—certainly, Wonder Woman seems to find them so in this image. But the use of masculinity could also at times reflexively reproduce power relationships that the feminist movement had worked to critique—such as, for example, the tendency to see women as brainless, sexualized phallic-substitutes. These conflicts were exacerbated, Reed argues, by the fact that queer women performing masculinity quickly received institutional support and accolades that had long been denied feminist artists (241).

Reed positions Eisenman at the center of these debates because of her success and because she has been vocally ambivalent about presenting her work in a lesbian or feminist context (242–243).[19] Reed quotes Eisenman as declaring, "I was born to be an artist, not a female or lesbian artist" (242). In a similar vein, the Jack Tilton Gallery includes the following statement from Eisenman next to a reproduction of *Wonder Woman*:

> I have a problem with having my work seen primarily as feminist. I am a feminist, but in a way that I don't even think about. It seems like second nature. I think we're all feminists by now. We know it's right. But I'm not making "feminist art" any more than I'm doing "lesbian art." I mean those things are there in the work because they're part of my life. But I spend more time watching TV every day than sleeping with my girlfriend. (Eisenman)

In more recent interviews, Eisenman has said that she feels increasingly that "subject matter is beside the point" and that she is more interested in technique than in what a painting is saying (Berry 7). These statements, as Reed notes, tend to denigrate collective politics in favor of avant-garde individualism (242). This point is made a good deal more painfully by Laurie Weeks's predictably playful prose tribute to Eisenman, in which the artist is figured, not nearly ironically enough, as a semidivine cyberpunk seer:

> So she [Eisenman] turns her unconscious into theater, plucking elements from the tsunami of cultural input swamping her nervous system, and detaches them from their underlying, normative logic to recast them as actors in fields of wide open possibility, like kids released from church into the wilderness. She effects some kind of phase shift that dematerializes the force field of our prescribed reality—agreed? (9)

It goes on like that for pages, a torrent of recycled pomo sludge burbling up exhausted reflex hiccups redolent with the same old revelatory insights as ever.

To be taken as an individual, it seems, requires a withering conformity. Thus, Eisenman, in discussing her focus on skill and technique in painting, admits, "It's scary because you are giving birth to this thing and you don't want it to be a mutant" (Berry 9). Lady Gaga would perhaps beg to differ—but in any case, avant-garde individualism as normative demand couldn't be expressed much more concisely. For

Marston and Hippolyte, perhaps, the cold statue of Diana can become a living, breathing bond through the power of faith and love. But for Eisenman, birth and art have to be approached more cautiously. Who knows what queer thing Alice might say, or be, if she weren't carefully kept in her place as ego accouterment?

Marston's queer Wonder Woman was a utopian vision, which reached out for identification and sisterhood across genders. Eisenman's is, according to her own assertions, just another way to say, "Hey! I'm avant-garde!" In eschewing lesbianism and feminism as constricting, she ends up trapped with the most limiting identity of all—that of genius. There's a gleeful rush in seeing Wonder Woman flaunt it ecstatically, but what an exhausting pose to have to maintain forever.

BEING TRUE TO WONDER WOMAN

At the beginning of this chapter, I suggested that the vast majority of Wonder Woman material post-Marston is superfluous. Now that I've discussed some of those latter-day iterations, I'd like to clarify what I meant by that.

First of all, when I say that the material is superfluous, I don't mean that it is completely worthless or uninteresting in its own right. As I've said, I think Nicole Eisenman's *Wonder Woman* illustration is very funny—it's also ingenious and, not least, skillfully and intriguingly rendered. Gail Simone's run on *Wonder Woman* was witty and entertainingly written. Even the Azzarello/Chiang series, which I loathe, is competent genre product—which puts it head and shoulders over the vast majority of mainstream superhero comics produced today. The same goes, more or less, for any number of other takes on the character. Darwyn Cookie's luscious, cartoony Wonder Woman cheesecake in *New Frontier* (2004–2005) is pleasing to look at. Denny O'Neil and Mike Sekowsky's 1968 determination to turn Wonder Woman into Mrs. Peel was energetic and had some great retro-constructivist-hippie art. The zombie Amazon fighters in the Wonder Woman animated film from 2009 are spectacularly creepy. Dara Birnbaum's seminal video-art piece *Technology/Transformation: Wonder Woman* (1978) shows Lynda Carter spinning into Wonder Woman over and over on a tape loop, which is pretty entertaining. And so forth. I'm sure I could find something worthwhile in even Robert Kanigher's run or Greg Rucka's if I had to.[20]

So when I call various versions of Wonder Woman superfluous, I don't mean that nobody could possibly like them or that they shouldn't have been created. What I mean is that, for the most part, they don't have anything particularly to do with Marston/Peter. They don't engage with Marston's themes; they don't build on his ideas; they don't reference or incorporate or think about Peter's art. They're about Wonder Woman the icon, but they don't have much, or anything, to do with Marston/Peter's comics. Certainly this is the case for the work discussed in this chapter. Azzarello/Chiang build their series on refuting Marston's legacy, but their take on that legacy is so impoverished that I wouldn't be surprised if they never read the original comics. Gail Simone deals directly and explicitly with Marston's themes of pacifism, but her handling of those themes is not related to Marston's even by negation. Nicole Eisenman's queering of the character, as I said, strongly suggests that she did not know the character was queer in the first place. It also seems significant that Eisenman, who is an accomplished visual mimic, makes no effort to reference Peter's art in her drawing.

It is possible to make too much of the disconnect. Wonder Woman has over the years largely retained the costume that Peter designed for her. She remains, as Marston made her, a feminist icon. She remains (again, as Marston made her) a sexual icon, at least if the occasional *Playboy* spread is to be trusted. Anyone who writes or draws Wonder Woman is making use of some of the elements that Marston and Peter created, even if they're getting those elements second- or third-hand. Indeed, those elements, in garbled form, have arguably been the very things that have tripped up so many latter-day Wonder Woman creators, who have been unable to untie the numerous knots—of feminism and bondage, pacifism and violence, gayness and heterosexuality—that Marston left scattered behind him.

But even granted such continuities, it's still hard to ignore the extent to which Marston and Peter have been obscured by the character they created. This happens with other creators as well—Superman today doesn't have a whole lot to do with the quasi-socialist, capitalist-thumping, high jumper that Joe Siegel and Jerry Shuster made. In

Marston and Peter's case, though, it seems especially sad, since, as I said in the introduction, the original comics are so much more interesting and vital than virtually anything that has been done with the character since. Even when Marston's *Wonder Woman* is explicitly discussed, his art, his thought, his conclusions, and his arguments are not available as a resource. Jeffrey A. Brown, for example, notes that *Wonder Woman* exemplifies the contradiction in presenting the action heroine as both empowered autonomous hero and sexual fetish object. But he seems mostly unaware of how passionately, intelligently, and thoroughly Marston and Peter thought about, and through, those contradictions.[21] At this stage, Wonder Woman the icon is just another female superhero with a few slightly unusual quirks. *Wonder Woman* as written by Marston/Peter, on the other hand, seems after seventy years like it has hardly been touched. My fondest hope for this book is that it encourages some people, whether Wonder Woman fans or otherwise, to go back and read those original comics. If enough do, perhaps someday Marston and Peter's legacy will be recognized not in a slew of indifferent Wonder Woman product but in any work created in the spirit of feminism, of peace, of queerness, and of love.

NOTES

INTRODUCTION

1 Jeffrey A. Brown discusses Wonder Woman's dual role as feminist icon for girls and fetish symbol, pointing to a toy Wonder Woman lamp owned by his daughter and the prevalence of sexy fetish Wonder Woman Halloween costumes (239–242).

2 The *Comics Journal*'s "Top 100 Comics" included Will Eisner's *The Spirit* (at 15), Jack Cole's *Plastic Man* (at 32), and C. C. Beck's *Captain Marvel* (at 79) but not *Wonder Woman*. A 2011 poll of comics' critics and professionals conducted by Robert Stanley Martin at *The Hooded Utilitarian*, a blog that I edit, had *The Spirit* at 18 out of the 115 top comics. *Plastic Man, Captain Marvel*, and *Wonder Woman* did not make the list.

3 Along with *Wonder Woman*, other second-tier comics from the era would probably include Simon and Kirby's *Captain America* and the early *Batman* comics. Mike Madrid (31) argues that Sheena, Queen of the Jungle, was actually the first female superhero. Whether or not Madrid is correct, Wonder Woman remains popularly considered the first female superhero, which is sufficient for the point I am making here.

4 Just to be clear, I am not saying that all comics-centered approaches are automatically inferior or uninteresting. Geoff Klock's *How to Read Super-Hero Comics and Why*, for example, is very much centered on superhero comics' intertextual history, and it is great. For that matter, Les Daniels's historical approach to Wonder Woman is useful and entertaining. My point is simply that comics-centered approaches to Marston/Peter tend to be interested in the character's historical importance, which is not the focus of this study.

5 Even scholars routinely claim that the lasso in the early comics is a lasso of truth. Call, for example, whose discussion of the early Wonder Woman comics is in most respects excellent, says that the lasso "compelled those bound

by it to speak the truth" and links it to Marston's scientific work on the lie detector (28). The lasso did compel people to speak the truth—but only as a subset of compelling them to do anything the wielder commanded. The lasso became a lasso of truth rather than a lasso of command only after Marston's death.

6 Biographical information about Marston has been taken from Bunn; Saunders 41–44; and Daniels 11. Ken Alder also includes extensive biographical information throughout his book, focusing especially on Marston's polygraph experiments.

7 Attributions are dicey since Marston (or "Charles Moulton") was credited in some cases for scripts he did not write. However, as best I can tell, Marston's last issues appear to have been *Wonder Woman #28*, *Sensation Comics #79*, and *Comics Cavalcade #29*.

CHAPTER ONE

1 The cover illustration is by Murphy Anderson and Jack Adler, both longtime artists for DC comics.

2 Marston passed away in May 1947; the story was published in *Wonder Woman #28*, with a cover date of March–April 1948.

3 Other writers who have made similar points about the centrality of bondage in *Wonder Woman* include Lillian Robinson (53), Lewis Call (35), and Jeffrey A. Brown (236). Brown insightfully notes that for Wonder Woman bondage is a "core weakness" since she loses her powers when a man welds her bracelets together.

4 Call (30) also notes the discomfort that *Wonder Woman* bondage has caused among feminists. There are many feminists who are not embarrassed by bondage, of course. As just a couple of examples, see Bright; and Friday.

5 Susie Bright (39) explicitly rejects the feminist argument that rape fantasies are the result of patriarchal brainwashing and implicitly suggests that they can be a way to work through, or at least an adjunct to working through, the trauma of sexual assault. See my essay "When Rape Is a Fantasy."

6 Alyssa Rosenberg provides a good example of the feminist case against *Twilight*; Laura Miller of the feminist case against *Hunger Games*. N. Berlatsky, "'Twilight' vs. 'Hunger Games,'" is a fuller discussion of my own take on both series. Laura Davis et al. summarize some feminist objections to *Fifty Shades of Grey*. See also Minou Arjomand et al., a roundtable on the *Fifty Shades of Grey* series that includes my own lengthier take on the books.

7 For a fairly pure version of the "it's all bad" approach, Frederic Wertham is the notorious example in comics. A smart version of the "it's all good" approach is Call's take on Wonder Woman, which sees the character as promot-

ing consensual and healthy BDSM relationships (27, though there are a couple of minor caveats on 55–56).

8 See, for example, Pamela Regis, who argues that Modleski's sweeping conclusions about romance fiction are based on too small a sample of works (6). For other more positive assessments of romance fiction, see Sherrie Silman, who answers yes to her title question, "Can Feminists Learn from Romance Novels?"; and Patricia Zakreski, who argues that popular romance writer Jennifer Crusie "uses the structure of romance narrative as a way of challenging what she sees as ideological 'lies,'" particularly around patriarchal and feminist essentialist notions about women. See also my own essay "The Regency as Feminist Utopia."

9 Janice Radway comes at these issues from an anthropological perspective. In interviewing a group of romance readers, she found that the women often saw the act of romance reading as a kind of protest or independence, in that they, who were always positioned as caretakers of others, were taking time to care for themselves. She also sees the romance plot itself as providing fantasies of care, and she notes that romances analyze women's needs accurately but could potentially be seen as defusing those needs or deflecting them from actual social change (213). Though somewhat different in emphasis, these arguments have significant overlap with Modleski's, as Radway acknowledges (7).

10 The *Wonder Woman Archive Edition* attributes the story to Murchison. However, Daniels indicates in his discussion of Murchison's scripting that Marston often co-wrote the scripts or worked closely with Murchison (74).

11 Interestingly, Regis identifies the Persephone myth as a central mythological archetype for romance novels (35).

12 In addition to Masson, Gale Swiontkowski (57–63) and Ward (101–118) both discuss Freud's changing positions on incest and their implications.

13 As some disparate examples of the continuing impact of Herman and Hirschman's work, see Jay Peters and Lenard Kaye, who cite the authors repeatedly in a paper on childhood sexual abuse among older women in institutional settings; Emma Miller, who discusses Herman and Hirschman's views in a consideration of child sexual abuse in Iris Murdoch's novels; and the interview with Herman for UC Berkeley's "Conversations with History" series (Herman, "Case of Trauma").

14 It is perhaps worth noting here that in *Sensation Comics #26* from February 1944, Wonder Woman is confronted with a mysterious impersonator who turns out to be, literally, her mother, Hippolyte. The mother-double is not an uncanny threat, however. Instead, she acts as Wonder Woman's protector and ally, saving her repeatedly. Mothers for Marston are virtually never frightening, except perhaps through their absence. A woman who is like her

mother is twice a woman, which, for Marston, makes her twice as good. I would argue, therefore, that Brian Attebery's suggestion (89) that Marston sees something "alarming" in Queen Hippolyte, or in mothers in general, is a decided misreading of the comics. (This misreading may be the result of the fact that Attebery tries to situate Marston in relation to contemporary pulp science fiction, rather than in relation to the Greek legends and psychological literature that seem to have been much more direct influences on his work.)

15 In contrast, in *Wonder Woman #11* (winter 1944), Wonder Woman's bracelets are welded together by the evil hypnotist Hypnota. Marston has Wonder Woman clearly state that it is only when a man chains her bracelets that she is rendered helpless (9C). Later, when it is revealed that Hypnota is a woman cross-dressing as a man, Wonder Woman explains again that her strength is only gone when a man binds her (16C). Marston was able to explicate the bondage rules when he wanted to. He just decided not to in *Wonder Woman #16*. For more on *Wonder Woman #11*, see chapter 3.

16 Portions of the following discussion are adapted from N. Berlatsky, "Edward, Daddy."

17 Ken Gelder (68–69) summarizes readings of Dracula that foreground incest. See also N. Berlatsky, "Wurdulak."

18 Melissa Ames summarizes some feminist objections to *Twilight* (39–40).

19 Portions of the following discussion are adapted from N. Berlatsky, "Villainy, Thy Name Is Woman."

20 The ambivalent relationship between masochism and feminism is discussed more fully in chapter 2.

21 Saunders (36–71) and Bunn both provide detailed accounts of Marston's theories.

22 Angelides argues at one point that Freud did not believe that sexual abuse was fantasy but rather "remained so committed to a belief in the reality of widespread child sexual abuse that he was driven to seek an explanation for why most people are not hysterical" (156). This argument seems problematic for two reasons. First, to make sexual abuse as common as Angelides suggests here effectively normalizes it; if it happens to everyone, then it is not really abuse and not really harmful. Second, Angelides's argument seems to directly contradict Freud's stated reason for abandoning the seduction theory, namely, that "such widespread perversions against children are not very probable" (*Complete Letters*, 264). Perhaps the truth is that Freud's thoughts on the frequency of sexual abuse varied, as did the theoretical weight that he was willing to give to that abuse.

23 The only real contender is Dr. Psycho, who is also seen in some ways as a rapist. See chapter 3.

CHAPTER TWO

1 There are some exceptions that test the rule. Wolverine (he of the foot-long claws) does actually use them to cut bread—in *Mini Marvels*, an all-ages humor strip utilizing elementary-school incarnations of the Marvel heroes, written and illustrated by Chris Giarrusso. There are also adult superhero comics in which there is little violence. One instance is the Wonder Woman story "She's a Wonder" by Phil Jimenez, in which our heroine is presented as an international humanitarian worker, going around the globe delivering speeches, encouraging relief efforts, and punching nobody. When I spoke to a group of students at Randolph Macon University in 2009, they uniformly (and not without reason) found this story boring to the point of incomprehensibility.

2 See, for instance, Morrison's story in *Animal Man #7*, "The Death of the Red Mask," for an example of a narrative in which the hero tries to resolve conflict without violence.

3 Some of the material that follows is adapted from N. Berlatsky, "The Amish Plot against the Superheroes," and N. Berlatsky, "Spider-Dove."

4 In that same essay, Niebuhr actually strongly endorsed pop wisdom in matters of war and peace. As he said, "One is persuaded to thank God in such times as these [that is, during World War II] that the common people maintain a degree of 'common sense,' that they preserve an uncorrupted ability to react against injustice and the cruelty of racial bigotry" (111)—though, of course, the idea that Marston and Peter were fighting racial bigotry is a bit of a stretch given their caricatures of the Japanese or, indeed, given their caricatures of blacks and Jews. In particular, see the grotesque depiction of Africans in *Wonder Woman #19*.

5 See, in this context, Jeet Heer's essay about Obama as comics fan.

6 Wonder Woman's mischievous enjoyment of power here puts pressure on Julie D. O'Reilly's suggestion that Wonder Woman lacks autonomy. O'Reilly argues that female superheroes such as Wonder Woman have to "prove their merit to a sanctioning institution" (274). Thus, Wonder Woman has to win at Amazon games in order to prove herself a hero, whereas Superman simply dons a costume. O'Reilly sees this as giving Wonder Woman a limited kind of heroism. Perhaps, though, it is simply a kind of heroism in which playing with your companions (whether by riding on kangaroos or forcing them to stand on their heads) is an enjoyable pleasure in itself and in which community and autonomy are not necessarily at odds. From Wonder Woman's perspective, after all, Superman becoming a hero by just putting on a costume might well seem sad or even pathetic—certainly less empowering than competing with, and triumphing with, your sisters.

7   Ben Saunders interestingly notes that Wonder Woman's cheerfulness separates her from most later female superheroes, who tend to be "moody, haunted, erratic and often untrustworthy" (156).

8   Valcour argues that "the love in loving leadership clearly did not represent sexuality or romantic emotions" (82). The link Marston draws here between training, motherhood, and genital stimulation seems like it calls Valcour's "clearly" into question.

9   See also *Emotions of Normal People*, in which Marston specifically says that psychoanalysts are wrong about the abnormality of the Oedipal complex and that "*passion felt by children of both sexes toward the mother is a natural and wholly desirable type of love response*" (303, italics in original).

10 The original lyric is "Money won't change you / but time will take you on," from the song "Money Won't Change You," originally released by James Brown in 1966.

11 See also Connell 213; Kilshaw 184; Barrett 77.

12 For a relevant discussion of gender in John Carpenter's *The Thing*, see N. Berlatsky, "Fecund Horror," and also N. Berlatsky, "What 'The Thing' Loses by Adding Women."

13 For one popular account that links Rosie the Riveter and Wonder Woman as examples of the improved position of women during the war, see Faludi 66. Against this interpretation, many researchers argue that there was little improvement in the status or image of women during the war—for example (in a British context), Plain 20. For a summary of some of the debates around American women's status, see Honey 2. Marston and Peter actually address the backlash against women's improved status in *Wonder Woman #5*, June–July 1943, in which the dwarfish misogynist Dr. Psycho creates an ectoplasmic construction of George Washington to falsely denounce women war workers. (See chapter 3 for a further discussion of Dr. Psycho.) Interestingly, if the war did not substantially affect the image of women, some explanations of *Wonder Woman*'s initial popularity, and *Wonder Woman*'s initial feminism, may need to be rethought. For one example of such an explanation, see Ben Saunders (37, 156), who suggests that *Wonder Woman* was dependent on the "wartime milieu." In contrast, Lillian Robinson seems closer to the mark when she says that it was Marston's death, not a loss of wartime idealism, that put an end to *Wonder Woman*'s feminism.

14 Sacher-Masoch had a complicated relationship with feminism. On the one hand, articles in *Auf der Höhe* (*At the Pinnacle*), the Leipzig magazine he edited, "show a clear pattern of support" of women's emancipation, according to Barbara Hyams (147). At the same time, however, Sacher-Masoch himself was capable of writing an article for his own publication in which (taking up

a misogynist trope that is with us yet) he blamed the decline of literature on novels written for women. Hyams concludes that Sacher-Masoch combined a "preoccupation with the war between the sexes" with "guarded support of political and social equality for women" (147). That support seems very guarded indeed at the conclusion of *Venus in Furs*. Hyams also notes in reference to Sacher-Masoch's oeuvre, "While the playful inversion of social norms and cultural values, taking on subordinate roles for the pleasure of it, can be an effective strategy for social criticism, it can also become another expression of hegemony" (150).

Thus, Gaylyn Studlar (interpreting Deleuze interpreting Sacher-Masoch) says that sadists "use fantasy for the specific aim of increasing their aggressive power to act. On the other hand, she says that masochistic "fantasy is aesthetically savored purely for itself" (24–25). In other words, for Sacher-Masoch/Deleuze, the imagined female power in masochism is not so much imagined *female power* as it is *imagined* female power. The fantasy is not alluring because it is about strong female; rather, strong females are alluring because they are a fantasy. Studlar does not follow the logic out, but it seems clear that, if this is the case, an actual feminist political program would undermine the whole masochistic appeal of feminine power—an appeal that is, precisely, its unreality. Powerful women are beautiful just so long as they are a childish dream. They are appealing because they are, like unicorns or dragons, so entirely improbable. No wonder Sacher-Masoch's support for feminism was ambivalent.

15 Again, Studlar's discussion of masochism as fantasy is relevant here (see note 14).

16 For complementary discussions of the place of fetishism and masochism in the original Siegel and Shuster *Superman*, see Eric Berlatsky, "Between Supermen"; and Noah Berlatsky, "Superthing."

17 Portions of the following discussion are adapted from Berlatsky, "Can Wonder Woman Be a Superdick? (Part 2)."

18 Irigaray has written extensively about incarnation, which she sees, in Rine's summation, as having "the potential to confound the traditional religious oppositions of divinity and humanity, spirit and flesh, body and Word" (6). Irigaray sees this potential as unrealized; male Christian discourse, as Rine says, "maintains a schism between the embodied and the divine, asserting a theology that only conceives of the male word becoming male flesh" (6). Marston's vision of Diana becoming Diana(s) can be seen as one possible answer to Irigaray's prayers: a pagan, female incarnation that collapses the binary between divine and human, individual and individual, and (as a comic) between body (or image) and word.

CHAPTER THREE

1 Peter Hegarty and Brian Mitchell Peters both write from something like Mad-dox's perspective, albeit in a more queer-positive vein. Peters, in particular, suggests that queer readers (whether gay men or lesbians) find a "subtextual gay text" in *Wonder Woman* comics (4). For Peters, that queer subtext is em-powering rather than (as it is for Maddox) funny. But whether empowering or not, the intent, or recognition, is with the reader, not (or at least not necessar-ily) with the creator.

2 Wertham is discussed in many histories of comics; for example, G. Jones 277; and Hajdu. Bart Beaty argues convincingly that Wertham's negative influence on the comics industry has been overstated (see especially 205).

3 Though Robbins does not discuss this aspect of the comic, *Wonder Woman* *#19* also happens to be hideously and inexcusably racist. In large part as a re-sult, it is probably the single worst Marston/Peter comic. I discuss it at length in N. Berlatsky, "Bound to Blog: Wonder Woman #19."

4 The famous first line of *Pride and Prejudice* reads, "It is a truth universally acknowledged, that a single man in possession of a good fortune, must be in want of a wife." Note that the reader's complicity in knowledge and ignorance is doubled by the irony; Austen says that men in possession of a good fortune must be in want of a wife, but she actually means that they aren't necessarily. Thus, the reader knows a truth unavailable to the characters, making the mi-lieu seem more "real" and further investing the reader in the novel's insight.

5 *Wonder Woman #5* is not numbered in the same manner as the rest of the *Wonder Woman* comics. The first part is numbered 1A, 2A, etc., but rather than being numbered 1B, 2B, the second part (and subsequent parts) are simply numbered 1, 2, 3. In this case, therefore, the page number "11" refers to the second part. Further page-number references to this comic will specify the part of the comic for clarity.

6 See Russo for a discussion of Sedgwick's sexuality.

7 I am indebted to Derik Badman's essay on Harry Peter's style for drawing my attention to the mysterious pink topiary in this panel.

8 For a fuller discussion, see chapter 1.

9 Ben Saunders (49–50) precedes me in intimating that Marston and the "psy-chologist" here may be one and the same.

10 For instance, Lamb quotes Elizabeth Marston's granddaughter Susan Gruppo-so as saying, "Grandmother once said to me: 'Maybe that's just the way things should be—everyone should just get along.'" The suggestion is that Elizabeth and Olive were tolerant of each other and so were able to live together. This, of course, neatly elides the extraordinarily close relationship between the two women (who named their children after each other). It also skirts the pos-

sibility that Elizabeth and Olive's relationship may have prompted them to an interest in other kinds of tolerance.

11 Information in this paragraph is taken from Jill Lepore, *The Secret History of Wonder Woman*, New York: Alfred A. Knopf, 2014. Because of the timing of release, I was unable to see a final printed copy, and used a preview version without page numbers.

12 See also Bart Beaty (201) on Wertham's convincing reading of the homosexual subtext of Batman and Robin's relationship. Along the same lines, see Kripal's claim that "the difficult truth is that Wertham is a complex and often frankly convincing read" (165).

13 Sharon Marcus to the author, email, September 16, 2011; quoted by permission.

14 "A Boy Named Sue" is a Shel Silverstein song made famous by Johnny Cash, who recorded it in 1969.

15 The discussion of Pussy Galore is adapted in part from N. Berlatsky, "Jack Hill and Rape."

16 Eve Sedgwick's *Between Men* discusses at length the way in which homosexual desire is routed through competition over, or supposed desire for, women. Sedgwick focuses particularly on English nineteenth-century literature, but her insights can often be applied to Western culture more broadly.

17 I have some additional discussion of Susie Bright in Berlatsky, "Susie Bright and the Haters."

18 The following discussion is adapted in part from Berlatsky, "Bound to Blog: The Private Life of Julius Caesar."

19 A "Mary Sue" is a character who represents an idealized image of the author. It is a term often used in discussions of Internet writing and Internet fan fiction.

20 This is the origin of the Amazon's giant space kangaroos. Before this point, they rode giant bunnies. As far as I know, Marston never provided an origin for the giant bunnies.

21 Dr. Poison, a woman dressed as a man, is the villain in *Sensation Comics #2*. In *Wonder Woman #28*, Dr. Poison returns, along with fellow female-to-male cross-dressers Hypnota and the Blue Snowman.

22 The Blue Snowman appears first in *Sensation Comics #59* and returns in *Wonder Woman #28*.

23 My discussion of *Solaris* is fleshed out more fully in Berlatsky, "Lies Real Enough to Love."

24 Butler points out the Orientalist overtones of Kristeva's list of matriarchal comparisons (121).

25 Some of this section is adapted from Berlatsky, "Bound to Blog: Wonder Woman #1."

26 The painting can be seen at http://commons.wikimedia.org/wiki/
File:Gustave_Courbet_014.jpg.

27 Courbet did specifically connect women's reproductive organs and creativity
in his (in)famous pornographic painting *The Origin of the World*. I discuss
this painting in Berlatsky, "The Origin of Catwoman's Ass."

CONCLUSION

1 I discuss Delany, *League of One*, Kanigher, and many other later iterations
of Wonder Woman in the series "Only One Can Wear the Venus Girdle," at
my blog *The Hooded Utilitarian*. See http://hoodedutilitarian.com/category/
series/only-one-can-wear-the-venus-girdle/.

2 For examples of positive reviews, see E. Cole; and Thompson, "Review."
Thompson reconsiders the series in a March 26, 2012, review but continues
to praise Azzarello and Chiang for their creativity and professionalism ("She
Has No Head!")

3 Some parts of the following discussion are adapted from N. Berlatsky, "Only
One Can Wear the Venus Girdle." I discuss later issues in the run in N. Berlatsky, "Wonder Woman's Violent, Man-Pandering Second Act."

4 As I've mentioned before, in Marston's conception, the lasso caused people
to submit; it could be used to force confessions, but only as a subset of its
more generalized power of control. Sometime after Marston—probably in the
1950s—the lasso's power was changed from submission to truth, and it has
remained so up to the present.

5 *Hippolyte* ends with an *e* in Marston/Peter, but subsequent authors, including
Azzarello, have tended to end her name with an *a*.

6 Azzarello/Chiang are effectively depowering Hippolyta here; before she could
make life on her own, now she cannot. This depowering could be seen as in
line with Richard J. Gray II's argument that supeheroines in contemporary
film are allowed to be powerful, but only up to a point. That point, Gray
argues, is when toughness starts to detract from sex appeal. In this case,
Hippolyta's self-sufficiency meant she could do away with men altogether, a
state of affairs that, Azzarello seems to have felt, violated what Gray calls "the
delicate balance between sex appeal and strength" (81).

7 Rape-revenge narratives are discussed more fully toward the end of chapter 1.

8 Gordon also notes that women's disempowerment tends to increase the likeli-
hood of women abusing their children, not to decrease it (63). As I mentioned in chapter 1, Steven Angelides raises some objections to the argument
that feminism aids victims of abuse on the grounds that anti-incest feminism
desexualizes children, which he argues can have damaging consequences.
Angelides never really grapples with the way in which his critique fits into the

narrative of feminists as castrators, and I think that Azzarello and Chiang, by making that link clear, do more to undermine Angelides than he does to support them. In any case, Angelides's critique is based, as he says repeatedly, in queer theory, and as we'll see, one of Azzarello and Chiang's innovations is to leech the queerness out of *Wonder Woman*.

9   My thanks to Vom Marlowe for pointing out the Hephaestus rape legends.

10   Ben Saunders discusses some of these contradictions and relates them to *Wonder Woman* (39–41). Josine H. Blok discusses them in more depth (1–3, 431), arguing that "paradox appears at the heart" of many Greek discussions of the Amazons (434).

11   Andrea Dworkin's *Right-Wing Women* is an extended discussion of the ways in which liberal men have often been every bit as misogynist as right-wing men.

12   Parts of the following discussion are adapted from N. Berlatsky, "Gail Simone Hearts Diana Sue."

13   The Green Lanterns are a group of space warriors/protectors/superheroes from different worlds. Each is equipped with a superscientific ring that projects green energy into any form they choose. Like the Khund, the Green Lantern Corps are DC characters of long standing. As this suggests, Simone's plots are littered with obsessive references to DC history and continuity porn, for better or worse.

14   Russell states in his essay "The Future of Pacifism" that he believes that "some wars are worth fighting" and gives as an example not only World War II but the American Revolution. Coincidentally, Russell's essay appeared in the same 1943–1944 issue of the *American Spectator* as William Marston's essay "Why 100,000,000 Americans Read Comics."

15   Noddings bases her maternal morality in large part on an evolutionary behaviorism that I find dubious, to put it mildly. Among other things, she never convincingly explains why an evolutionary basis of care is necessary for her ethics, when historical or cultural claims seem as if they would work just as well. However, for my purposes here, the evolutionary aspects of her theories are largely beside the point, and so I have avoided discussing them in detail.

16   Of course, many women side with their own without any particular sorrow and even with glee, just as many men do. Noddings is presumably describing the ideal of her ethic, rather than actual observable behavior.

17   Remember, the one instance in Marston/Peter in which Wonder Woman does convert particular men into her own servants, it is specifically under the orders of Aphrodite—who has to convince a reluctant Wonder Woman to take on the task. See chapter 2.

18   Thanks to Sharon Marcus for bringing this piece to my attention.

19 Reed reproduces Eisenman's *Wonder Woman* (242) but does not provide an analysis of it. My discussion is, however, informed by his comments on the artist more generally.

20 Again, I have blogged about a whole range of latter-day Wonder Woman iterations: http://hoodedutilitarian.com/category/series/only-one-can-wear-the-venus-girdle.

21 Jeffrey A. Brown deals with Marston directly (235–237) in his chapter on Wonder Woman and female action heroes (233–246). Again, though Brown talks about Marston, he doesn't engage with his ideas to any meaningful extent. For example, Brown sees the fetishization of women as undermining the role of empowered action heroine. But for Marston, this was the point; fetishization and bondage play in Marston is meant deliberately to question or destabilize the (in Marston's view, masculine) action narrative of violence and force.

WORKS CITED

Alder, Ken. *The Lie Detectors: The History of an American Obsession.* New York: Free Press, 2007.

Allison, Anne. *Permitted and Prohibited Desires: Mothers, Comics, and Censorship in Japan.* Berkeley: University of California Press, 2000.

AM Azure Consulting. *Disc Based Personality Assessment: History and Current Status, and the Fascinating Life of William Marston.* 2011. http://www.amazureconsulting.com/files/1/74900324/DISCPastAndPresentAndWilliamMarston.pdf.

Ames, Melissa. "Twilight Follows Tradition: Analyzing 'Biting' Critiques of Vampire Narratives for Their Portrayals of Gender and Sexuality." *Bitten by Twilight: Youth Culture, Media, and the Vampire Franchise.* Ed. Melissa A. Click, Jennifer Stevens Aubrey, and Elizabeth Behm-Morawitz. New York: Peter Lang, 2010. 37–54.

Angelides, Steven. "Feminism, Child Sexual Abuse, and the Erasure of Child Sexuality." *GLQ: A Journal of Lesbian and Gay Studies* 10.2 (2004): 141–177.

Ariès, Philippe. *Centuries of Childhood: A Social History of Family Life.* London: Pimlico, 1996.

Arjomand, Minou, Noah Berlatsky, Jane Gallop, Hillary A. Hallett, Claire Jarvis, Bethany Schneider, and Marianna Torgovnick. "Virtual Roundtable on 50 Shades of Grey." *Public Books.* June 5, 2013. http://www.publicbooks.org/fiction/virtual-roundtable-on-fifty-shades-of-grey.

Attebery, Brian. *Decoding Gender in Science Fiction.* New York: Routledge, 2002.

Austen, Jane. *Pride and Prejudice.* 1813. Project Gutenberg. August 26, 2008. http://www.gutenberg.org/ebooks/1342.

Azzarello, Brian, and Cliff Chiang. *Wonder Woman #7.* May 2012.

Azzarello, Brian, Cliff Chiang, and Tony Akins. *Wonder Woman Volume 1: Blood.* New York: DC Comics, 2012.

Badman, Derik. "A Peter That Never Existed." *Hooded Utilitarian.* May 14, 2012. http://hoodedutilitarian.com/2012/05/a-peter-that-never-existed/.

Barrett, Frank J. "The Organizational Construction of Hegemonic Masculinity: The Case of the US Navy." *The Masculinities Reader.* Ed. Stephen M. Whitehead and Frank J. Barrett. Malden, MA: Blackwell, 2001. 77–99.

Beaty, Bart. *Fredric Wertham and the Critique of Mass Culture.* Jackson: University Press of Mississippi, 2005.

Berlatsky, Eric. "Between Supermen: Homosociality, Misogyny, and Triangular Desire in the Earliest Superman Stories." *Comics Forum.* March 11, 2013. http://comicsforum.org/2013/04/11/between-supermen-homosociality-misogyny-and-triangular-desire-in-the-earliest-superman-stories-by-eric-berlatsky/.

Berlatsky, Noah. "The Amish Plot against the Superheroes." *Hooded Utilitarian.* September 9, 2010. http://hoodedutilitarian.com/2010/09/the-amish-plot-against-the-superheroes/.

———. "Bound to Blog: The Private Life of Julius Caesar." *Hooded Utilitarian.* September 6, 2009. http://www.hoodedutilitarian.com/2009/09/bound-to-blog-the-private-life-of-julius-caesar/.

———. "Bound to Blog: Wonder Woman #1." *Hooded Utilitarian.* April 2, 2009. http://www.hoodedutilitarian.com/2009/04/bound-to-blog-wonder-woman-1/.

———. "Bound to Blog: Wonder Woman #19 (Black and White and Startlingly Offensive All Over)." *Hooded Utilitarian.* November 2, 2009. http://hoodedutilitarian.com/2009/11/bound-to-blog-wonder-woman-19-black-and-white-and-startlingly-offensive-all-over/.

———. "Can Wonder Woman Be a Superdick? (Part Two)." *Hooded Utilitarian.* May 25, 2011. http://www.hoodedutilitarian.com/2011/05/can-wonder-woman-be-a-superdick-part-2/.

———. "Comics in the Closet, Part 1." *Hooded Utilitarian.* October 18, 2009. http://hoodedutilitarian.blogspot.com/2009/10/comics-in-closet-part-1.html.

———. "Edward, Daddy." *Hooded Utilitarian.* April 11, 2012. http://hoodedutilitarian.com/2012/04/edward-daddy/.

———. "Fecund Horror." *Gay Utopia.* December 20, 2007. http://gayutopia.blogspot.com/2007/12/noah-berlatsky-fecund-horror_12.html.

———. "Gail Simone Hearts Diana Sue." *Hooded Utilitarian.* May 17, 2009. http://www.hoodedutilitarian.com/2009/05/gail-simone-hearts-diana-sue/.

———. "Jack Hill and Rape." *Hooded Utilitarian.* March 27, 2008. http://hoodedutilitarian.com/2008/03/jack-hill-and-rape/.

———. "Lies Real Enough to Love." *Hooded Utilitarian.* January 9, 2011. http://hoodedutilitarian.com/2011/01/lies-real-enough-to-love/.

———. "Only One Can Wear the Venus Girdle, You Patriarchal Dipshit." *Hooded Utilitarian.* April 23, 2012. http://www.hoodedutilitarian.com/2012/04/only-one-can-wear-the-venus-girdle-you-patriarchal-dipshit/.

———. "The Origin of Catwoman's Ass." *Hooded Utilitarian.* June 28, 2012. http://

www.hoodedutilitarian.com/2012/06/the-origin-of-catwomans-ass/.

———. "The Regency as Feminist Utopia." *Hooded Utilitarian*. October 30, 2013. http://www.hoodedutilitarian.com/2013/10/the-regency-as-feminist-utopia/.

———. "Spider-Dove." *Hooded Utilitarian*. November 4, 2012. http://hoodedutilitarian.com/2012/11/spider-dove/.

———. "Superthing." *Hooded Utilitarian*. February 12, 2012. http://hoodedutilitarian.com/2012/02/superthing/.

———. "Susie Bright and the Haters." *Hooded Utilitarian*. June 23, 2012. http://hoodedutilitarian.com/2012/06/susie-bright-and-the-haters/.

———. "'Twilight' vs. 'Hunger Games': Why Do So Many Grown-Ups Hate Bella?" *Atlantic*. November 15, 2011. http://www.theatlantic.com/entertainment/archive/2011/11/twilight-vs-hunger-games-why-do-so-many-grown-ups-hate-bella/248439/.

———. "Villainy, Thy Name Is Woman (Bound to Blog): Wonder Woman #28." *Hooded Utilitarian*. May 1, 2012. http://hoodedutilitarian.com/2012/05/villainy-thy-name-is-women-bound-to-blog-wonder-woman-28/.

———. "What 'The Thing' Loses by Adding Women." *Atlantic*. October 13, 2011. http://www.theatlantic.com/entertainment/archive/2011/10/what-the-thing-loses-by-adding-women/246648/.

———. "When Rape Is a Fantasy." *Atlantic*. June 17, 2013. http://www.theatlantic.com/sexes/archive/2013/06/when-rape-is-a-fantasy/276933/.

———. "Wonder Woman's Violent, Man-Pandering Second Act." *Atlantic*. February 5, 2013. http://www.theatlantic.com/sexes/archive/2013/02/wonder-womans-violent-man-pandering-second-act/272871/.

———. "Wurdulak." *Hooded Utilitarian*. September 18, 2007. http://www.hoodedutilitarian.com/2007/09/wurdulak/.

Berry, Ian. *Nicole Eisenman: The Way We Weren't*. Saratoga Springs, NY: Francis Young Tang Teaching Museum and Art Gallery at Skidmore College, 2010.

Blok, Josine H. *The Early Amazons: Modern and Ancient Perspectives on a Persistent Myth*. New York: Brill, 1995.

Boesel, Chris, "The Apophasis of Divine Freedom: Saving 'the Name' and the Neighbor from Human Mastery." *Apophatic Bodies: Negative Theology, Incarnation, and Relationality*. Ed. Chris Boesel and Catherine Keller. New York: Fordham University Press, 2010. 307–328.

Bright, Susie. *Sexual Reality*. Santa Cruz, CA: Bright Stuff, 2008.

Brown, Jeffrey A. *Dangerous Curves: Action Heroines, Gender, Fetishism, and Popular Culture*. Jackson: University of Mississippi Press, 2011.

Brownmiller, Susan. *Against Our Will: Men, Women, and Rape*. New York: Simon and Schuster, 1975.

Bunn, Geoffrey C. "The Lie Detector, *Wonder Woman* and Liberty: The Life and

Work of William Moulton Marston." *History of the Human Sciences* 10.1 (February 1997): 91–119.

Butler, Judith. *Gender Trouble*. New York: Routledge, 1990.

Call, Lewis. *BDSM in American Science Fiction and Fantasy*. New York: Palgrave Macmillan, 2013.

Clover, Carol J. *Men, Women, and Chain Saws: Gender in the Modern Horror Film*. Princeton, NJ: Princeton University Press, 1992.

Coakley, Sarah. *Powers and Submissions: Spirituality, Philosophy and Gender*. Malden, MA: Blackwell, 2002.

Cole, Eliot. "Review: Wonder Woman #8 by Brian Azzarello and Cliff Chiang." *Bleeding Cool*. April 22, 2012. http://www.bleedingcool.com/2012/04/22/review-wonder-woman-by-brian-azzarello-cliff-chiang/.

Cole, Herbert. "Sleeping Beauty." 1906. *SurLaLune Fairy Tales*. Last updated September 30, 2007. http://www.surlalunefairytales.com/illustrations/sleeping-beauty/colesleep2.html.

Collins, Judy. Introduction. *Wonder Woman Archives Volume 1*. By William Marston and H. G. Peter. New York: DC Comics, 1998. 5–7.

Collins, Suzanne. *Catching Fire*. New York: Scholastic, 2009.

———. *The Hunger Games*. New York: Scholastic, 2008.

———. *Mockingjay*. New York: Scholastic, 2010.

Connell, R. W. *Masculinities*. Cambridge, UK: Polity, 2005.

Core, Philip. *Camp: The Lie That Tells the Truth*. New York: Delilah, 1984.

Daniels, Les. *Wonder Woman: The Complete History*. San Francisco: Chronicle, 2000.

Davis, Alan, and Mark Farmer. *JLA: The Nail*. New York: DC Comics, 1999.

Davis, Laura, Gina Barreca, Meg Barker. "The Debate: Is the Submissive Relationship in *50 Shades of Grey* Degrading to Women?" *Independent*. July 4, 2012. http://blogs.independent.co.uk/2012/07/04/the-debate-does-the-sadomasochism-seen-in-50-shades-of-grey-degrading-to-women/.

Dawn of the Dead. Dir. George Romero. United Film Distribution Company, 1978. Film.

DeJean, Joan. *Fictions of Sappho, 1546–1937*. Chicago: University of Chicago Press, 1989.

Deleuze, Gilles. "Coldness and Cruelty." *Masochism*. New York: Zone, 1991. 9–138.

Dworkin, Andrea. *Right-Wing Women: The Politics of Domesticated Females*. New York: Perigee, 1983.

Early, Frances H., and Kathleen Kennedy. Introduction. *Athena's Daughters: Television's New Women Warriors*. Ed. Frances H. Early and Kathleen Kennedy. Syracuse, NY: Syracuse University Press, 2003. 1–10.

Eisenman, Nicole. "*Wonder Woman 1996*." *Jack Tilton Gallery*. Retrieved July 27, 2012. http://www.artseensoho.com/Art/TILTON/eisenman96/ei2.html.

Elfenbein, Andrew. *Romantic Genius: The Prehistory of a Homosexual Role*. New York: Columbia University Press, 1999.

Eliot, George. *Middlemarch*. 1871–1872. Project Gutenberg. May 24, 2008. http://www.gutenberg.org/ebooks/145.

Elshtain, Jean Bethke. *Women and War*. New York: Basic, 1987.

Esterson, Allen. "Jeffrey Masson and Freud's Seduction Theory: A New Fable Based on Old Myths." *History of the Human Sciences* 11.1 (1998): 1–21.

Faludi, Susan. *Backlash: The Undeclared War against American Women*. New York: Three Rivers, 2006.

Firestone, Shulamith. *The Dialectic of Sex: The Case for Feminist Revolution*. New York: Bantam, 1970.

Fischer, Craig. "Emotional Hands: Ditko, Anxiety, Repression." *Thought Balloonists*. June 28, 2009. http://www.thoughtballoonists.com/2009/06/nervous-hands-ditko-anxiety-and-repression-.html.

Fleming, Ian. *Goldfinger*. 1959. Las Vegas, NV: Thomas & Mercer, 2012.

Freud, Sigmund. "The Aetiology of Hysteria." April 21, 1896. Trans. James Strachey. *The Assault on Truth: Freud's Suppression of the Seduction Theory*. By Jeffrey Moussaieff Masson. New York: Farrar, Straus and Giroux, 1984. 251–282.

———. *The Complete Letters of Sigmund Freud to Wilhelm Fliess, 1887–1904*. Trans. and ed. Jeffrey Moussaieff Masson. Cambridge, MA: Harvard University Press, 1985.

Friday, Nancy. *My Secret Garden: Women's Sexual Fantasies*. New York: Pocket, 1973.

Fried, Michael. "Courbet's 'Femininity.'" *Courbet Reconsidered*. Ed. Sarah Faunce and Linda Nochlin. New Haven, CT: Yale University Press, 1988. 43–53.

Frisch, Marc-Oliver. "DC Comics Month-to-Month Sales: April 2012." *Beat*. June 6, 2012. http://www.comicsbeat.com/2012/06/06/dc-comics-month-to-month-sales-april-2012/.

Fussell, Paul. *The Great War and Modern Memory*. New York: Oxford University Press, 1975.

Gelder, Ken. *Reading the Vampire*. New York: Routledge, 1994.

Giarrusso, Chris. "The French Bread." *Mini Marvels: The Secret Invasion*. New York: Marvel Comics, 2009.

Gleaves, David H., and Elsa Hernandez. "Recent Reformulations of Freud's Development and Abandonment of His Seduction Theory: Historical/Scientific Clarification or a Continued Assault on Truth?" *History of Psychology* 2.4 (1999): 324–354.

Goldfinger (Special Edition). Dir. Guy Hamilton. MGM, 1965. DVD, 2002. DVD.

The Good War and Those Who Refused to Fight It. Dir. Judith Ehrlich and Rick Tejada-Flores. First Run Features, 2011.

Gordon, Linda "The Politics of Sexual Abuse: Notes from American History." *Feminist Review* 28 (Spring 1988): 56–64.

Gray, Richard J., II. "Vivacious Vixens and Scintillating Super-Hotties." *The 21st Century Superhero*. Ed. Richard Gray II and Betty Kaklamanidou. Jefferson, NC: McFarland, 2011. 75–93.

Grimké, Sarah. "Rights and Responsibilities of Women." *The Libertarian Reader: Classic and Contemporary Writings from Lao-Tzu to Milton Friedman*. Ed. David Boaz. New York: Free, 1997. 92–93.

Gubar, Susan. "'This Is My Rifle, This Is My Gun': World War II and the Blitz on Women." *Behind the Lines: Gender and the Two World Wars*. Ed. Margaret Randolph Higonnet, Jane Jenson, Sonya Michel, and Margaret Collins Weitz. New Haven, CT: Yale University Press, 1987. 227–259.

Hajdu, David. *The Ten-Cent Plague: The Great Comic-Book Scare and How It Changed America*. New York: Macmillan, 2008.

Halberstam, Judith. *Female Masculinity*. Durham, NC: Duke University Press, 1998.

Hanley, Tim. *Wonder Woman Unbound: The Curious History of the World's Most Famous Heroine*. Chicago: Chicago Review Press, 2014.

Hauerwas, Stanley. *Dispatches from the Front: Theological Engagements with the Secular*. Durham, NC: Duke University Press, 1994.

Heer, Jeet. "Obama the Comics Fan?" *sans everything*. November 10, 2008. http://sanseverything.wordpress.com/2008/11/10/obama-the-comics-fan/.

Hegarty, Peter. "Queerying Lesbian and Gay Psychology's Coming of Age: Was History Just Kid Stuff?" *The Ashgate Research Companion to Queer Theory*. Ed. Michael O'Rourke and Noreen Giffney. Burlington, VT: Ashgate, 2009. 514–544. http://www.academia.edu/3039054/Queerying_lesbian_and_gay_psychologys_coming_of_age_Was_history_just_kid_stuff.

Hergé. *The Adventures of Tintin*. Vol. 1. New York: Little, Brown, 1994.

Herman, Judith Lewis. "The Case of Trauma and Recovery: Conversation with Judith Herman, M.D." Interview by Harry Kreisler. Conversations with History: Institute of International Studies, UC Berkeley. 2000. http://globetrotter.berkeley.edu/people/Herman/herman-cono.html.

Herman, Judith Lewis, with Lisa Hirschman. *Father-Daughter Incest*. Cambridge, MA: Harvard University Press, 2000.

Honey, Maureen. *Creating Rosie the Riveter: Class, Gender, and Propaganda during World War II*. Amherst: University of Massachusetts Press, 1984.

Hyams, Barbara. "Causal Connections: The Case of Sacher-Masoch." *One Hundred Years of Masochism: Literary Texts, Social and Cultural Contexts*. Ed. Michael C. Finke and Carl Nieker. Atlanta: Rodopi, 1994. 139–154.

Irigaray, Luce. "Divine Women." *Sexes and Genealogies*. Trans. Gillian C. Gill. New York: Columbia University Press, 1993. 55–73.

————. *Key Writings*. New York: Continuum, 2004.

————. "This Sex Which Is Not One." *This Sex Which Is Not One*. Trans. Catherine Porter. Ithaca, NY: Cornell University Press, 1985. 23–33.

I Spit on Your Grave. Dir. Meir Zarchi. Cinemagic Pictures, 1978.

James, E. L. *Fifty Shades Darker*. New York: Random House, 2011.

————. *Fifty Shades Freed*. New York: Random House, 2011.

————. *Fifty Shades of Grey*. New York: Random House, 2011.

Jarrell, Randall. "The Death of the Ball Turret Gunner." *The Complete Poems*. New York: Farrar, Straus and Giroux, 1969. *Poets.org*. http://www.poets.org/viewmedia.php/prmMID/15309.

Jarvis, Christina S. *The Male Body at War: American Masculinity during World War II*. DeKalb: Northern Illinois University Press, 2004.

Jewett, Robert, and John Shelton Lawrence. *Captain America and the Crusade against Evil: The Dilemma of Zealous Nationalism*. Cambridge, UK: Eerdmans, 2003.

Jones, Gerard. *Men of Tomorrow: Geeks, Gangsters, and the Birth of the Comic Book*. New York: Basic, 2005.

Jones, One of the Jones Boys. "How Do You Solve a Problem Like Diana?" *Hooded Utilitarian*. May 2, 2012. http://hoodedutilitarian.com/2012/05/how-do-you-solve-a-problem-like-diana/.

Kilshaw, Susie. *Impotent Warriors: Perspectives on Gulf War Syndrome, Vulnerability, and Masculinity*. Oxford, UK: Berghahn, 2009.

Klock, Geoff. *How to Read Superhero Comics and Why*. New York: Continuum, 2002.

Kripal, Jeffrey J. *Mutants and Mystics: Science Fiction, Superhero Comics, and the Paranormal*. Chicago: University of Chicago Press, 2011.

Kristeva, Julia. *Desire in Language: A Semiotic Approach to Literature and Art*. Ed. Leon S. Roudiez. Trans. Thomas Gora, Alice Jardine, and Leon S. Roudiez. New York: Columbia University Press, 1980.

Lacan, Jacques. *Écrits: A Selection*. Trans. Bruce Fink. New York: Norton, 2002.

Ladenson, Elisabeth. "Lovely Lesbians; or, Pussy Galore." *GLQ* 7.3 (2001): 417–423.

————. *Proust's Lesbianism*. Ithaca, NY: Cornell University Press, 1999.

————. "The Special Issue That Shagged Me." *GLQ* 7.3 (2001): 371–376.

Lamb, Marguerite. "Who Was Wonder Woman?" *Bostonia*. Fall 2001. http://www.bu.edu/bostonia/fall01/woman/.

Lee, Stan, and Steve Ditko. *Amazing Fantasy #15*. August 1962. Rpt. in *Essential Spider-Man Volume 1*. New York: Marvel Comics, 1998.

Leed, Eric J. *No Man's Land: Combat and Identity in World War I*. Cambridge: Cambridge University Press, 1979.

Lewis, C. S. *The Lion, the Witch, and the Wardrobe*. 1950. New York: Macmillan, 1970.

————. *That Hideous Strength*. 1945. London: Bodley Head, 1965.

Maddox. "Unintentionally Sexual Comic Book Covers." *The Best Page in the Universe*. http://www.thebestpageintheuniverse.net/c.cgi?u=uscc_part1.

Madrid, Mike. *The Supergirls: Fashion, Feminism, Fantasy, and the History of Comic Book Heroines*. Minneapolis, MN: Exterminating Angel, 2009.

Marcus, Sharon. *Between Women: Friendship, Desire, and Marriage in Victorian England*. Princeton, NJ: Princeton University Press, 2007.

———. "Wonder Woman vs. *Wonder Woman*." *Hooded Utilitarian*. May 7, 2012. http://hoodedutilitarian.com/2012/05/wonder-woman-vs-wonder-woman/.

Marston, William. *Emotions of Normal People*. New York: Harcourt, Brace, 1928.

———. *The Private Life of Julius Caesar* (alt. title *Venus with Us: A Story of the Caesar*). New York: Universal, 1943.

———. "Why 100,000,000 Americans Read Comics." *American Scholar* 13.1 (1944): 35–44.

Marston, William, C. Daly King, and Elizabeth H. Marston. *Integrative Psychology: A Study of Unit Response*. London: Kegan Paul, Trench, Trubner, 1931.

Marston, William, and H. G. Peter. *Wonder Woman Archives Volume 1*. New York: DC Comics, 1998.

———. *Wonder Woman Archives Volume 2*. New York: DC Comics, 2000.

———. *Wonder Woman Archives Volume 7*. New York: DC Comics, 2012.

Martin, Robert Stanley. "The Top 115." *Hooded Utilitarian*. August 5, 2011. http://hoodedutilitarian.com/2011/08/the-top-115/.

Masson, Jeffrey Moussaieff. *The Assault on Truth: Freud's Suppression of the Seduction Theory*. New York: Farrar, Straus and Giroux, 1984.

Melville, Herman. *Benito Cereno. The Piazza Tales*. 1856. Project Gutenberg. May 18, 2005. http://www.gutenberg.org/files/15859/15859-h/15859-h.htm.

Merton, Thomas. *Thomas Merton on Peace*. New York: McCall, 1971.

Meyer, Stephenie. *Breaking Dawn*. New York: Little, Brown, 2008.

———. *Eclipse*. New York: Little, Brown, 2007.

———. *New Moon*. New York: Little, Brown, 2006.

———. *Twilight*. New York: Little, Brown, 2005.

Miller, Emma, "'We Must Not Forget That There *Was* a Crime': Incest, Domestic Violence, and Textual Memory in the Novels of Iris Murdoch." *Journal of Literature and Trauma Studies* 1.2 (Fall 2012): 65–94.

Miller, Laura. "'The Hunger Games' vs. 'Twilight.'" *Salon.com*. September 5, 2010. http://www.salon.com/2010/09/05/hunger_games_twilight/.

Modleski, Tania. *Feminism without Women: Culture and Criticism in a "Postfeminist" Age*. New York: Routledge, 1991.

———. *Loving with a Vengeance: Mass-Produced Fantasies for Women*. 2nd ed. New York: Routledge, 2008.

———. "Q&A: Tania Modleski, Feminist Film Critic." *Lazy Scholar*. March 24,

2010. http://thelazyscholar.com/2010/03/24/interview-tania-modleski-feminist-film-critic/.

Moore, Mark. "Pacifism Is Not Passiveism." *The John 3:30 Group*. September 11, 2008. http://markmoore.org/330/archives/2008_09_01_archive.html.

Morrison, Grant, Chas Truog, and Doug Hazlewood. *Animal Man, Book 3: Deus Ex Machina*. New York: Vertigo, 2003.

——. "The Death of the Red Mask." *Animal Man #7*. New York: Vertigo, January 1989.

Mulvey, Laura. "Visual Pleasure and Narrative Cinema." *Film Theory and Criticism: Introductory Readings*. Ed. Leo Braudy and Marshall Cohen. New York: Oxford University Press, 1999. 833–844.

Mungello, D. E. *Drowning Girls in China: Female Infanticide since 1650*. Lanham, MD: Rowman and Littlefield, 2008.

Niebuhr, Reinhold. "Why the Christian Church Is Not Pacifist." *The Essential Reinhold Niebuhr: Selected Essays and Addresses*. New Haven, CT: Yale University Press, 1986. 102–120.

Noddings, Nel. *The Maternal Factor: Two Paths to Morality*. Berkeley: University of California Press, 2010.

Obama, Barack. "Remarks by the President at the Acceptance of the Nobel Peace Prize." *Whitehouse.gov*. December 10, 2009. http://www.whitehouse.gov/the-press-office/remarks-president-acceptance-nobel-peace-prize.

O'Reilly, Julie D. "The Wonder Woman Precedent: Female (Super)Heroism on Trial." *Journal of American Culture* 28.3 (September 2005): 273–283. http://cuwhist.files.wordpress.com/2012/03/the-wonder-woman-precedent-female-superheroism-on-trial.pdf.

Ortega, Terese. "Wandering around Wonder Woman." *In Sequence*. February 9, 2008. http://www.insequence.org/2008/02/wandering_around_wonder_woman_1.html.

Peters, Brian Mitchell. "Qu(e)erying Comic Book Culture and Representations of Sexuality in Wonder Woman." *Comparative Literature and Culture* 5.3 (2003). http://docs.lib.purdue.edu/clcweb/vol5/iss3/6.

Peters, Jay, and Lenard W. Kaye. "Childhood Sexual Abuse: A Review of Its Impact on Older Women Entering Institutional Settings." *Clinical Gerontologist* 26.3–4 (2003): 29–53.

Plain, Gil. *Women's Fiction of the Second World War: Gender, Power, and Resistance*. New York: St. Martin's, 1996.

Radway, Janice A. *Reading the Romance: Women, Patriarchy, and Popular Literature*. Chapel Hill: University of North Carolina Press, 1991.

Raymond, Janice. *The Transsexual Empire: The Making of the She-Male*. New York: Teachers College Press, 1994.

Reece, Charles. "On Second Thought I Really Don't Like Wonder Woman, Part 1." *Hooded Utilitarian*. May 23, 2012. http://hoodedutilitarian.com/2012/05/on-second-thought-i-really-dont-like-wonder-woman-part-1/.

Reed, Christopher. *Art and Homosexuality: A History of Ideas*. New York: Oxford University Press, 2011.

Regis, Pamela. *A Natural History of the Romance Novel*. Philadelphia: University of Pennsylvania Press, 2003.

Reynolds, Richard. *Super Heroes: A Modern Mythology*. Jackson: University Press of Mississippi, 1992.

Richard, Olive (pseudonym of Olive Byrne). "Our Women Are Our Future." *Family Circle*. August 14, 1944. 14–17, 19.

Rine, Abigail. *Irigaray, Incarnation, and Contemporary Women's Fiction*. New York: Academic, 2013.

Robbins, Trina. *The Great Women Superheroes*. Northampton, MA: Kitchen Sink, 1996.

———. "Re-inventing Wonder Woman—Again!" *Hooded Utilitarian*. April 30, 2012. http://hoodedutilitarian.com/2012/04/re-inventing-wonder-woman-again/.

———. "Wonder Woman: Lesbian or Dyke? Paradise Island as a Woman's Community." *Girl-Wonder.org*. May 2006. http://girl-wonder.org/papers/robbins.html.

Robinson, Lillian. *Wonder Women: Feminisms and Superheroes*. London: Routledge, 2004.

Rose, Lionel. *The Massacre of the Innocents: Infanticide in Britain, 1800–1939*. London: Routledge & Kegan Paul, 1986.

Rosenberg, Alyssa. "A Condemnation of Sparkly Vampires." *Atlantic*. November 19, 2009. http://www.theatlantic.com/magazine/archive/2009/11/a-condemnation-of-sparkly-vampires/7792/.

Rowling, J. K. *Harry Potter and the Sorcerer's Stone*. New York: Scholastic, 1997.

Russell, Bertrand. "The Future of Pacifism." *American Scholar* 13.1 (Winter 1943–1944): 7–13.

Russo, Maria. "The Reeducation of a Queer Theorist." *Salon*. September 27, 1999. http://www.salon.com/1999/09/27/sedgwick/.

Sacher-Masoch, Leopold von. *Venus in Furs*. 1870. *Masochism*. New York: Zone, 1991. 143–271.

Sandifer, Philip. *A Golden Thread: An Unauthorized Critical History of Wonder Woman*. n.p. Eruditorum, 2014.

Saunders, Ben. *Do the Gods Wear Capes?* New York: Continuum, 2011.

Schor, Naomi. "Male Lesbianism." *GLQ* 7.3 (2001): 391–399.

Sedgwick, Eve. *Between Men: English Literature and Male Homosocial Desire*. New York: Columbia University Press, 1985.

———. *The Epistemology of the Closet.* Berkeley: University of California Press, 2008.

Serano, Julia. "Performance Piece." *The Gay Utopia.* December 2007. http://gayutopia.blogspot.com/2007/12/julia-serano-performance-piece.html.

———. *Whipping Girl: A Transsexual Woman on Sexism and the Scapegoating of Femininity.* Emeryville, CA: Seal, 2007.

Shakespeare, William. *The Winter's Tale.* 1623. Project Gutenberg. July 2000. http://www.gutenberg.org/cache/epub/2248/pg2248.html.

Showalter, Elaine. "Rivers and Sassoon: The Inscription of Male Gender Anxieties." *Behind the Lines: Gender and the Two World Wars.* Ed. Margaret Randolph Higonnet, Jane Jenson, Sonya Michel, and Margaret Collins Weitz. New Haven, CT: Yale University Press, 1987. 61–69.

Silman, Sherrie. "Can Feminists Learn from Romance Novels?" *Feminspire.* September 19, 2013. http://feminspire.com/can-feminists-learn-from-romance-novels/.

Silverman, Kaja. *Male Subjectivity at the Margins.* New York: Routledge, 2001.

Simone, Gail, Terry Dodson, and Bernard Chang. *Wonder Woman: The Circle.* New York: DC Comics, 2008.

Solaris. Dir. Andrei Tarkovsky. 1972. Criterion Collection, 2002.

Steinem, Gloria. Introduction. *Wonder Woman.* By William Marston and H. G. Peter. New York: Holt, Rinehart and Winston, 1972.

———. Introduction. *Wonder Woman: Featuring over Five Decades of Great Covers.* New York: Abbeville, 1995.

Stoltenberg, John. *Refusing to Be a Man: Essays on Sex and Justice.* Rev. ed. London: UCL Press, 2000.

Stryker, Susan, and Stephen Whittle. Introduction to chapter 10. *The Transgender Studies Reader.* Ed. Susan Stryker and Stephen Whittle. New York: Taylor & Francis, 2006. 131.

Studlar, Gaylyn. *In the Realm of Pleasure: Von Sternberg, Dietrich, and the Masochistic Aesthetic.* Urbana: University of Illinois Press, 1988.

Swiontkowski, Gale. *Imagining Incest: Sexton, Plath, Rich, and Olds on Life with Daddy.* Danves, MA: Rosemont, 2003.

The Thing (Collector's Edition). Dir. John Carpenter. 1982. Universal Pictures, 2004.

Thomas, Jamaal. "Azzarello and Chiang's Excellent Adventure." *Funnybook Babylon.* May 11, 2012. http://funnybookbabylon.com/2012/05/11/azzarello-and-chiangs-excellent-adventure/.

Thompson, Kelly. "Review: Wonder Woman #5." *Comic Book Resources.* January 19, 2012. http://www.comicbookresources.com/?page=user_review&id=4371.

———. "She Has No Head!—Is the Destruction of the Amazons the Destruction of Feminism in DC Comics?" *Comic Book Resources.* March 26, 2012. http://

goodcomics.comicbookresources.com/2012/03/26/she-has-no-head-is-the-destruction-of-the-amazons-the-destruction-of-feminism-in-dc-comics/.

"Top 100 Comics." *Comics Journal* 210 (February 1999): 34–108.

Twitchell, James. *Forbidden Partners: The Incest Taboo in Modern Culture*. New York: Columbia University Press, 1989.

Valcour, Francine. "Training 'Love Leaders': William Moulton Marston, Wonder Woman and the 'New Woman' of the 1940s." MA thesis, Arizona State University, May 1999.

Ward, Elizabeth. *Father-Daughter Rape*. London: Women's Press, 1984.

Watterson, Bill. *Calvin and Hobbes*. Kansas City, MO: Andrews and McMeel, 1987.

Weeks, Laurie. "Eat Me." *Nicole Eisenman*. Ed. Beatrix Ruf. Zurich, Switzerland: JRP/Ringier, 2011. 6–13.

Weil, Simone. "*The Iliad*, or the Poem of Force." 1939. *War and the Iliad*. Trans. Mary McCarthy. New York: New York Review of Books, 2005. 1–38.

Wertham, Frederic. *Seduction of the Innocent*. New York: Rinehart, 1953.

Williams, Linda. *Hard Core: Power, Pleasure, and the "Frenzy of the Visible."* Berkeley: University of California Press, 1999.

Wolk, Douglas. *Reading Comics: How Graphic Novels Work and What They Mean*. Cambridge, MA: Da Capo, 2007.

Woolf, Virginia. *Three Guineas*. 1938. New York: Harcourt Brace, 1966.

Wright, Bradford, W. *Comic Book Nation: The Transformation of Youth Culture in America*. Baltimore: Johns Hopkins University Press, 2001.

Yoder, John Howard. *The Politics of Jesus*. 2nd ed. Grand Rapids, MI: Eerdmans, 1994.

Zakreski, Patricia. "'Tell Me Lies: Lying, Storytelling, and the Romance Novel as Feminist Fiction." *Journal of Popular Romance Studies*. April 30, 2012. http://jprstudies.org/2012/04/tell-me-lies-lying-storytelling-and-the-romance-novel-as-feminist-fiction-by-patricia-zakreski/.

INDEX

ABOUT THE AUTHOR

Noah Berlatsky is a freelance writer whose work has appeared in the *Atlantic*, *Salon*, *Slate*, *Reason*, and *Splice Today*, among other venues. He edits the comics and culture website *The Hooded Utilitarian*.

CPSIA information can be obtained at www.ICGtesting.com
Printed in the USA
BVOW03s0426260215

389372BV00001B/21/P